Civilization in Overdrive

Civilization in Overdrive
Conversations at the Edge
of the Human Future

KONRAD STACHNIO

Clarity Press, Inc.

© 2020 Konrad Stachnio
ISBN: 978-1-949762-28-0
EBOOK ISBN: 978-1-949762-29-7

In-house editor: Diana G. Collier
Cover design: R. Jordan Santos

ALL RIGHTS RESERVED: Except for purposes of review, this book may not be copied, or stored in any information retrieval system, in whole or in part, without permission in writing from the publishers.

Library of Congress Control Number: 2020942814

Clarity Press, Inc.
2625 Piedmont Rd. NE, Ste. 56
Atlanta, GA 30324, USA
https://www.claritypress.com

Interviews

PREFACE vii

INTERVIEWS:

1. Alexandr Dugin 1
2. Alain de Benoist. 18
3. Andrei Raevsky 27
4. Carine Hutsebaut 36
5. Catherine Austin Fitts 45
6 Douglas Rushkoff. 68
7. Erik Davis 77
8. Sheikh Imran Nazar Hosein. 92
9. Rabbi Joel David Bakst 103
10. Jack Rasmus. 123
11. John Perkins. 141
12. Mikhail A. Lebedev, PhD 149
13. Paul Craig Roberts. 157
14. Richard Falk. 164
15. Tim Draper. 191
16. Thomas Campbell 197
17. William Binney 217

INTERVIEWEE BIOGRAPHIES 231

INDEX 237

Preface

When I started working on this book, the idea seemed a little crazy—even to me. Because here, I was embarking on a journey to answer the question of what our future would look like. We live in exceptional times full of chaos, full of rapid changes that take place so quickly that we don't stop to even think about them, treating the world more and more as a simulation that we can no longer influence. "Reality has long since outrun fiction," as a friend of mine once said.

In such conditions, aiming at answering how our future will look may seem like madness, like something impossible. But this was a deliberate madness that I imposed upon myself, just to see if it was possible to achieve. I truly didn't know where this path would lead. However, I knew that in order to start seriously at all, I had to fully immerse myself in the areas I was studying: NBIC (Nanotechnology, Biology and medicine, Information sciences, and Cognitive Sciences), AI (Artificial Intelligence), geopolitics, religion, philosophy, sociology, and economy. Not so much to sink into it, as to be able to synthesize it.

It took me hundreds of hours to prepare for the conversations with my guests.

I did not want to create an easy book where my interlocutors would repeat clichés and already trending messages. I also didn't want to create another politically correct book. That was precisely why I invited such diverse people to talk with me.

Such diversity is what freedom of speech and real discussion are all about. Everything else is—for me—more or less a mental prison, the Thought Police à la 1984. It is these sometimes extremely divergent points of view that are, in my opinion, the narrow and dangerous paths that can lead you to the truth, when at some point you see how everything in some strange and unexpected way intertwines into one whole.

I knew that in order to study the subject in depth, I had to talk to people from various worlds, from various cultures, who sometimes almost appeared to each other as species from different planets. Only in this way did I think I could manage to pick out some particles of truth.

When I started my work, I also thought that I knew more or less where it would lead me. How wrong I was. As each conversation progressed, my own views began to change, directing me to tracks I would never have thought of. And this is probably the biggest reward, that these conversations changed me that they led me straight to the rabbit hole and into a world whose existence I could never have forseen.

At some point, I decided to stop.

While I had permission for further interviews, I felt that there was nothing to add and the next conversation would just be venturing toward "entertainment."

I regard this book as bearing witness to the very special times in which we lived. A testament from a former world where nothing will remain as it was.

Did I succeed? You will have to judge for yourself.

—*Konrad Stachnio*

Aleksandr Dugin[*]

"What is important is to be against modernity."

KONRAD STACHNIO: You said in previous interviews that we were dealing with some kind of satanic agenda emerging in our world. Do you mean a globalist agenda—even a "satanic agenda" in a Hollywood fetish way or some other, real satanic agenda?

ALEKSANDR DUGIN: First of all, I am a follower of traditionalism. Traditionalism is a special kind of philosophy that regards religious understanding of reality and the vision of the traditional societies as absolutely legitimate, not overcome, not abolished or destroyed by modernity. So, traditionalism considers there's no such thing as progress. So, all the narrative of modernity is put into time in a historic perspective. So, for modernity to believe in what our ancestors believed is the sign of sheer stupidity—because they believe in time, and if you don't believe in time, you are an idiot. So, if you are not modern, you are crazy—a dangerous Nazi—and you are completely, completely mad and need to be re-educated or marginalized or put outside of society. That is really important, and traditionalism—instead of this intellectual attack of modernity—tries to affirm quite the opposite. So, if God exists, and if we believe in His eternity that doesn't belong to the past, then God exists always, God exists now, God will exist after, after our death. So, after this modernity ends, God will persist, continue to persist and so that is a kind of belief in eternity. It is incompatible with modernity; it is completely incompatible.

If you believe in eternity you are a dangerous idiot. You should be re-educated and eliminated. And that is the main narrative of modernity. Traditionalism opposes this narrative, the strong belief in eternity when it is

---

[*]ALEKSANDR DUGIN is one of the best-known writers and political commentators in post-Soviet Russia. He is considered to be one of the most contentious thinkers of the modern world.

out of mode, when it is impossible, when it is prohibited. So, we are dangerous freaks, traditionalists or religious orthodox Christians, or Muslim people, or the Hindu, or Buddhist. Because we all believe in metaphysics and we are acting on the base of this belief. So, in our lives, modernity is satanic, because Satan is not something new. Satan is also an eternal creature and Satan leads the war against Christ, against God always—but now, he is winning. This is not a new idea that he is fighting God. The new turn in sacred history is that now he is winning, and his victory is so great and so big and so extensive that it affects everyone. Satan is inside of us, Satan governs our thoughts, our societies. So, we live inside of Satan, not outside of him. So, Hollywood productions, artificial intelligence, technical development, the ideas of enlightenment, progress, modern science, materialism and all political theory of modernity are all purely parts of a satanic plan to destroy civilisation based on no belief in God. That is my belief, and believing in God, believing in traditional societies, I have no other concept that would fit better than the concept of satanic paradigm in order to qualify modernity. Modernity doesn't believe in God and thinks that is normal; for me, it is absolutely abnormal. If we reject God and eternity, if we are founding our civilisation on negation, refusing to believe in the eternity, we are following the satanic plan, we are part of it, consciously or unconsciously. And that is my understanding of what is going on with Western civilisation during the enlightenment and in the time of modernity.

So, it is much broader than some Hollywood phenomenon, than gender politics or liberalism, or globalisation. They are all parts of this plan but not the essence. So, I don't blame, for example, some specific persons or peoples or countries or civilisations. I blame Satan, or I put the responsibility on him, precisely on him, and I regard everybody who is involved in modernity and as well in post-modernity much more… I consider them to be some kind of technical details of the great satanic mechanism that tries to lead the final battle against the saints, against church, against eternity, against heaven and God. And I sincerely believe in it and I am constructing my political, geopolitical, social, sociological, philosophical, anthropological and my theories of multipolarity precisely on this basis. I am not distinguishing that; I don't separate my belief from my thought. To believe and to think, for me, is one and the same.

KS: Slavoy Zizek said the future elite will be those who will be able to live without technology in a world where everything is dependent on it. So who will those people be, taking this into your traditionalist concept of understanding?

AD: First of all, I think technology it is not a technological problem, it is a metaphysical problem. So, the technic is not the accident in our lives; in our civilisation, it is the essence. The technical approach, the very essence of technic is alienation from man and the ambience around him. So, when you have a kind of stick—if you use the stick in order to have plants or have bananas, you are inside of a technological circle. Because, you introduce between you and the world some kind of tool, a kind of weapon—a kind that doesn't belong absolutely to outside or inside. It is a kind of organ, and this is kind of prosthesis. And the stick is already the destiny, the metaphysical destiny. Taking the stick in our hands, we are on the way, we are starting to go to a modern, technological civilisation that is a kind of end of this way of alienation between ourselves and the world around us. I am following Heidegger and that metaphysical way of thinking, because I think that the world, die Welt in German, is a kind of existential creation of the human being. Not of the human being as an individual entity, but as I would call it, Dasein. So, the world means absence of animals, or stones, or vegetables. They are but they don't exist because they don't create or constitute a better world around them. They have no idea what the world is. Only humans, being based on the Dasein construct, constitute the world. It is our decision to put something between us and this world. It is Logos, and this Logos in some special situation could turn into the stick, into the instrument, into the technic. Into something that separates, not unites. So, there are two ways to understand Logos. One Logos could include ourselves and the world inside of Dasein. And that would be called—following once more Heidegger—fundamental ontology. Fundamental ontology is trying not to go out from the limits of the existing being, then out of Dasein and understanding the process of creation of the world, of the constitution of the world, inside of our existential horizon.

The problem of Western civilisation—it has a metaphysical problem—is that it has given too much importance to the Logos first, then to the technics afterwards. So, we have lost the key to interpret correctly what the technic is, not only to use it positively or negatively. That is a problem. For example, if you consider Australian aboriginal civilisation, you see persistence. Evil for Australian natives is a kind of absolute sin. Why? Because it kills at a distance, without coming into contact, without returning to the point of starting, to the starting point that is metaphysical sin and crime. For example, for the Maori to have richness, it is a crime and a sin, it is a damned path that should be destroyed in order to save the balance, to grant a balance of civilisation. And when we put all our force and all our belief and confidence into the Logos and into the techniques, we destroy this balance, so we destroy the world and we destroy ourselves. We turn into mechanical robot figures, and we're dehumanizing ourselves. So that is the problem. So, the technology—the technics—is not one problem among others; it is the most subtle problem. And we could not solve this situation by trying to bypass technology. That is an illusion. We need to return to the point when we have committed the most important error, when we have lost our way and when we have lost this balance, this sacred balance between the world, ourselves, God, the Sacred—and we need to restart the last three or four hundred years of our history. This modern period of this history is absolutely wrong. We have lost our way, we have lost ourselves in the forest in a way. We are lost and need to return to the starting point—if it is yet possible—in order to follow our way. Because what is going on now is the result of this moment of being lost, and the results are not the reasons, so we could not fight against the consequences. We need to cure the reasons for what is going on.

Some elite are completely engaged in this technological version and Slavoy Zizek is part of it because he is modern, he is progressive, he is in favour of communists. He is a little detail of this satanic plan, pretending that he is thinking. No, he is not thinking, he is just repeating a so-called critical distance. But it is a very short distance, not real distance, as the only real distance, only traditionalists could have. If you don't agree with Guenon or Evola, you have nothing to say to anybody. So, you are a part of an automatic, mechanistic process. In order to solve real problems, we could not only refuse technology; it is not enough. No elite will accept that. Because the elite is always ahead of the others so all this orientation is going to the abyss. And Slavoy Zizek is financed by George Soros and he defends him. So that is absolutely simulacrum. He is not danger, he is not a philosopher, he is one more of Soros' marionettes and puppets, and he is a part of this establishment playing at ecology, playing on liberalism, on leftism, leftism liberalism criticising traditionalism, pretending it to be nationalism, racism, and so on. That is a part of ecological thinking. I agree with this thinking only under the condition that we return to the roots of the problem. And the correct roots of the problem are explained by Guenon and by Heidegger and Dasein philosophy. We have all the choices possible now in order to really solve the problem, and we need nothing more but we don't want it—and we are still playing Satan's game repeating all the parts, all the abstract details, all the narratives going in the same direction. What we need is an absolute metaphysical alternative in order to solve the slightest, the smallest problem.

KS: Yes, but what is the practical solution, the alternative? People take technology and the modern world for granted. They even don't suspect any other world could exist. So how can you survive in this modern world without technology? Transhumanists argue that by technology, we will be able to, for example, cure cancer. So, how can we live right now without these advanced technologies which offer us help in many ways?

AD: All these arguments are valid only if you think survival relates to the end of the life of humanity. But if you don't agree with that, no argument of this kind is valid. So, for example, life is part of the being, not the whole. Only in modernity do they put all meaning, all the ontology, into life. But if you are Christian or traditionalist, you believe life here on the earth is the much more extensive form of being, and to die properly and to die in a good way, maybe it is much more than surviving. It is not necessarily, but to die—or to be or not to be—is the question of life or not life. It is the question of modernity, and for traditionalists, there are some much more important things than life and death—that is sacred, that is God. If cancer reminds you of your finitude and of your immortal soul, maybe it is the way by which God puts you on right path and teaches you to do the right things. And if we follow this way, he will cure us by a miracle—or maybe if we die, we die as normal, decent, believing people. Because on the pretext of making life, material life better or easier, they steal our souls, they pervert our minds and that is an absolutely satanic plan.

Why survive? Nietzsche said: you like to liberate yourselves from slavery but have you something for which you should be liberated? Maybe you try to survive but it is an animalistic instinct. We humans, we need the goal. Survival for what reason? Survival, or to be liberated, or to be free—to do what? Not anything, because we are free. We shouldn't be free; we are living, we live here and in the afterlife. Our souls cannot die and in putting all the attention on the material side of things, we are damaging ourselves. It is obvious that for modernity, the soul doesn't exist. So, my narrative sounds like the words of crazy people. But for the believer in God, it's a completely different situation. So the idea to survive, to cure in a material way some natural diseases or artificial diseases—all that represents is a completely crazy attitude and a deep misunderstanding of the nature of the human, because the soul cannot be killed. Modernity pretends there is no such thing as the soul but it is only pretence, it is lies.

So, the idea of technology, post-humanism, is based on lies, on metaphysical lies. For example, it's based on premises that the afterlife, God, eternity don't exist and are fairy tales of the past, but not the special teaching that is in contact with present and with the future. Because for us, the future comes from eternity and the only basis to exist in the future for humanity or soul, for everything in the world, is based in God. If God, for example, will not want to save humanity, no one can. But all this is the question of principles, not of consequences. That is my position and I am explaining what I believe in.

KS: But is there any chance to reverse this technological trend? Because all of this is more or less ideological thinking, but we are dealing with so-called

"reality"—real technology being implemented in our environment, in our lives on a daily basis. How can a modern, Western individual try to reverse this trend?

AD: First of all, there is no sign of that political elite or natural way of things in the West, but at the same time in the East, there is no sign of this reversal. There are many signs of the intensification of the same technological process. There is no sign of return; there are many signs of acceleration of the process. And it seems to be fatal, to be kind of irreversible, so we could not seriously, realistically consider the possibility to stand up and say stop. But what is interesting is that the human being is absolutely free and that is a new idea for progressives and liberals. Because they are fighting for liberty, destroying or misunderstanding, misinterpreting the real existing liberty of man and his dignity, because the man inside of his heart could always say yes or no. He could pay with his life, his comfort, he could pay by great suffering. But that is the part of his immense—I would say absolute—freedom. So, if you don't agree with this course of things, they are completely artificial—that elites are following some plans, satanic plans. Satan inspires the idea that God doesn't exist and therefore we should rely on ourselves, we need to go to progress, everything is material, everything is calculated, only money and technology is Dasein, and so on. But these are concepts first of all; after, they turn into the reality but it is an ideological struggle. That is the struggle not of the armies but of the minds, of the concepts, and these concepts appear as something natural, inside of the things, as reality. Not ideas, but they are the ideas put into the reality, but they organize satanic plans. So, we all live not only in a satanic concept, we all live in satanic themes, because this satanic concept has entered into reality. Our economy, our technology, our political system, our ideas, our education, our way of life; all that is a part of this artificially created matrix, I would say, satanic matrix. How to liberate from the matrix?

First of all, we need to know it is always possible, because we are free and if one of us, only one of us, is against that, then not everything is lost, there is some hope. If one, only one—is against the matrix. So, if there are two or three in the name of Christ, as Christ has said in the Evangelists, so I believed him. Those, those whom the God is, can always win. It is quite incredible if we consider what one person or one decision or one soul can do against all this huge humanity, huge laws, economic transactions, these programs, TV stations, gay rights, globalisation problems, processes, political elites serving as puppets for these new world government masters—but it is always possible. So, first of all, nobody can deprive us of the alternative of this freedom, nobody.... And being freed by God, we could lead resistance in any sense on any level, maybe political, economical, spiritual, in the field of art, in the field of philosophy, in the field of everyday life. If we see that something is a lie, we should say: that is a lie. If we see something that is merely an illusion, we need to call it an illusion and I think now, we are approaching the last moment, the last battle. There is a kind of call there, a call that we need to interpret not in only the religious sense. It is the call for humanity to return to our roots, to our freedom and we need to interpret this call, maybe in our tradition. For you Polish, it would be—I presume—the Catholic tradition. Because Catholics are absolutely incompatible with the modern world. Because in the Catholic tradition, you should be Catholic or modern; you could not be a modern Catholic. It is a kind of schizophrenia, so either Catholic or modernist. So, either secular or for Christ, or Christian identity or antichristian identity—that is, modern identity. They try to say if you are Catholic, you should fight against Muslims or Orthodox. They say the same for Muslims; that is the satanic plan. But the call of transcendence, this call is directed toward Polish people as Catholics, in order to reaffirm Polish identity. That could be anti-Russian, anti-Muslim, pro-Muslim, pro-Russian. That is not important. What is important is to be against modernity. The same for us Orthodox Christian people, the same for Muslims, because everybody is a loser in the globalist game.

So now, for example, being geopolitically anti-American, now we see what is going on. This Orange Revolution inside of the United States, this absolutely indecent attack against Trump, against his supporters, I can feel it myself. Because some Americans hear the call, the call to be against what is going on, to be against the trend. Maybe in a reduced part, maybe not so profoundly, metaphysically based as it should be, but they certainly hear the call. And I think that is the moment, so we need to transcend what divides us, people of tradition, people of identity, people defending what we are, and we need to together return to the point where this negative process started and try to re-think everything, to put it under question. For example, we need to put aside anything appearing to be taken for granted. Nothing is taken for granted. We are risky beings; the human being is living in risk. To be human is dangerous; not to be a dangerous human is dangerous. To be human as such is very dangerous and you cannot be human and be innocent. It is danger, we are living in danger, we need to respond to the challenges and that way is hard. That is our way and I think it is always possible. So, I think defence of tradition, of identity, defence of the sacred, of eternity, of the sincere and profound belief in God in the sacred, is our current level that could reverse nevertheless—with the help of God—this kind of situation. I am absolutely sure that only we can; they cannot, they are falling into the abyss and that is absence of power, and not the power to slide into the abyss, to fall. That doesn't demand the force. Consider Obama; he is sliding, and he is very happy. Regard Trump; he tries to climb on the wall, he tries to reverse things and that is very hard for him, because to slide is easy and to climb the mountain is hard. The same for liberals, they don't make efforts. They oppose us because we are calling on everybody in humanity to make an effort, to think, to act and behave as free beings and not as mechanical elements of the matrix. So, I think the reversal of this situation is quite possible. We could not predict how it will look if we will, but certainly it will be something other than is happening now.

KS: What do you think about the current migrant crisis in Europe? In the future, those people will be looking for jobs, but it seems there won't be jobs for them—not enough, at least. So, perhaps one of the ways for them to survive will be as part of criminal organisations. Because as Bill Gates said, if artificial intelligence becomes more powerful in one or two decades, it will make so-called simple jobs disappear. So, what will happen with all those people in this new reality? On the other hand, the optimist claims there won't be simple jobs for them, but the market will create new segments and demand. Now, people work in factories but in the future, people will be working in areas using compassion, the sharing economy, passion etc. But I don't think this is the real scenario for that many people.

AD: I think the problem with immigrants is not so much an economic one. The idea is to destroy European identity and to make what the French call the Great Replacement. That means they try to replace the European population with an extra European population, destroying two identities not just one. By changing the ambience and by changing the place, the Muslims coming to Europe are conserving only the artificial identity of Islam. It is not the real Islam, it is an artificial, Salafi Islam, a kind of sect, a kind of heresy of Islam. So, they are modernizing by doing that. That is the way to modernize traditional people, to make the Muslim first and Salafi after that. After the first part of modernisation, they will be equals—as European moderns. But at the same time Europeans lose their identities, they become robots; they will end being Polish, French, or German and become everybody—Europeans. So, Europeans immigrants are trying to imitate them, but Europeans in that situation will lose their identity, they will be replaced by immigrants and after that, everybody will be replaced by robots. So, Muslims and immigrants—that is not (going to be) for a long time. That is precisely why globalists don't bother to give the jobs to immigrants. The immigrants are the weapons, are tools, coming to Europe to destroy you, to destroy your identity, maybe to start a civil war in order to create a kind of emergency situation. And after that, the matrix will be imposed on all of you and instead of gay rights, you will have robots' rights and so on. That is a very important phase. So, if we let things go as they're going, immigrants will destroy European society—and destroying themselves in the process—this is not in favour of them. They never will create a Caliphate or Islamic State because their countries are falling apart. So, they are coming to Europe with the idea of a Caliphate out of depression, out of frustration. Because they have lost their possibility to create their State—Islamic or not—they are coming to Europe in order to maybe save their illusion. So, nobody will create a Caliphate in Europe. It is impossible, including in the Arab, Muslim world. They are losing all their battles for that, precisely because it is an artificial goal imposed on them by globalists. So, they are coming here to kill you, to replace you and nothing else. And after, they will be killed, and globalists will replace them. So, globalists will replace all of us; we are in the same situation. Using 3D printers, they will print newborn babies and there will be no Muslim babies or European babies anymore. They will be 3D-printer babies and that is the technology and that is normal, and that is good for transhumanists. They declare that as their goal and finally, that is the logical conclusion of modernity. Modernity was always wrong from the very beginning and now we're arriving at the end. So, Muslims and immigrants are parts of this anticipated scenario. Where are the other elements? It is a kind of soup, a kind of plate they're preparing. There is a kind of Muslim, there are Europeans, there are Americans, there are Russians. The others are technologists, there are ecologists, there is Zizek—and everything should turn on this plate finally, when everybody will be too tired to defend their own identity in the mixture. This mixture will no longer be human once we awake in the mechanical, virtual world with no way out. So that is the matrix.

KS: But do you really think those people who are building this new technological world and environment—like Elon Musk for instance—are aware of what are they're doing, or maybe doing this only to help humanity? Are they too blind to see what they're building? Elon Musk usually says AI is very risky, and we need to make some effort to avoid this risk, but at the end of the day, he is still doing it. Are those people just insane in some way?

AD: No, not at all. They are sane but in their specific manner. They are sane as the followers of the trend. They are bearers of some paradigm, the paradigm of progress, of materialism, of social development, of liberation, it is a more or less technological scientific development that's natural in itself. So, they are not absolutely crazy, they have no bad intentions, they are sincere and are sometimes brilliant people personally. But there is something much deeper than their will. They are part of the trend and that trend is discernible to its sources. For example, if we consider how it all began, we see the idea of liberation of the individual from any kind of links with the collective identity would be an idea from the beginning of modernity—the liberation of man—and this liberation has led to a liberation from moral responsibilities, national identity, religious identity. But that was liberation from God and from what's sacred, and they finally have come to the conclusion of it lying. Because the last identity, collective identity, is human identity. And if we are consequent—and those people mentioned before are consequent more than others—they think, if we need to liberate individuals from any kind of collective identity, we need to stop, destroy, reconstruct or transform human identity because it is collective.

Gender politics is the sign, because that is liberation of the individual from gender identity, which is collective, and the next step is liberating individuals from human, collective identity and that is the open way to artificial intellect and the cyborgs—and that is logical, that is the result of liberalism and if we accept this logic, we need to accept them, because they are more developed, they are ahead of us, if we follow that line. If we don't follow that line in a whole inner self, then for us, the people who are working on artificial intelligence or who are liberals, or who are missionaries or who are bourgeoisie or who are communist, or everybody who belongs to this modern paradigm are on the same line—and it is not so important how progressive they are, because the people who now promote artificial intelligence are more intelligent than others. They are more intelligent because that is artificial intelligence; it is the paradigm we are living in. The robots are revelations of our mechanical soul, our pretended mechanical nature. So, they first turned us into robots and after that, they can declare that now, we're coming to (a state of) robot rule. That is not a completely new, unexpected, satanic, turn of modernity. That is the normal terminal station of the way we have been travelling for many centuries now in Europe. That is the end—terminal—station; welcome to the terminal station. We are arriving at the last point of our destination. In modernity, we are ourselves robots. So, the matrix began to be introduced some centuries ago and that was beginning of the de-Christianisation of Europe and implementation of the modern way of thinking and doing, and now we are already cyborgs. Because we use not only material technology, computers or credit cards or trains or so on. We are also using mental technology, implemented on us. We are thinking for example about survival, democracy, gay rights, Russian hackers, Muslim invasions or we are in the justice to destroy the monumental status for founding fathers in the United States. All these are kinds of programs, ways of thinking, trends, artificially created in our minds, in our brains, and we are following them as we are robots already. So, artificial intelligence doesn't present a huge danger for robots. We are already robots in some way, so we will not perceive change. This change will be very smooth because we are half robots already. So, everybody will become that way without noticing that. So that is their way to organize.

KS: But this system offers people the chance to become some kind of God. For example, they're planning that the consciousness of the individual will be part of some kind of swarm awareness, a collective consciousness where everyone sees, hears, talks telepathically and feels as everyone, where your privacy and private thinking is gone. So, first of all, who will you become in that situation? Isn't it this gap between the outside and inside world that makes us human? But it seems people do not see this as a problem but as an advantage. Who is going to be controlling this system?

AD: I think there is a difference between soft and strong artificial intelligence. So, the difference is that strong AI is based on neural networks that could decide what to do. So, that is the real competitor to so-called human intelligence. So if they refuse to recognize the existence of the soul, of God, of eternity and of the radical subject or radical interiority—and they have dedicated many writings to the concept of the radical subject—so if a being refuses to recognize what is radical subjectivity that is the soul, immortality, eternity and God, radical interiority, then we are already half robots. So, we are dealing with a kind of mirror reflection of ourselves. Strong artificial intelligence is exactly the same; this is not radical subjectiveness that could represent interiority or imitate interiority. So the problem is that what is really interior—since all the rest is exterior because that is mechanical inside our organisms—what is really interior, what is inner in ourselves, that is the process of thinking. If strong AI is implemented, so there will be interiority of that completely self-sufficient system. So humans will be a kind of sub-robot, some mark I type of robot that is, for example, iPhone 4, something like iPhone 4 that hardly anybody will use.

So, no more jobs for Muslims, no more jobs for Europeans. But the jobs will be distributed by the cyborgs. Because this kind of modern intelligence or rationality of modernity could be theoretically imitated and artificially created in a strong version, and in a version that exists already. So I think this shift from the modern situation of humanity to the post-humanity and to strong artificial intelligence will be unnoticed by humanity, because we are partly inside of it and I think nobody will control that. Nobody, because this will give the control initiative to strong AI. Because that will be exactly what we are now. It will be not something new, because now we are awaiting the possibility of thinking to be something other than we are ourselves. We are living inside of the matrix already, so we don't think by ourselves, we are trendies; we are following the trends, and in that situation, there is not much difference between strong artificial intelligence that will guide us in the future or now when our political elite, TV stations, Internet and programs already define our tastes à propos what we need to sell, to do, to admire and what for.

So, I think what is going on is a kind of revelation of apocalypses—that everything is now manifested. Now it is clear, because before, in the epoch of the first traditionalists, that was a kind of forecast, kind of a fantastic way, fantastic things. Now it is the dystopian reality of the traditionalist. Not of Orwell, because it's not from the left side from communism that it's come; it has come from the mainstream. That is a kind of important turn in history. For example; Huxley against Orwell. Huxley was right being traditionalist, and Orwell—for whom I have sympathy, but I am rather on the side of the bad guy described by him—I like him more than the small protester. If you are in a difficult situation, try to be great at least! But nevertheless, Huxley is equally right and 1984 is not in the Soviet Union or in communist China or North Korea; it is in Washington, it is in Brussels, it is in Europe. So welcome to this new liberal totalitarianism.

KS: Do you believe artificial intelligence will rule the world on its own or be controlled by some elite? I spoke with my colleague who's involved in so-called futurism and the sharing economy, and he said AI isn't risky to humans at all. The risk is on the side of those using AI, not in AI itself. The risk is that a few people will be in control of the system. And are we dealing with a biogenetic situation, where the future elite will be biologically different from us, not only because they are extremely affluent but because they will be a very different biological organism than we are now? They are mixing our DNA with all sorts of things. So, who knows what the final result of these experiments will be? They even try to create a new genome from scratch, a totally new genome itself. You once said simulacrum cannot create real life, that life can be created only by God, not by simulacrum. So, what is your view on this?

AD: So, first of all, concerning the elite ruling AI. The idea of strong AI supposes this kind of intellect is equal to the human intellect. So, the term strong AI supposes it is equal to human intelligence. So, if we are speaking about strong AI, given the possibility of the speed of re-working information gathered everywhere, it is absolutely clear this strong AI—being equal by qualitative parameters—will be much stronger than humans. Because humans are limited and this strong AI will be unlimited, working with much greater speed. So, nobody could control strong AI. Weak AI, it is possible to control, and it will be elite operators or administrators, elite programmers who could control that.

But when neural networks are capable of constructing their languages, which they are already beginning to be, then that will be the end of manipulators. So, the only real subject of the ruling class will be a kind of personalized strong AI that in my opinion will coincide with the antichrist. So, that will be a kind of collusion. So the antichrist will not so much be human, and now we are approaching that moment and at the same time—concerning the second question about biogenetics—it is obvious nobody except God could create life, but we could destroy life or pervert life. I don't think we could really create life from nothing, but we could manipulate life, we could pervert life and biogenetical weapons can fulfil this task. Because it is the logic of liberalism in liberating the individual from any kind of collective identity. If we are strong supporters of this liberation process, we would propose—and now transhumanists have already proposed it—we will propose to combine, to ameliorate genes and the genome, to create better species of entities. Partly computers, partly genetics, because for example, the eye of the eagle sees wider and better than eye of the man. Or the eye of the owl sees during the night so we will improve the eye of the human in order to see, for example for some bodyguards to make their positions covert during their defence of big bosses. They need eagle eyes or owl eyes in case they are working at night. And all the rest, we could improve—the capacity to run, to hit, to fly for example. I think that is quite possible, but that is not creation of life, that is perversion of life, disfiguration of life. That is the use of a sacred thing as life in completely satanic purposes. So, I think maybe we could be witnesses of this turn, but that it's a trend; it could happen, or it could not happen if we resist. By itself, it will happen. So, going as it is, following the same line, it will arrive, absolutely, or God will destroy everybody with us and he will be right. Or elsewhere, we'll start a great resistance, revolt and war against the status quo. Not against one people or other people, including not against political enemies. We need to start the war against Satan. It is a sacred war and that is the last war of humanity, and I think that is the essence of the call. So, we need to be prepared, it is going on, it is arriving.

This is interesting. Recently, I made an appearance on Alex Jones' show, InfoWars, and just before it, one hour beforehand, I saw the David Lynch film: *Twin Peaks 3,* where there is a person absolutely identical in his discourse to Alex Jones! I was in some way, somehow, inside of the David Lynch film, appearing, speaking with Alex Jones! When I was speaking, I had the feeling it was a kind of parody, someone already in some film declared this thing I am declaring now, but is a kind of postmodern game of reflection, of mirrors. We are on one side in the Ukraine; on the other side, it is mixed and confused, but everything is very serious and I think we have the right to raise the questions as you have asked; it is very serious and essential.

KS: Right now, I see a very strange situation in Europe, like some sort of Hollywood Tarantino scenario. I mean Islamic, so-called ISIS will be fighting with Nazis against so-called corrupt globalism. I see that kind of scenario. What are your thoughts about it?

AD: This certainly could happen. I cannot foresee the future, much less make statements about the timing of the process. I think theoretically, there are only two solutions for the future; either the end, or the war. So, war is an alternative. The end means the other alternative. So, if everything will go the way it's going now, that will signify the end. This appearance of humanity as humanity—because maybe it will be replaced by something other—that is the end. At the same time, we could not imagine the alternative, to be realist, something that could be a kind of new utopia. So, we stop that, we return to tradition and we are a happy and free and harmonious society. I am sorry that will not happen, including if we win, because we are in such a deep catastrophe, there is no easy way out. So, the end, or war. I prefer war to the end.

I prefer to resist, battle, struggle and fight. Fight for the alternative, including what is impossible. But it is our dignity to defend what is true and what is sacred in situations when we have zero chance to win. And we fulfil by such a fight our destiny, with zero chances and God will decide who is right and who is wrong. So, in that situation, as kind of intermediary scenarios, it could be easily as you have mentioned. For example, migrants against nationalists, but they will create the way to globalism and to this antichrist to rule from that, because this civil war in Europe is planned. For example, what is going on in Charlottesville in the United States is the same situation we have seen in other countries. That is the Arab Spring scenario, Ukrainian scenario, Georgian scenario, Russian scenario. That is the way to organize a completely senseless, completely crazy, stupid battle against the radicals of two sides in order to hit the other goal, not for one of them to win, but to struggle against them and in that situation, to put away Trump or impeach Trump and so on. But the same situation could be in Europe. That will not be the war I have mentioned. I have mentioned the Sacred War, the Sacred War between eternity and time that went wrong. Time has lost its normal, correct line, time has lost itself; it is in an impasse, in a dead end, and eternity and its fighters should put time on the right side and save the time itself that went astray, that went in the wrong direction. That is not a metaphysical idea, that is a practical idea and we oppose our war to their war, because you have described the scenario of their war. Alain Soral, French philosopher, sees that very well. So, we need our war, our war with left or right against the system; it is our war, and the part of extreme left and extreme right against themselves is their war. And they use that artificially in order to reach, to achieve some concrete goals. So, we need to be intelligent because I think only our global, radical opposition could be comparable to strong artificial intellect. We would be weaker, but we will be intelligent as well as this strong AI, and maybe a little bit more so. But we will be weaker in that situation and need to prepare the next generation for this war that's our task and mission.

KS: Would you agree the marriage between power and politics is over? Political parties seem more akin to discussion clubs than real entities that can control anything. Looks like the true control is now somewhere else, crucial decisions are made somewhere else, in places of big, international capital. So, what is the practical way for simple individuals to resist this new emerging world, if the political parties lose their power and capacity to control the situation? You have said if I understood you correctly, that people need to gather and create some kind of global movement to resist?

AD: Not necessarily movement. I agree about political parties, but that depends. In normal situations, they are completely out of the question, not clubs for discussing ideas but only groups to achieve their individualistic, material goals. So, they have nothing to do with ideas and discussion; these are out of the question. But from time to time, there appears some political force that represents something more. So, we shouldn't exclude that. In Russia for example, party life doesn't exist; it is absolutely of no importance who is in parliament. The only important thing is where is Mr. Putin. If Mr. Putin is in his place, that is more or less normal. If he is absent, chaos begins. So, nobody, no ideas, no voters, no election, nothing in Russia makes sense; this is out of the question. The same for most of Europe except for some special situations when a kind of alternative force or figure appears—could be half alternatives, half system, for example, and as strong as Trump—that need our support. Such a politician could appear in Poland, could appear in France, and we need to support them, but it is not normal, it is the exceptional situation of an emergency. Normally, we could not enter in this field because it is already completely manipulated and dominated by this artificial intelligence, political artificial intelligence when everybody knows right from the beginning, all the endings. But I think that we could use these facilities of communication, this knowledge of the English language in order to straighten the network. Because there is a kind of network of call, network of opposition, network of resistance. And for example, speaking with Alex Jones who is an American patriot; I am discovering that we have so many things in common, being on the other side of a geopolitical struggle. I know of Polish people who hate me very much, thinking I am a Russian imperialist. I am a kind of Russian imperialist but have absolutely nothing—and never said any words—against Polish people. It is asymmetric. Asymmetric.

So I like Polish culture, but that is how we need to avoid being classified. For example, you are a Russian nationalist, Polish nationalist, American imperialist, French, German. We need to go beyond that little by little. Because the danger, the enemy we are dealing with is against both of us. So, continuing our eternal and holy course, we could miss the point to organize the resistance. So we need to be at least in contact on the global level, people who share some concerns in order not to create—as we have no means to create something important—but in order to exchange ideas, because ideas do matter. Ideas do matter, really, and that is the only thing that really does matter—ideas. So, I think that this exchange of ideas could lead us—or maybe followers—to some organisation, some conclusion in the emergency situation. Because if we are prepared now in the situation of global conflict, there will be a kind of window of opportunity for us to act. For example, if you consider what is going on with American traditionalists, they were absolutely unknown, absolutely unknown in United States and in the world. Now, they are the center of attention. They were small groups of some interesting people trying to challenge the mainstream discourse. Now they are in all the newspapers and magazines of the world. So there are some windows of opportunity, but for example, when Steve Bannon was really important—it's not now when he is the Trump advisor—was at the time he read Guenon and Evola; that was the most important, but he was isolated, an unknown person. But what he read when he read Guenon and Evola, what he was reading, that was important. So, what he has been discussing which his friends, with different people—that was really important. So, all of us can have a chance to be in the right place in the right moment. Maybe not, but we need to be prepared, because from time to time, it happens when there is a kind of window of opportunity to change something, to influence the situation.

Take my example as well. I was absolutely marginalized, and from time to time, more and more, I am marginalized. Then I am put in the center of discussion, after that marginalized once more to the point where I have some position of influence in Russia. After that, I have been put on the periphery and I return. But it doesn't matter; we need to be prepared, and we need to act when there is a possibility and we are prepared for it. When we are ready, this possibility appears. If it doesn't appear, that means we are not ready; that is the idea.

KS: So, you are saying we are living in some kind of satanic matrix where a satanic agenda is ruling the world. But are those ruling us aware of the fact they are worshiping some metaphysical evil or a form of real evil? Or

they are just unaware, puppets and actors of someone? For example, Jacques Attali the former French president's advisor, wrote a book called *A Brief History of the Future*. Here, he described the future of the world and this future looks almost exactly like what is going on right now in our world. People like Elon Musk will be the new idols.

AD: So as far as I am concerned, I think that man is a worshiping being. If the man doesn't worship God, he worships the Devil, knowing or unknowing; that will be a kind of unholiness in favor of the Devil. So, if you are atheist you are a Satanist, and how much does the atheist who doesn't believe in God understand that he worships the Devil? At the same time, I don't think the root problem is Satanism. Satan and Satanism are two different things. Satanism is very marginal, very small movement, a kind of Broadway theatre that tries to inspire fear that is an esthetical, psychological dimension. It is so ridiculous and so marginal and so small, we should leave it completely outside of our interest. It would be too easy if we could connect such extravagance—little, small and finally completely innocent, I would say, groups of these Broadway spectacles. Including if they made bad things, because what makes liberals, globalists—they are huge bad things. So, I am against if you torture animals, for example; absolutely, that provokes my hatred. But if you kill a hundred thousand innocent people in Iraq or Libya or Syria, I consider nevertheless—for all my pity for innocent, poor animals—I am rather on the side of the people killed with a smile by the people with good jackets, black ties and who are not torturing any animal. They are simply killing humanity. So, I think, the real Satan is not in the circles of some extravagant groups or Broadway spectacles. So, people that have never tortured animals or never put on horns, put on the devil mask, considering themselves maybe a completely decent person, they commit their crimes on a major scale.

So, I think real Satanism is globalism, atheism and modernity. So, if you are modern, you are worshiping the Devil because modernity is a process, it is an ideology, it is a paradigm. They try to replace God by man, and that is Satanism. Satan doesn't want worship for himself; for him, it is enough if the man worships his ego. That is Satanism. Satan lives in this moment when we think we don't need to worship anyone. That is the worship of Satan and not a formal cult. I think people like Jacques Attali and others who consciously follow that line are not the cause of that; they are evildoers, they are evil followers and they didn't initiate that process, they're simply servants of the terminal station, they are small train station servants doing their job. That is nothing personal to them, they didn't initiate that, they didn't start the worship of the Devil. They are simply following the main line, the mainstream road. Maybe some step ahead of it, but they are not the reason for the evil—they are just details.

Alain de Benoist*

"History is, by definition, always an open-ended story."

KONRAD STACHNIO: What part do you think the State and political parties are going to play in the future? Is there still a place for them?

ALAIN DE BENOIST: Political parties have already lost some of their importance. In liberal democracies, they have turned into plain electoral engines. However, it is worth noting that Emmanuel Macron has been elected President of the French Republic this year without the support of any political party (and thereby rejecting the traditional left-right divide). At the same time, the States currently see their leeway restricted. They have lost entire sections of their sovereignty (political, economic, financial, budgetary, military etc.). This tendency should deepen in the coming years, but it would probably be a mistake to interpret this as the harbinger of the disappearance of the political sphere.

KS: How do you envision the future cultural landscape? Do you consider our current times as the times of the so-called "high culture"?

AdB: The culture of the few past centuries seems to have come to the end of its potential. In a way, we can speak of the end of a world. However, the end of a certain world does not mean the end of the world, as such. It is probable that a new culture will emerge. The question remains to know whether it is going to develop into a multipolar or unipolar world.

---

*ALAIN de BENOIST is a French journalist, political philosopher, and founder of the GRECE think tank and the larger cultural movement, the European New Right, launched in 1968. For over forty years Benoist has had a massive impact on the philosophical and ideological understanding of the political situation in Europe.

KS: What do you think will happen to all the "superfluous men" generated by our current globalised, technological world?

AdB: The current evolution of the work environment seems to be drifting towards a generalised precariousness and a multiplication of "superfluous men" (Claude Lefort)—people who are not needed by the economy anymore. The fundamental assessment is that we are producing more and more goods and services with the help of less and less workforce, while robotics and AI are in constant development. By 2050, most of the jobs that will not be complementary with AI will become virtually non-existent. The gap between the "connected," who benefit from globalisation, and the "peripheral," who are victims of a triple exclusion—political, social, and cultural—is bound to widen. All this outlines quite terrifying prospects.

KS: In the future, what could take over the role of "traditional community" protecting the individual?

AdB: Liberal modernity has grown on the ruins of organic community bonds which stood in the way of an ever-expanding market. Karl Marx was right when he noted that capitalism is far from being "conservative" or "patriarchal"—on the contrary, it demands a perpetual transformation of social relations aiming towards a "reification" (Verdinglichung, in Georg Lukács's term) of the social cohesion induced by the fetish of merchandise. The preserving of social cohesion—whose primary function is to protect the individuals and give meaning to their collective presence in the world—is one of the biggest challenges of our modern world. This can only be achieved through a systematic promotion of "localism." We have to recreate spaces (of modest size, to begin with) freed from the predominant ideology (which, as we all know, is always the ideology of the dominant class).

KS: What could become a new "life purpose" in a society of people deprived of work, such as those living on guaranteed income? How do you imagine a new economic system?

AdB: How one feels about their life fundamentally depends on the existence of (relatively) stable markers providing a sense of purpose, whether individual or collective. The free market society resulting from liberal capitalism has largely contributed to the progressive disappearance of these markers. The situation is further aggravated by the prevailing individualism and allergy to differences manifested by all the greatest universalist, religious, and profane ideologies—whether these differences pertain to one's culture, lifestyle, or gender.

KS: How do you imagine Man's process of adaptation to the emerging technological environment?

AdB: This is a very difficult question. To begin with, we would have to determine whether it is our task to adapt to our technological environment, or whether our role should be to make use (assuming, of course, it is still in our power) of technology to address our needs. The same question is valid for the economy: is man at the service of the economy, or is the economy at man's service? All that we can establish is that throughout history, technological transformations (the steam engine, the internal combustion engine, the automobile, the plane, contraception pill, the internet, etc.) have had a definitely stronger impact on people's everyday life than any political or social revolution ever had.

KS: What impact do you think Islam will have in the future?

AdB: Islam is currently a growing religion, but it is difficult to know if its expansion has been caused by strictly religious factors or has more to do with political ones. The Middle East's destabilisation (for which the Western powers are the first to blame), the rise of radical Islam, the multiplication of terrorist attacks, the immigration problem—all these have to be considered and carefully analysed. In addition, we should not forget about the always-decisive demographic factors: one third of births in France occur in populations from a migrant background. The strength of Islam is, in the end, only a consequence of the the non-Islamic population weakness. Only 4% of the population in France are Catholic churchgoers.

KS: Will we have to deal with the division of society into separate castes and an even greater increase of social inequalities?

AdB: Yes, this seems quite obvious to me. Since the Trente Glorieuses (30 glorious years of rapidly rising living standards in France following the end of WWII), the gap between the people and the elite keeps widening. Capital income always grows faster than labour income. We are not a society shaped like a pyramid any more, where wealth accumulated at the top and ended up going down towards the pyramid's base; we are now looking at an hourglass-shaped society where the wealthy grow wealthier and wealthier, while the poor grow poorer and poorer (and more numerous). Industrial capitalism has been replaced by speculative and financial capitalism. One of the most striking consequences of this evolution is the progressive disappearance of the middle class, which kept expanding until the 1970s. The middle class is now slowly downgrading and most of its members wind up among grassroots classes.

KS: In this new system, is the individual going to fully become a product and inevitably a part of a commercial system?

AdB: Of course. There is no other way, as long as commercial and merchant values are prevailing and dominating all the other ones. The only remedy is to accept that economy is not destiny, to recognise the limits of the reign of quantity, and to put an end to the logic of profit, utilitarianism, and the axiom of benefit—in short, to "decolonize the symbolic imagery" (Serge Latouche) by bringing the economy back to its subordinated place.

KS: What would it mean for us to abolish the gap between our inner world and the outside world through technology? Was it not specifically that gap separating us from the outside world that constitutes us, up until now, as human beings? What will happen if this gap disappears?

AdB: In a world of screens, the gap between one's inner world and the outside world keeps shrinking. It takes an invasive form and resembles a capture of the internal by a limitless external: the external world itself does not have an outside. Here we can speak of "globalitarism." Georges Bernanos saw the modern world as a "conspiracy against inner life." We could also mention "distraction" in the Pascalian sense of the term. Today, entertainment has taken over distraction, but we went even further. What is actually disappearing is firsthand experience, replaced by spurious relationships ("friends" on Facebook and other social media) and flows of images which mainly consist of "special effects" and illusions.

KS: Isn't the fight for preserving diversity in a world that aims towards standardisation and unification a lost cause, condemning the individual to a definitive loneliness and total alienation?

AdB: I do not believe that the fight for preserving diversity is condemning to solitude, let alone alienation. On the contrary, it is the standardisation of the world, the eradication of specific ways of life, the religion of human rights, the politically correct, the mass anonymity, etc. that condemn to solitude. Nonetheless, the risk of total standardisation is not that imminent. People will always have a vast disparity in their aspirations which, in some cases, will generate conflicts. Globalisation itself should be regarded as dialectics: on the one hand it standardises, on the other it creates new fragmentations.

KS: In this future society, do you think there will still be a place for "sanctity"? Or is it going to be fully replaced by "Man"?

AdB: Humanity cannot make sense of their own existence if it is not in relation to something that surpasses them. A society that would entirely abolish the boundary between the sacred and the profane still seems highly unlikely, even if our secularised societies sometimes struggle with grasping the difference between the sacred and the taboo.

KS: Do you think we are dealing with some kind of fatalism or are there still different paths for our future to unfold?

AdB: We have many reasons to be pessimistic, but fatalism is not reasonable. Nothing is ever written in advance and we are always wrong when we imagine the future as a simple extension or enhancement of current tendencies. History is, by definition, always an open-ended story.

KS: In the end, do you think the boundary between the world considered as real and the virtual world will disappear completely? Or maybe, is the definition of what we consider "real" going to change?

AdB: It is indeed one of the big questions worth asking. Here, I would refer you to Jean Beaudrillard's work on the virtualisation of the real and the advent of the "hyperreal." It is true that the boundary between the real and the virtual, the authentic and the inauthentic, tend to fade. We are getting close to the point where, as would Guy Debord say, "the real is only a moment of the false."

KS: In the future, how do you envision the development of movements such as trans-humanism, as well as the role of science as such?

AdB: The notion of trans-humanism is equivocal. In some regards, it is based on real scientific work, but it also refers to science-fiction. It is one thing to improve the human being; to transform it is another and it is still a third and different thing to surpass it. The threatening idea here would be the incapacity of humanity to control what it has created. It reminds us of the fundamental law of technology, as formulated by Friedrich Georg Jünger (Die Perfektion der Technik): whatever becomes technically possible will be actually carried out. In other words, one does not stop technology. At the same time, we can already see that some machines are not only as good as man in performing tasks—in many domains (and there are going to be even more of them) they are already performing better. The question is therefore to know who controls whom: is the ruler the one who ultimately decides? Tomorrow, who will decide?

KS: In our current times we witness more and more infantilism and wishful thinking as a reaction to the inability to adapt to the ever-expanding technology which is replacing our natural environment. As a result of this impotence, individuals start to behave more and more like primitive man in respect to their natural environment which they used to control. Therefore, we encounter a return of superstitions, magical thinking, etc. as a reaction to the ever-expanding technological environment. Even intellectuals who realise the speed and the extent of the current expansion more and more resort to superstition and magical thinking. In this regard, we witness a certain standardisation of primitivism. Is the decline of culture and humanity a condition for the expansion of technological environment?

AdB: You are right to speak of "infantilism" to characterise our contemporaries, but I do not agree with your interpretation of it as a resurgence of the "primitive." Traditional societies have always been very far from infantile. Of course, I see what you mean when you allude to "magical thinking." For many people today, new technologies are more or less incomprehensible: the phone, the television, the internet, the smartphones, etc. all have a "magical" side to them as no-one really understands "how it works." But it does not matter—what matters is that the daily usage of all of these machines separates us further and further from direct experience. We live more and more vicariously. We see all kinds of landscapes on our screens, but we do not have any direct contact with nature. Facebook accords us hundreds of "friends" who are, in fact, nothing more than ghosts. In these conditions the real itself becomes "hyperreal" (Jean Baudrillard). The virtual replaces the real because it seems more real than reality itself. Guy Debord would say that today, "the truth is only a moment of false." People from traditional ("primitive") societies have, in fact, always had a very acute sense of the real which was a fundamental condition for their survival. They had their beliefs, but they never lived in an illusion.

KS: The process of assimilation with the technological system does not require people to develop certain personality traits such as empathy, etc. People are more and more dehumanised, for example through "wearing masks" on the internet. Moreover, the lack of ability to identify with another human being results in cruelty and violence. As a result of assimilating with the technological system, people are more and more robotised and mechanised. The technological system itself is not ruled by any ideology, but by technical necessity. In this world, technology becomes culture and culture turns into a procedure. In these conditions, people start to develop traits of a depersonalised personality. Considering all this, would it be fair to assume

that future AI, being created (in our image) could have a psychopathic character? It would not be able to feel fear, empathy, guilt, etc?

AdB: The reign of technology unmistakably leads to a weakening of social cohesion which, usually differentiated, is replaced by a uniform procedure. Social life itself becomes procedural. It seems evident, therefore, that individuals ultimately become depersonalised—despite the fact that individualism has never been as pronounced as it is now. But we must be even more thorough in our analysis. Throughout centuries, technology has made human life easier. We have created machines that execute certain tasks as well as people and today some of them are even more efficient than people in performing them. AI is the royal path of the future; at the same time, this is where the danger lies. In an abstract manner, AI contributes to the mechanisation of life and to the traceability of individuals thanks to the algorithmic organisation of ever more numerous areas of life. It also enables machines to compete with functions that are not solely manual anymore. This, in turn, poses the question to the decision-maker: is the machine better placed to decide, as it can treat its information better than a human being could? What will happen when machines can decide by themselves and will be able to not only reprogram themselves or repair themselves, but also create each other mutually? In this scenario, machines will be able to reproduce themselves using a language that we will not be able to understand anymore. In this scenario, the human being become increasingly useless and superfluous.

In the workplace, we can already notice widespread structural unemployment (no longer linked with economic cycles). It is caused by the fact that we are producing more and more goods and services with less and less workers. The capitalist system is therefore confronted by one of its major contradictions; on the one hand, the capital is on a constant lookout for efficiency gains that would enable it to face the competition, which leads to job losses and reduced overall working time. On the other hand, the system considers working time as the sole and only measure of its value. Therefore, efficiency gains result in job losses while it is precisely "jobs" that have, in the past, permitted for work to be the main driving force for the expansion of capital in the first place. This contradiction has remained hidden in the past as the increased production, as well as the extension of the market, managed to compensate for the decrease of the workforce. However, today's efficiency gains are such that process of innovation is faster than product innovation. With the IT revolution, the production of wealth keeps growing faster than the human workforce and, for the first time, more jobs are being suppressed than the expanding market is able to reabsorb. In this regard we can say that capitalism is approaching an "absolute historical limit."

KS: Will the global process, consisting of the unification of the world, people, and cultures, lead to a culminating point where all contradictory tendencies are eradicated? Would this extend to the point where the process of history itself is stopped and the world will only exist as a simulation that does not require any physical space? In such a setup, the system would reach its maximum and would start to collapse; the ultra-elites would be relegated to outsider status by history and the creation of the world would be occurring outside of man. Would you agree?

AdB: I am somewhat less pessimistic than you are. I do not believe either in the world's total unification, or in the final point of history (already imprudently predicted by Fukuyama). On the contrary, I believe that history is always open and that it is unpredictable (in that it can give rise to the worst just as well as the best). And the best proof of that is that futurologists have been unable to predict any of the greatest historical turning points of the past century. Moreover, I tend to believe that all social structures, even the most unified and "domesticated," preserve a dialectical dimension. The diversity of interests, not to mention that of values, will always result in clashes and conflicts.

A total unification of the world would demand a global authority which in itself remains—at least for the time being—a fantasy. As the world does not constitute a political entity, to call oneself a "citizen of the world" is devoid of meaning. While our current globalisation does indeed homogenise many things, it also keeps creating new fragmentations.

KS: How do you see Europe and France's position in the future in the context of mass migration and an increasing number of internal conflicts?

AdB: I am afraid it might take up a whole book to answer this question. To begin with, we have to realise that "Europe" and the EU are not synonyms. I, for one, am very "European" but very hostile to current European institutions. I believe that the European construction has, from the very beginning, occurred despite common sense. Four major mistakes have been made: 1) To have started from the standpoint of economy and trade instead of politics and culture. The idea behind it must have been that economical citizenship would automatically result in a political citizenship. 2) To have created Europe starting from above (The Brussels Commission) instead of starting from the bottom, according to the subsidiarity principle or the sufficient jurisdiction principle. 3) To have privileged a hasty expansion to incorporate ill-prepared countries instead of focusing on the deepening of the existing political structures. 4) To have never clearly defined Europe's borders, nor stated the purposes of the European construction: is it to create a Europe-market or a Europe-political power? A free-trade area or an autonomous force that would also constitute the centre of culture and civilisation? The European Union of today is more or less ruined, powerless, and paralysed. As it has not succeeded in conserving any of its initial purpose, it is as if struck with amnesia and drained of its energy. Social pathologies resulting from massive and uncontrolled immigration are bound to spread.

Western Europe is the most seriously affected. Therefore, I feel that the future is rather in the hand of Central and Eastern Europe, if not Russia.

Andrei Raevsky*

"The era of empires is now going away with the last one finally crashing down."

KONRAD STACHNIO: How do you see the future of extremist Islam a la ISIS in the context of the fall of "liberal democracies"?

ANDREI RAEVSKY: "Liberal democracies" created extremist Islam in the first place. Wahabism, which is the ideological movement which eventually gave birth to modern Takfirism was created by the USA, the Kingdom of Saudi Arabia and Israel. The U.S. really organized the Takfiris by bringing together the distinct groups, the Saudis financed it and Israel supported it. You know what the biggest enemy of extremist Islam is? Real traditional Islam, be it Sunni or Shia. By the way, the Takfiris reserve a very special hatred towards all those Muslims who do not share their views. In the West we are told that the genocidal nutcases a la al-Qaeda/ISIS/al-Nusra/etc hate "our way of life." That is true, but what is always forgotten is that they hate other Muslims much, MUCH more. The best and easiest way to get rid of these Takfiris would be to support Russia, China, Iran and Hezbollah who have done more to crush Takfiris than anybody else. And if folks in the West really want to hate Russia, China, Iran and Hezbollah, and they simply cannot imagine showing support for them, then—fine! At least stop helping the Takfiris! That won't happen, of course. So first the Empire will have to crash. Then its most obscene and ugliest by-products (I think of the pseudo-Islamic state, of course, but also Kosovo and the Zionist entity) will quickly die out as they only can exist as long as the Empire keep them alive.

*****ANDREI RAEVSKY is a Swiss-born military analyst. He worked as a specialist for the operational-level training of the General Staff of Swiss armed forces and with the UN Institute for Disarmament Research (UNIDIR) where he specialized in peacekeeping tactics and operations. Raevsky is the founder of the widely read blog, "The Vineyard of the Saker."**

KS: Could you elaborate on the Arctic Circle and possible conflict in this context?

AR: The Arctic will be the place of a major economic and political struggle not only due to its immense riches, but also thanks to climate change which had a major impact on the Arctic. However, I don't see any military conflict taking place there because basically the Arctic is "Russkies land": Russia is SO far ahead in Arctic civilian and military capabilities that it really leaves no chance for the western militaries at all. Simply put, Russia already has all she needs to fight a major battle in the Arctic. The Empire has almost nothing (true, a few units go and live in the Canadian north for a while, and some U.S. nuclear-powered submarines patrol under the ice, but should it come to a shooting war, both would be destroyed very soon).

KS: Are we currently dealing with the emergence of the Persian, Russian and Chinese empires, which in their nature are traditional empires? Do you think that events in the Middle East involving these parties have an eschatological and spiritual dimension, not just a utilitarian one? And can only these three combined empires fight the so-called great Satan—modernism? etc.

AR: No, not at all. The era of empires is now going away with the last one finally crashing down. Not only that, but there is no constituency in the countries you mention to return to an imperial model. The Iranians, Russians and Chinese people have come to realize that empires are deadly parasites for their "host-nation," which inevitably gets impoverished internally and hated externally. I strongly believe that what these countries want now is a 1) multi-polar world in which 2) relations between states are regulated by international law and 3) each country has the right to develop socially/economically/spiritually/ideologically/culturally/etc. as it wishes. Remember, even right now we have Iran, which is a Shia Islamic republic, Russia, which is a conservative neoliberal federation and China is a weird and unique blend of capitalism and Marxism. They are already totally different!).

KS: How do you see the future of Turkey and Saudi Arabia?

AR: For decades these two countries totally depended on the AngloZionist Empire. Now this empire is falling apart. So both Turkey and Saudi Arabia will have to manage a very difficult, and even dangerous, transition from the status of vassal state of the USA to being more or less independent regional actors. In the long term, this is better for both countries, as becoming a credible and more or less independent regional actor will imply that they ditch their current ideologies (Neo-Osmanism and Takfirism respectively). By the way, the Zionist entity known as "Israel" will face exactly the same problem, but exacerbated by an even more rabid (and racist) ideology: Jewish supremacism (whether of the secular, Zionist, or the religious Talmudic, type). In the past, these countries got away with murder (often literally) only because Uncle Shmuel would protect them. Now that this protection will gradually but inevitably die down, they will have to stop alienating all their neighbors and they will have to accept that they are but "one amongst equal" nations of the region. Either that, or they will simply implode in an orgy of violence (plenty of potential for that in all three of these countries)

KS: How do you imagine the future of the Arab world in the Middle East? What political model could work here realistically and what are the biggest challenges in your opinion?

AR: The Levant is inherently multi-cultural and multi-religious. Thus, any ideology which plans to impose itself on everybody else is destined to fail. The biggest challenge for that region is how to manage the transition of Turkey, Saudi Arabia and Israel from imperial vassals to civilized and independent nations. Frankly I am moderately optimistic in the case of Turkey, rather pessimistic in the case of the KSA, and very pessimistic in the case of Israel, which has the most narcissistic and even psychopathic culture of the three. In that latter case, the transition will only become possible by the total military defeat of the IDF (which, I am confident, will happen, sooner rather than later).

KS: Hezbollah's activity has recently been banned in Germany. How do you perceive Hezbollah's future and its relationship with the Orthodox Church?

AR: Hezbollah does not have an specific relationship to the Orthodox Church as a whole simply because while the Orthodox Church is One in Her faith, organizationally all local Orthodox churches are independent. However, it is clear that in both Lebanon and Syria Hezbollah has proven itself to be an objective protector of the Orthodox Church. This is why, for example, why Latin Christians (aka "Catholics") mostly left Syria forever, while Orthodox Christians mostly stayed. Not only that, but while there are no non-Muslims in Hezbollah (for a very logical reason, as this is an openly Muslim party), there are Christians in the Hezbollah-headed Resistance (Moqawama). In fact, the first person to sacrifice herself by blowing up a car at an Israeli checkpoint (during the invasion of Lebanon) came from an Orthodox family. Hezbollah has always declared that it will not seek to impose an Islamic rule over non-Muslims and, so far, Hezbollah has always delivered on that promise. Finally, both Arab

Christians and Arab Muslims fully realize that the only real danger comes from the "modern Crusaders," to use a term often heard in the Middle-East.

KS: Would you agree that we will be dealing with a Cold War between Russia and China? That this war will be much more dangerous than the original Cold War? Are we heading toward a greater escalation of the conflict where at its very beginning we might expect Hybrid Wars, Biological Wars, Cyber Wars between U.S.-China-Russia? Can these scenarios be used due to the lack of capability for open conflict? Due to the weakening of the economy and thus the funding of the U.S. military? Will the U.S. have to relocate its military resources from Europe to the Pacific as a result of a bad budget situation?

AR: No, I don't see that at all. Russia and China are now strategic allies and they work together towards the same goal of a multi-polar world. There will be no conflict between these two nations because what they really have become today are symbionts: they need each other like two puzzle pieces: precisely because they are so totally different that this makes them ideal partners. Now the U.S. will continue to wage a rabid ideological and economic war against both countries, not so much because the U.S. really hopes to prevail, but because that is all it can do anyway (and it is expedient for internal political reasons). But militarily it's now truly "game over," especially against Russia, and soon against China too.

KS: Do you think Europe will be heading towards consolidating with China and Russia or will it face an almost complete loss of importance? Are we dealing with the end of the so-called open societies?

AR: I believe that the EU as we see it today will implode, and that will result in a lot of "regime change" amongst most EU member states. Likewise, the loss of U.S. influence (which is still almost total today—the EU is still a U.S. colony) will also accelerate this trend. As a result, Europe (the continent, as opposed to the EU as an organization) will have to reinvent itself. It won't be the "good old 'White'" Europe" (most immigrants will stay and adapt, even if that takes time), but it will be a new kind of society, something which has already happened in the European past. And since Russia+China have so much more to offer than the EU, these European nations will eventually turn towards the East. I would say that for Russia this will be a very good development, but hardly a very important one: Russia sees her future in the South, the East and the North. As for the West, mostly what Russia hopes for is that it finally accepts the existence of Russia as a different civilizational model and stops trying to invade and subvert Russia. After 1000 years of western imperialism and overt and covert wars against Russia, that would be a most welcome change. And if you wonder—nobody in Russia has any desire or interest in invading anybody, least of all countries which only exist thanks to western financial aid and which, if left alone, only represent mostly irrelevant and poor nations that Russia does not want to feed (especially true of the three Baltic statelets, the Ukraine and Poland).

KS: Would you agree with Edward Snowden that now with the virus and its subsequent phases, will a so-called technological architecture of oppression be built?

AR: Yes. The way this works is like this: first, a state declares a national emergency, then the state develops new capabilities (legal and technological) to, supposedly, deal with the threat. But then these new capabilities stay engagement-capable forever. This is a real danger, not only in the West, but also for Russia and China (which has already gone a long way down that road).

KS: Do you think that big changes in human history have always caused conflict? So, are we waiting for a big conflict due to huge changes caused by this virus?

AR: Major conflicts typically result in major changes; the opposite, however, is not necessarily true. Pandemics can (and have) resulted in major changes without any wars. Right now (May 1st, 2020) the biggest danger is an AngloZionist attack on Iran. But that is not inevitable. Whereas the pandemic-induced changes have already begun, and a lot of them will be irreversible.

KS: Would you agree with the statement that the only chance for a U.S. victory is to wreck globalization? China is one of the great beneficiaries of globalization.

AR: I agree with your latter statement about China, but I don't agree with the former one: the so-called globalization did make it possible for the U.S. to plunder the planet of its most precious resources while peddling its worthless fiat currency. The problem is that in the past, the dollar was first backed by gold, then it was backed by oil, then eventually only by aircraft carriers. Now that the latter are little more than expensive sitting ducks for Russian and Chinese (and probably soon Iranian) hypersonic missiles, the dollar is really backed by nothing. Yes, right now the dollar is strong, it is a "safer" reserve currency in times of crisis, but that is only a bubble (just look at how the stock market is booming while the real economy is agonizing in free fall!). Sooner or later the dollar will tank, and there is nothing the U.S. will be able to do to stop it. It is just a matter of time.

KS: Do you think that if the economic system collapses, countries like Russia and China will have national military dictatorships or military socialism to deal with the chaos? Will Europe and the U.S. plunge into chaos without such management at this time?

AR: Russia will not become a dictatorship, the Russian people have absolutely no desire to lose all the precious freedoms they have obtained at great (even exorbitant) costs. The most likely evolution for Russia will be to become a uniquely Russian form of "authoritarian democracy," meaning that what the Russians call the "verticality of power" will remain strong, but people power will still remain crucial to the nation. I am not competent to speak about the possible future of China. As for Europe and the U.S., they are in very different positions: Europe needs to recover real sovereignty, while the U.S. (as a nation) needs to ditch the Empire and become a "normal" (if still very powerful and rich) nation. Both Europe and the USA will do infinitely better as soon as they will liberate themselves from the AngloZionist imperial yoke.

KS: Do you think that this is the final end of the capitalist-liberal west? Would you agree that when Europe and the U.S. realize that they can no longer exploit humanity, there will be a war?

AR: Yes. For all their other (mostly prescriptive) misguided opinions, Marx and Lenin were both quite correct when they declared that capitalism was not viable. Imperialism is the highest/latest/last stage of capitalism. For example, capitalism is both deeply immoral (it claims that the sum of our individual greeds will result in some optimal society) and deeply misguided (you cannot have infinite growth, which is a pre-condition for both usury and capitalism, in a finite environment: our planet). There is a very good reason why the original Jewish faith, Christianity and Islam all forbade usury. Our planet "forgot" this and now we are paying the consequences of our foolishness and arrogance ("we know better than God"). At the end of the day, capitalism is a satanic ideology which will either destroy mankind or vanish. Which of the two happens depends on all of us.

KS: What advice would you give to people in cities without jobs and without any prospects. Are we facing something like civil war scenario in Europe, the United States and the rest of the world?

AR: Violence is a distinct possibility, even if it is not certain. I don't have any special advice, especially for those who are weak, poor or otherwise fragile. I can offer a few basic suggestions:

1. If you can, move to a small town. Big cities will be the most dangerous, followed by isolated homes away from everything.
2. Try to prepare by reaching out to your family, friends, neighbors, etc. There is safety in numbers.
3. If that is legal where you live, try to legally arm and train (only the basics) your family and yourself in the defensive use of a firearm. Get as many weapons of self-defense and ammunition as you can reasonably afford (both will also become precious currencies in case of violence).
4. Don't freak out when you hear of crazy stuff happening in big cities. Think *locally* as your local conditions will determine your chances of survival and conditions thereof.
5. Try to "collect skills" (medical, agricultural, etc.) amongst your neighbors. Don't be caught off-guard alone.
6. If you need to relocate, do it *before* the crisis explodes as "bugging out" can be much more dangerous than hunkering down in the location you know best.
7. If you have any money you can set aside, deposit some in your bank, keep some cash in/near our house and get some gold/silver (even small amounts) and carefully hide that in separate location. Don't put all your eggs in the same basket.

KS: Are we heading towards the fall of liberalism, individualism, globalism and capitalism? Or maybe instead we are just entering the era of real "global management" of the kind we have never seen before? What do you think about the new ideological concepts that can be real alternative to this new emerging world?

AR: I believe that the former is much more likely to happen because the capitalism/globalist model is unsustainable. The pandemic is just the latest evidence of that, but there are so many other factors including economic, social, cultural, ecologic, economic, etc. etc. etc. Fundamentally, capitalism is built on growth. We live on a finite planet. Absolutely ANYTHING which requires infinite growth will act like a malignant tumor for the planet and for humanity. Until we manage to colonize our solar system (which ain't happening anytime soon!) we need a stable, no-growth economic system. Everything else will just degrade the environment we live in. The tree huggers are right: we need sustainability, desperately!

KS: We are now entering an environment very similar to that before World War II: trade wars, currency wars, and Great Depression. How do you see, in this context, the situation in the Middle East in the long run?

AR: The Zionist entity (aka "Israel") is built on two core principles: racism and violence. That is not something viable in the long run. In fact, the worse "Israel" acts, the stronger the Arabs become (anybody familiar with dialectical materialism will see that the Zionist entity did create its own contradiction in the form of Hezbollah and Iran). Besides, Israel is vitally dependent on the USA, which is now agonizing (and the EU is all talk, it can't defend Israel either). No, Ayatollah Khomeini was right—the Zionist regime will inevitably disappear, and it will be replaced by a "one person one vote" single state which will not be based on racist delusions.

KS: How do you perceive the role of China, Russia and the U.S. in the post-virus world in the long run?

AR: Russia and China are in a symbiotic relationship which the Chinese call a "Strategic comprehensive partnership of coordination for the new era" and the Russian refer to as a "crucial alliance." These two countries (and others, such as Iran) will shape the future international system which will have the following characteristics:

1. It will be multi-polar.
2. Each country will be able to pursue its economic, social, political, religious, spiritual and cultural path. There shall be no "universal models" imposed on anybody.
3. Relations between countries will be organized according to international law, not violence.
4. The sovereignty of each nation shall not be infringed in any way.

As for the USA, assuming it does not break up into several successor states, it will become a major and powerful country, but also a "normal" one like, say, Russia.

KS: How do you perceive new movements in so-called megacities? Are we heading towards so-called urban terrorism? Will it be a combination of urban guerillas with technological dissidents able to resist ubiquitous surveillance? What do you think about the ideological concepts that they can adapt for their goals? Will these mobilized people of big cities remind us in their struggle of the people of Iraq or Afghanistan, for example? Can they be a real and threatening force to an increasingly militarized apparatus of the State or to Technocratism and so-called Hard power?

AR: Cities exist for a reason: civilization needs them and I don't see that changing. However, how our cities are organized might very well change. Working remotely make so much sense that this trend will only continue further. As for surveillance, it is just like every other technology: it will be used against people and people will learn the way to resist it. This is what all technological innovations have created in history—a response making it possible to defeat them. Like, say, universal snooping on email resulted in some people developing very strong encryption technologies. The cycle of "attack-defense" will only stop if/when humanity ends. Until then, this will never change. As for megacities, I think that they will happen more often in poor and struggling countries than in rich ones. Decentralization makes much more sense for advanced societies.

KS: In 2018, at West Point, Dr. James Giordano gave a lecture entitled "Neuroweapons." In it he noted that the currently developed sciences of neuro-imaging of the brain and data analysis from the brains of entire populations allow far-reaching social control and open entire populations to neuro-attacks, and ultimately neuro-wars. Similar systems are already being developed in the laboratories of private companies and are being tested in the civil market for employee control. Scientists from DARPA and related military agencies are beginning to mention openly that these systems will eventually lead to massive modification of the human psyche. Will the information war soon move from the media to a completely new, unexplored area of human unconsciousness? Will the psyche itself become the target of the attacks, which, as emphasized in military studies, "has no barrier" and will be taken over by those best prepared for this war? How do you imagine the resistance movement in this context?

AR: I am not an engineer, I am a military analyst. I cannot tell you who is researching what, where and why. But I DO know that, as of today, neuro-weapons are not deployed and forces have not been trained to use them. What can happen in the future I cannot predict, but right now this is not a reality.

KS: Do you think we are heading towards a global revolution?

AR: Yes, inevitably, as the face of our planet will very much change with the end of the last empire, the AngloZionist one.

Carine Hutsebaut*

"The coming generations are seriously detached from humankind, and that's a big problem."

KONRAD STACHNIO: Explain this idea of disconnected wiring in today's children.

CARINE HUTSEBAUT: I come from quite a stable family with a strict father who was an army officer, and a mother who stayed home most of the time with five children. So, a stable household. But how many stable households do we have now? A lot of children are cut off from binding with their mothers at around three months of age, and then that baby belongs to the state because you already have to go out to work! Before, one loan would have been enough to keep a family going with five, six, seven children, but now we see that even if you both work, it's not enough to get everything paid. So that's social destruction, where children, as soon as they are born, just don't know where they belong. In fact, the baby is not lacking anything, since everything is there for them, so they aren't hungry. The child is taken care of, and all the most expensive things are put into the nursery—but on an emotional level, it is cold. So, these children–I don't say all of them–but these children are already raised with disconnected wiring inside them. You can see it, of course, in shocking criminal cases. On a general level, the coming generations are seriously detached from humankind, and that's a big problem; they feel empty, and emptiness is one of the cruelest feelings that borderline people have, that emptiness they feel inside.

---

*CARINE HUTSEBAUT is a Belgian psychotherapist, criminologist, and author of the books *Child Hunters: Requiem of a Child-killer*, *Profile of a Serial Killer*, *Little Sinners: The Church and Child Trafficking*, *Profession: Profiler*, and *He is still amongst us*. Her work has been the basis and inspiration for the making of multiple movies.

And you can heal it easily, but it takes some courage. These people should send their children to go out and help in very damaged countries such as Africa, for instance. Leave them there for three or six months, and they will relearn the values of humanity. I have younger people in therapy who were lost on drugs and all that. The parents are desperate because the help given to them is not real help. The first thing I ask these parents is if they'd agree to send their son or their daughter for one month during school vacation to another country, where they'd have to help rebuild a cemetery or an elderly care facility in Hungary, or in Tunisia, free of charge? They have to cover the costs and fund a place to sleep. These kids are from all over the world and come together in small groups to do this work via a Christian organization that does this in Belgium, and they've been organizing it for fifty or sixty years already. And you see, when these youngsters come back, they've completely changed. They've been involved in something, and they were useful. Now, they're not useful, they're not doing anything. Anyway, it's the parents who give them too much of an impression that they are gods. All this plays a role in why people want to fill in that emptiness, and instead of doing it with reconstructive or creative things, for some reason, they take the easy way: porn.

KS: Yes, that's the really easy way, because you just get your laptop and click "enter," and that's it. End of story. You don't have to even go outside of your apartment.

CH: No. Absolutely not. And not only in the porn business. It's like that in Malaysia, all these "factories" where they're selling babies for adoption. It is horrific. Many young pregnant girls are immediately taken in, just as I described in my book, *Little Sinners: The Church and Child Trafficking*. It's a market like you just can't believe. These places know they have corrupt police and so they have all their people sitting in a pyramid. For these children, it's going to be even impossible to find their mothers. When a woman is pregnant and she's about to give birth, the adoptive mother is right next to her already. So the baby goes with the "mother" who buys the child, and there's no connection at all because all the papers are completed with "name unknown" for the birth mother. You have there a tremendous, profound cut in human life. It starts right there. These females who are pregnant are sometimes just twelve or thirteen years old, that's all, getting pregnant in little rooms everywhere. So you could just order a baby like you can order porn or a hamburger or your pizza. You can have everything; it's all for sale because of globalization. It's utopian to think like this, and it's destroying everything. In globalization and this new world order, you, as Konrad Stachnio, do not exist. You are the group. So if you want to take the initiative you are taking now, talking to people, writing a book and all that, well, you won't be able in a few years if this goes on. They take away your identity, and if you don't know who you are, then the biggest hole in a human being's existence is feeling. If they can't feel, they are lost. So, they need help to go back to a more profound, older feeling, the feeling of being alive. The love feeling comes later when you're okay with yourself, when you have a group around you. And this evolution that we now see means many people feel the unbearable emptiness of being nothing at all. That's the feeling. It isn't true, but that's the feeling they have. Then they dig deeper and deeper, and then they come to this lowest level where they are cutting themselves in order to feel, really feel, because they don't feel. Then in even lower levels, they are cutting up children, drinking their blood, imagining that they will live longer–to do what though, in their emptiness? Isn't it better to die early? It's just my impression. What we see is a psychopathic, sociopathic society. We are developing into that. You wouldn't imagine doing any of this if you lived in a small community of 3,000 people. For some reason, the human being needs a tribe.

When did they first start with all their serial killers in the United States? "In Europe, we don't have them." It's easier not to connect things, so that's what they say. "We don't have that." But in the United States, yes, they have them and they admit it. So, when did all that start? It started with the dissolving of the small cities, towns. It started there. And it started with the connection of people having a car, because then you could move around. With a horse and a carriage, it's much slower. Everybody would see you. But now, the anonymity of being in big, big cities, and the fact that you can take transport… If I want to kill a child, I'll just take a plane, and in six hours I'll be in New York. I'll kill a child, and then I'll come back. When do you think they will find me? I can do it in, say, 24 hours. Nobody will find me. So we have the possibility of transportation and the lack of social control, because when you had a small town and a car came in, everybody would have seen it. Now, nobody cares, in a city. You see thousands of people passing by. There is no social control at all, which means that children often are taken from the street in full daylight. And nobody sees it.

KS: But on the other hand, we have plenty, millions of cameras, everywhere. In London, for example, you have a camera on every street.

CH: Yes, it can be very useful to determine if somebody's alibi holds true or not. If somebody is suspected of a crime and they say, "I was sitting at home watching television, and working on my computer," well, they used to just leave it like that. But now, with cameras, they can see. Now, they can say, "This car was in the neighborhood of the crime, but he claimed he was at home." So it can be useful. But is this really the society we want to live in? Before you had this, other people were the cameras in these small, local towns; they kept you on track. Not these cameras. It's to give people the feeling that they're protected, that they're safe. Which is not the case at all.

KS: So emptiness, from your perspective, is the main reason for looking for fulfillment, such as in the porn industry or in other fields like pedophilia or whatever else?

CH: Yes. But that doesn't mean that everybody who has this tremendous emptiness is going in this direction. But you have a very clear cut between those doing good work all the time—the KISAs, Knights in Shining Armor, always helping people which is also a kind of filling in of emptiness, but the good side—and then you have the other side of the coin, the bad side. They couldn't fill in that emptiness without very strong death threats. Be it for themselves or projected on the victim–by proxy, we call it–it doesn't matter. It's one of the most exciting things for them, to have that godlike feeling. "You will remain alive if I tell you to. You will die when I tell you." That gives a tremendous adrenaline rush. When it's gone, they fall back into this tremendous black hole. And the reason for that is—most of the time—the first twelve years of their lives. The human brain is developing until age twenty-one, and it makes the connection between the right side, where everything is more material, rational, and all that, and the left side which is emotional. In younger years, bridges are built from one side of the brain to the other. In California, they tested adults who had been victims of child abuse and rape and torture in their childhoods, and there they saw these connections hadn't been built, or very few of them.

Is this an illness? No, it isn't. Everyone has a choice. It would be a bit too easy to say, "Yeah, but my connections," and all that. No, no. You always have a choice. It's about the pleasure they gain in torturing others, which in fact is a projection of what they have been in themselves. Many youngsters don't experience problems anymore. I don't mean all of them, but many, because the parents are always there to solve their issues. These kids do not learn how to cope with something going wrong. Then you come to this sociopathic level now, on the other hand, and that is quite scary. You never hear—in the mainstream media or on television—anyone speaking about the connection of sex and love, sex and respect. And this is not a coincidence. All of these programs you have all over the world now, from Love Island and all that, are bringing the level, the frequency of the human being down, down, down. Without knowing it, they make you stupid. Stupid, and you adapt to other norms. These norms, these lines are disappearing, and everybody's lost. So everything is allowed.

KS: This is my impression as well, that everything is allowed right now.

CH: For certain groups. For others, no.

KS: For certain groups, yeah, definitely. But it's becoming more and more….

CH: Evident.

KS: Yes, evident on every level, because people don't care anymore about anything.

CH: It is this minority that is now telling the majority how to think. It is this minority. I saw a manifestation some months ago in New York, with the "Chicken Dance." It is disgusting. It is a disgrace to humankind, to be there with your whole ass in the camera. It is so perverted. Our race is much higher than that; our frequencies are much higher, but they pull them down because they're especially bombarding the youth with all these things and giving the impression that this is the new normal. So we cannot put all the blame on the parents. The schools, media, all have their role in the destruction of humanity. Yes, there will still be humans, creatures, but is this humanity? There is a balance between rational thinking, feeling, and sexuality. It's all gone.

KS: If that is gone, then would you agree with me that everything on the dark web will be legitimized more and more in society? For example, twenty years from now, can you envisage pedophilia on YouTube, renting out kids to pedophile networks? "Okay, yeah, today I rented my kids to a bunch of pedophiles and made 2,000 Euros for just one day." That's a little futuristic and sick…but can you envisage things going that way?

CH: It is like that. This is not the future. We are in this already. But, no; pedophilia is the only thing that will shock people, because it has been examined by anthropologists who went into basic tribes in the Amazon, Central America, where they studied these groups. Everybody knows in these tribes that if you touch a child in an indecent way, you are immediately judged by the whole tribe. This is very important, not only for the criminal who touches a child, but especially for the child, because then the child will not stay in confusion for years. "What was this? Was I wrong? Did I do something bad? Am I a bad child?" You can get them out of this, eventually, out of their confusion of being raped. Immediately, the child sees that the whole tribe—society—will condemn the wrongdoer. The wrongdoer is expelled from the tribe for a year, two years, six months; it depends on the tribal elders.

Now, elderly people in all societies are disposable. Take their money and it's done. In other, more—mentally and not materially—developed tribes and groups, money has no meaning. What you now see is that everything is around money, and people try to buy their happiness with it. But that's not possible. It's already in the first book, *Child Hunters*. Many parents were renting their children to child sex abusers for the money. So how can you be surprised when these children grow up full of hate and emptiness and confusion? They feel, "There is something I have to feel, but I can't. I know it's there but can't reach it." And then they need something to put the fire in the ignition. Then for a moment, they feel. They feel scared because somebody can come in. They can feel excited. "I am God. Now I can do whatever I want." The little Hitlers, the little dictators… later on, they say, "There was nobody there for me," which is true. Yeah, there are organizations, sure, and all kinds of people knowing nothing about what a human being is and how vulnerable a child is. They think from their adult thinking, not from the thinking of a child. And then, yes, you come to a place where it is not acceptable but tolerated, because you can't do anything about it. But it is proven in our DNA, it is genetically proven, that humans will always reject child abuse. Always. That's the only point of light we have. Genetically, we will never accept child sex abuse.

KS: But then we have this case of PIE, an organization called Pedophile Information Exchange, actually run by a pedophile. I saw an interview with a guy around sixty years old on a TV documentary, *60 Minutes*. In this interview, this man said, "We should have access to children because we know better than anyone how to deal with them. We are more sensitive and have more compassion for them. We are more connected with them, so we should have normal access to kids."

CH: Yeah, sure. When you hear somebody say that, Konrad, ask them to explain, "How come when a child starts to have pubic hair, you don't love him/her anymore?" When these children start to have hair under their arms and in their pubic areas, they don't want them. So much for their love and compassion. I've seen hundreds of these people, follow hundreds of them, and it's pure, pure pedo talk. They never, ever talk about what the child feels. It is their entitlement, their right to take the child's sexuality. And why are our governments allowing this? Because they know that the younger a child is, the more they are sexually harmed, it's energetically beautiful. That's sexuality, not sex—I mean that when you break a child in this period, in these years, they are the perfect slaves. Because don't forget that from the moment you're born, you're followed in our system; you get assigned a number and a value. "This person will cost that much in psychiatric care." They all know that. "But we can exploit them for that much money." There is a price on all of us. They come into the home to see if you take good care of your child, and then when the child goes to school, they are followed with a fairly clear program designed to keep them down. Everything is noted down in books from the moment you're born, so the authorities have access to children they can use for "murder tasks," for the army. There's already a whole book on you in the social system. When they need stupid men to join the police, they are selected based on who they have been from birth. "Is this a good slave, somebody we can use to take risks, to enter a burning building?" They know all this. They know. So don't talk about cameras in the streets. We are all followed up, and whenever they can use us, they will. And we are not even aware of it. I wonder how many have false diplomas and surround themselves with an aura of an all-knowing professor? But it's not that piece of paper that shows that you're a good professor. It is the things you do and what you stand for. But we are all blinded by that. Uniforms, doctors' clothes, stethoscopes. All these are symbols for us of, "this is somebody who knows what he's doing," while maybe every night, he rapes his child. The outer, visible things, we are too attached to them. Look at what people do. Look how people speak. Listen. What kind of words do they use? This is all true, what they are saying, because our society has become such a lie. It's difficult to live in it. A big challenge.

KS: Friends who are much younger than me feel the same. They feel that something really, deeply wrong is going on with other young people. They don't have connections with other young people. There is no common language.

CH: No. But connections are becoming lost everywhere. It is partly due to age, but also there are people of the same age where all this is still in turmoil. Many people of your age cannot talk about what's going on in the world because they don't give a shit. There is a disconnection between you and people of your own age already, and then you also have disconnections with your parents. All these generations seem to disconnect completely from one another.

KS: Yeah, that's true. But right now, there is a movement toward drugs.

CH: I know. To legalize it.

KS: Maybe to fulfill this emptiness which we talk about? People feel empty, and that's why they are looking for drugs, for dance. I see this very widely, that there are a lot of parties right now involving drugs, drawing a lot of

people to them. Maybe that's one of the few things they can do, just dance and take drugs, to feel connected to others?

CH: I'm wondering why more people don't go back to the basic, most vulnerable human need to just be there, connecting to each other, doing something good for somebody else? Everybody's thinking "me, me, me, I, myself." Yet it is something children learn from the age of four, to have empathy and compassion for another child. It is getting stuck there, getting stuck already in nursery. It's not all the fault of the parents. It's the system. It's absolutely the system, and it's no accident. No, this is not a conspiracy. Just look around you. Everybody sees it, everybody feels it, but nobody can put their finger on it. "What is this? What is going on?" Now you're not even dead and they're fighting for your heritage. You're not even dead. So the connection of mother to child is broken. The connection of child to father is seriously broken. Many women are single parents. You need a male in the family, but what do they do with the males? They make them into females. And it goes on and on, and from one day to another.

It is like the thing with the frog. If you take a frog and you have boiling water and just throw the frog in, immediately it leaps out. But if you put the frog in cold water, put the fire under the pot, then it gets warmer slowly, slowly, and by the time it feels "Whoa, this is going wrong," it's too late. It can't jump out. And that's what they do with the whole system. Slowly, slowly heating the water. For most people, it will be too late to react. I'm sorry. "It's okay. We have everything. We have food, we have peace, we have a little sun now in Belgium. Everything is peaceful. Why should I bother?" Well, there are some people, like you and others–many others, more and more–who stand up for those who don't, because they can't, because they are not aware, because they are cowards. It doesn't matter. We need people to stand up. But these people have to be honest. We can turn this around quite fast by learning to say no to those who do not deserve a yes. When they come to my door with their smart meters rubbish, I say, "I don't need one." "Yes, but this is a smart—" "I don't want smart things," I say, and I slam the door. I don't want them. Say no. People have to learn to say no, and they know inside–not even deep inside–they know inside this is not okay. But they're afraid, and they're already slaves, and "I don't want trouble, so okay." And then they feel bad. Remember one thing, Konrad. People need to know this. There are consequences in every decision you make. If you say, "Yes, I'll let them put the smart meter in," you will be frustrated. You will end up hating yourself because you did not have the courage to say, "No, I don't want it." That's the consequence of your decision. When you say, "No, you are not coming in. This is my house. My meter is working perfectly, and I don't want to contribute to the system of smart meters" and then you slam the door, you know there could be consequences. You're not even sure, because that was six months ago. Well, I never saw them back. I think they would start with the sheep. The "sheepest" sheep who will say, "yes, yes." They avoid those who say no, and more and more people are doing this. If I know the consequence could be that I get a fee or something, or even if it's a trial, I don't care. But at least I've been honest with myself and told the truth, and that's it. There are always consequences in every decision you make. Take the consequences along with your decision. It's not that difficult.

Catherine Austin Fitts*

"The war is not between the U.S. and China. The war is between the people who want complete central control and the people who want freedom."

KONRAD STACHNIO: Elon Musk said that people have to connect themselves with the machines, we have to connect our brains with machines, because otherwise we're going to be totally irrelevant in the future. How would you comment on that?

CATHERINE AUSTIN FITTS: What I would say is there's a new video out with Rupert Sheldrake called *The Rebirth of Nature*. He talks about how, literally for the last several hundred years, we've been in a mode which he describes as the machine model. I think what Musk is saying is, if you want to keep the machine model going, you need to accelerate your composting of human beings. [Laughs.] Instead of allowing human beings the freedom to access all dimensions and all living intelligence, you need to hook them up to the machine to keep the machine going. It really comes down to: are we creative beings who have sovereignty and freedom, or are we compost for a centralizing machine?

If you look at the technology battle that's been going on for the last 20 years, the people centralizing control are trying to stop everybody from resonating with life and each other and the divine intelligence, and get everybody to resonate in the machine. And of course, the big fight we're having now is Mr. Gates and his syndicate want to basically inject you—I call it the injection fraud. They want to inject you with enough technology that they can have the equivalent of

---

*CATHERINE AUSTIN FITTS is the president of Solari, Inc., publisher of the *Solari Report*. Catherine has designed and closed over $25 billion of transactions and investments to date and has led portfolio and investment strategy for $300 billion of financial assets and liabilities.

a Microsoft operating system within you and plug you right into the machine. Musk was just jumping the curve. Gates is being a little bit more subtle, but Musk was basically saying, "I want to slap a Neuralink in you and hook you up." It's one way you can go. If you want to run the machine model on a centralized basis, the economic thing to do is to say, "I have robots, I have humans; the integration is going to be a cyborg. Let me basically redo my human systems to fit the robots in, so they don't have to create new laws, new taxation systems, new labor systems. I'll just integrate them in together, and then we'll see who's more productive for what." If you're running a machine and trying to make the machine produce as big a dividend as possible, if the planet's a REIT—do you know what a REIT is? A real estate investment trust. What you're trying to do is create—during slavery, they used to call it a whipping machine—create the most productive whipping machine you can come up with. Then it makes sense. But it's a slavery model.

I think Musk is basically—the problem with a highly centralized group of people is they tend to talk to each other. You always say people who play in a rigged game get stupid. But to me, it's a vision which is contradictory to reality and how life works and what intelligence really is. If you look at the ability we have to think and create in a hyper-dimensional fashion, I just think Musk is missing—the speed of processing is not the only form of intelligence.

KS: How can we survive in that kind of environment? We don't have too many choices as normal individuals, normal people. They are orchestrating these scenarios, this environment for us.

CAF: I completely disagree that you don't have too much choice. I think they have a vision. I can't say that Gates's vision is the same as Musk's vision, but I think the vision of continuing the machine model is fundamentally psychopathic and insane. It won't work. It will fail. Absolutely it will fail. It's contradictory—if you look at the intelligence of the universe and the way life works, I can see why they feel they need to keep the machine model going. The problem is, the machine model needs to die. It doesn't work. It's not going to work. It's never going to work. You can accelerate the composting of the human race to get it to work, to extend its life some more, but ultimately it's a liquidating model. It's a draining model. It's not economically anywhere near as wealth-producing as a freedom model.

Now, we could have another conversation about how you can use artificial intelligence intelligently within a living model. That's a different conversation. But the model they're progressing on—have you ever read Carl Jung? Carl Jung has a great story. I'll tell it. I was in the city of London at an investment conference, and a British money manager stood up in the middle of this huge investment conference with the portraits looking down on us of the ancestors, and he told this story. This story was as follows—and if you go to Solari, you can find it. The title of the section is "Karma means you don't get away with anything." Anyway, he tells the story of a woman who came to see Jung, and she walks into Jung's office and she says, "I'm not going to give you my name because I'm only going to come once. I believe if I confess and tell my story, by confessing to you, I will clear my sins and be able to come back into society." Here was her story. Jung said she was dressed as a very wealthy person. She was clearly from the upper echelons of society. What she told Jung is how, as a young woman, she had gone to medical school. She was from a very wealthy family. She'd gone to medical school, become a doctor, and then had fallen in love with her best friend's husband. She couldn't reconcile the tension, so, being a doctor, she knew how to do it—she killed her best friend. She murdered her. Subsequently, she married the best friend's husband. She said from that moment on, everything went wrong. She had these beautiful wolfhound dogs; they died. She was an accomplished horsewoman; she couldn't ride them anymore. They'd buck, they'd throw her off. It went on and on. Her husband died right after she married him. She was pregnant. She had her daughter after her husband died. Her daughter hated her, and as soon as she could run off, as soon as she was old enough to run away, she ran away. She had no idea where her daughter was. She told Jung wherever she was, the birds would stop singing. She said the birds knew.

If you look at how intelligence—our intelligence is shared. All life is intelligent, and we share intelligence. There is some level, there's a spiritual level, where everything is known. There are no secrets. The name I put on top of it is, "Karma means you don't get away with anything," it's one of the greatest destroyers of our economic productivity right now—wherever we are, the birds have stopped singing for us. They know. All these lies and all this corruption, we think we're all being creative—you can double down on the force and you can double down on the lies to keep it going and keep it going, and that's what we're in. We're in a big double down. The centralizers are trying to stay in control. The problem is if you have a highly centralized model where the centralizers are in control and everything is secret, and the official reality is a complete science fiction story, that wastes an enormous amount of energy, and it keeps everybody deeply, deeply dumbed down. You're talking about a very energy-expensive and wasteful economic model.

The problem is, if you and I were to try to dream up the perfect models for a living system, we would unleash a huge wave of creativity—it could be very chaotic. A lot could go wrong. But one thing I can assure you is the people who would end up leading us would not be the people who are centralizing control.

The problem for the centralizers is how can they stay in control. If you have as many legal and financial and ethical liabilities—one of the reasons they're being so extreme right now is, if you look at what was coming out over the last two or three years, people like you bringing things to light—they can't keep a lid on the secrecy. They need much more invasive power and force to keep a lid on the secrecy. It's not working. And it's never going to work. If you really study physics, whether it's the biophysics of humans or other living beings, or how the different dimensions work, how spiritual intelligence works, it's just never going to work. It's hard to say it in a geopolitical analysis, but if you go back through history and you look at every time they've tried to centralize control, the same thing happens. It falls apart.

KS: Yeah. We have this example of the Soviet Union, when everything was centralized. But they have technology right now on the global scale. They have satellites. They have this global mind which is emerging right now, and everyone will be interconnected. It looks like it will be the end of privacy; we'll have none at all.

CAF: Here's my little message. If you look at how our intelligence works, if we absolutely use and access all of our intelligence, individually and collectively, there's not enough technology to overwhelm that. Now, obviously, we can all be slaughtered and killed. You can slaughter seven billion people, ultimately, with this technology. One of my favorite lines is from John Rappoport. He says hopelessness is an op, and it's planet-wide. Because one of their most important marketing tools is to be able to persuade you that 1,000 people should be able to control seven billion people because it's hopeless, it's too late, they've got it all locked down, there's nothing you can do. [Laughs.]

I have a wonderful Solari report with Thomas Meyer, who's an anthroposophist from Basel. It's on the story of Gideon, which is my favorite Bible story. I came to the story of Gideon because I had watched this phenomenon happen so much when I was in Wall Street in Washington, and I just saw it again and again. Then when I read the story of Gideon, I said, "Okay, that's it." The story of Gideon—I won't go through the whole thing. It's really worth studying the story because it's very marvelous. Gideon and his army come down the side of the mountain with lights and pitchers, light and vibration, to try to throw the Midianites out of Israel. The Midianites are very dangerous, big people. They have lots of weapons. The Midianites jump up in the middle of the dark and attack each other because they're so hateful and suspicious. One of the reasons I'm absolutely convinced the machine model will fail is because if you look at the factionalism—to hold a major global organization together requires lots of different attributes, but it requires a shared vision, a shared culture, a shared something. If you look at the machine model, it produces lots of psychopaths who are like the scorpion and the frog. They have to kill, they have to take. The Midianites will kill each other. Now, I don't underestimate the billions of people they can kill in the meantime before they implode or before they kill each other, but my vision is we need to continue to work on a new model. The machine model and the central banking warfare model, which is the financial component of the machine model, has been going on for 400 or 500 years. When an entire planet has to change an economic model that is that big and deep and involves that much stuff, it's very hard to do. It's a very messy process.

But my vision is we've got to come up with alternatives because when the machine model fails, the question is, how are we going to do this? If you look at one of the reasons that the people who are running the machine model get so cranky, it's because it's much harder to run the planet and govern all the resources than we think. I've spent a lot of time on the inside; it's a big job. It's a hard job, and I think that people running it feel very unappreciated in certain respects. The rest of us have to go to the brain damage and trouble of saying, okay, how do we do a better job?

KS: What kind of model do you propose: Sharing Economy, Universal Income or something like this? Do you think universal income is something realistic?

CAF: It's a much longer conversation, but I think it is absolutely imperative to reengineer the financial system bottom-up so that it can conform to places. I'll use the United States as an example. In the United States, if you want to learn about the transportation industry, it's real easy to find a lot of statistics and data, and the government data is organized around "here's how all the money works in transportation," or to get the annual reports for all the transportation companies and see how their money works in transportation. But if you said, "I want to see how the money in the county of New York works," particularly the government money or the public money, there's remarkably little disclosure, or of what's available, most people don't know where it is. So people are voting for their congressman or their senator or even their president without looking at the sources and uses of taxpayer money and how it's been spent and used.

In Latin America, when they got into real trouble in the '80s, everybody that started got sit in a room and said, "We're going to do the budgets." It's called participatory budgeting. They sat down and said, "We have to learn how the money works here." And it's not just the money; it's the time, the resources, all the human energy within a place. It has to be contiguous to life because life works in places. It works in environmental ecosystems. So you need to map out and understand your financial ecosystem contiguous with your environmental ecosystem, and they need to be harmonized. In fact, if you could literally—and it's very easy to do, theoretically—if you had a way of investing or trading in your place, you could then create a financial system where everybody could make a fortune healing the environment. Describe any ill—are communities environmentally toxic? Are they ugly? Are people poor? Is there inequality? All those things can be solved, not because people want to make the world better, but because they can make money making it better. In other words, they can align their financial incentives. Right now, too many people—if I were to take the average person with a stock portfolio and look at their stock portfolio, what I could show them is basically how they are financing their own prison and their own environmental destruction. But you could create systems that allow them to see what it is they're financing, how it impacts them and their family, and literally give them opportunities to make money solving whatever problem you define as we having. But to do that requires financial transparency, particularly with respect to government money, and the ability for everybody to participate in equity participation.

It's really funny; I worked with the top strategic planners for one of the largest corporations in America, and after the explosion of privatization and things opened up with technology in the '80s, they were trying to figure out how they could get all the different parts of the corporation to coordinate and work together and collaborate. I was sitting with the strategic planners and I said, "Look, you've got 125,000 software developers. Let's make a tool on your intranet, the internal internet, called Let's Help Bob." The chairman's name at the time was Bob. So the tool was Let's Help Bob, and the idea was see how all the different intellectual capital could connect to increase the value of the stock so Bob could please the shareholders. The strategic planner said, "This is fantastic! This is such a great idea. We're going to go back and propose it." So they go back, and they work in the chairman's office so they can immediately access the highest people. They proposed it. They came back the next month and said, "They hated the idea." I said, "Why?" They said, "All the employees would want stock." I said, "So? That's good, right?" "No." [Laughs.] They wanted to keep them out of it. The problem with letting everybody in to understand how the money works and participate in making the pie bigger is then a few people can't come in and rape the pie all for themselves. Over time, you're going to evolve a system where the people who create value are the people who are going to get it, as opposed to the central bankers. If what you're worried about is generating the biggest centralized dividend, you end up with a much smaller pie.

Anyway, you have to realign your financial system with your living systems and your environmental systems. We have designed the system to keep it place-blind and to have nonaccountability on much of the government money. The books in America are run on a secret basis. You're not allowed to see how the money works on tax money. It's quite extraordinary. I can explain it in great detail because I've spent a lot of time mapping out the system. If you go to missingmoney.solari.com and read "The Real Game of Missing Money," you'll learn all about it. But essentially, if a few central bankers can take all the tax dollars, spend it totally secretly, and then use the central banking machine to turn the spigot on and off to manipulate, you're never going to get an environmentally healthy world, let alone a healthy civilization. But you will produce a centralized dividend.

KS: For example, there is one Italian writer, Roberto Saviano. He wrote the book *Gomorrah* **about the mafia, Camorra. I saw an interview with him a few weeks ago. I was really astonished because he said that the whole European financial system is based on mafia money because the mafia is pumping huge amounts of money to Liechtenstein, Luxembourg, and now London. He said that London right now is offshore heaven for mafia money. He said basically that this financial system in Europe cannot even work, cannot even proceed without this money. It will collapse. He said that the amount of money which they're giving to the financial system is the same as crude oil. Cocaine in the same amount as crude oil.**

CAF: Right now the financial system is addicted to dirty money. I have an online book called *Dillon Read & The Aristocracy of Stock Profits,* and I explain how the whole thing works. The important thing to understand is that organized crime is very, very integrated with the intelligence agencies. Remember, if you look at how the financial system works, all the money is aggregated and goes through a central point, so all of this is run from the very top. In other words, the mafia is simply an integrated part of the game. What's very interesting is historically, the mafia had more power than they have now, and it's really been the telecommunications and NSA and the Five Eyes that have been able to shift the balance of power between the guys who do the street level crime versus who's running the money through the SWIFT system or who's running the intelligence through the Five Eyes system. So there's constant flow back and forth between who controls the power in the system. But the system is very, very dependent on organized crime cash flows. What's interesting is if you map out how the money works within a neighborhood in the United States, it's amazing how they coordinate the lines between whether they're trying to sell you pharmaceuticals or whether they're trying to sell you illegal drugs. It's optimized on an integrated basis. They're just trying to harvest that place for the most money, and the line of what's legal is moved back and forth to optimize the full pod. It's quite remarkable. Especially in the '70s and '80s, the intelligence agencies very much took on a much more aggressive, intimate role with organized crime, and from what I read of NATO, it was the same here in Europe.

KS: But do you think we are dealing with a collapsing of the global financial system? Or this is not a realistic scenario? I saw a few interviews with you, and you said that we shouldn't believe in this "reset" scenario.

CAF: The dollar was starting to collapse. The dollar was in real trouble. What you're watching with COVID-19 is an effort to extend the dollar, but then accelerate the new system. They want to go to an all-digital currency for retail. Not necessarily for wholesale, but for individuals in transactions, they want a digital system, but they want to integrate it into your body. They want complete control. This is really a control system. Currency as we know it will go away. Crypto is not a currency; it's a credit system. So if you're chipped or they use whatever the technology is and you depend on your chip to access the money system, then they can turn your money off and on. They can increase it, they can decrease it. It's not a currency in the classic sense; it's a credit system. But it's a complete control system, and to me, it's really a slavery system. And it's completely illegal under current law. That's why they keep trying to promote all these injectables as vaccines, because under the law, a vaccine is a medicine. If it's a medicine, then you are under a different set of laws than if it's a poison or nanotechnology or gene-altering therapy without consent. So they're trying to define it as a vaccine, which it's not because it's not a medicine, because they want to slip through that legal pipeline. But it's fraudulent, what they're trying to do.

KS: So are we dealing with some sort of "Hotel Auschwitz" like you said in one interview?

CAF: That was John Rappoport's expression. We were talking and John was talking about the difference between previous genocides and the friendly fascism version. He said, "Think of it as like Hotel Auschwitz." I couldn't stop laughing. I was just cracking up. [Laughs.] He went into this whole long riff. It's a wonderful video. I have it up on Solari, this whole long riff about how pleasant things are in Hotel Auschwitz while you're getting your gene-altering poison.

KS: So this is like a modern slavery system? We are going this direction?

CAF: That's where they want to go. I'm not going. I don't have to go—one of the things I keep trying to say, because you have to remember, I litigated with the Department of Justice for 11 years, and they were free to break every law. Everyone told me I had no chance. And I can see why they said that. Within the machine model, I had no chance. It took 11 years, it took 36,000 hours of free time—that's my estimate, because it kept going with the taxes afterwards. But essentially, we won. We won because life has many dimensions, and the material model is—it's a much bigger, more intelligent universe. And miracles just kept happening. It was amazing. The Midianites ended up killing each other. So we were really lucky. It came down to the last—I'll tell you, there were 12 tracks of litigation, 18 audits of investigation. The last trial on the last day, there were three different groups of attorneys. There was the Department of Justice, the HUD Inspector-General, and then the private whistleblower, who's this professional snitch. We're standing in court, and they're fighting with each other in open courtroom because it's gotten so bad, and they've clearly lost. So the three of them are screaming, and one says, "You don't know that's true!" The guy yelled, "Yes, I do! I have a document. Fitts said it was true." Then they all agree, "Oh, well, if Fitts said it's true, I'm sure it's true." My attorney looked at me and he said, "You're the only person they trust." [Laughs.] It was pretty funny. So the Midianites killed each other.

Here's the thing. What everybody wants is a pathway to stay alive through this, and the reality is we're not all going to make it out alive of this. No, we're not. If you look at what's been going on, what we're watching in the United States is mercenaries and crisis actors and paid professional organizers drop into a place with businesses, being targeted by those mercenaries and local officials and police, being targeted and murdered. These are professional assassinations. These are hits, and there are people who are dying. If you watch it, I'll bet you a dollar that all of the ones I've seen—whenever local people capture them on video, those are professional hits. I think it was in the Bronx, a two-car team working a policeman, and they run him over. It was a professional hit. That's what it looked like to me. Anyway, there's going to be real physical violence going on. There's going to be real disaster capitalism. If you look at the fires in California, if you look at Katrina, we've seen disaster capitalism all over the world. People get killed. This is dangerous.

It's funny—I use the example of the swine flu. They were trying to mandate a vaccine that was really dangerous in I think 2010, and finally it got so bad—I didn't think that they would mandate it in my state, but I wasn't sure. I called a friend of mine who lives about 3 hours away who's got a big family, and they've got a ton of guns. I said to him, "Franklin, I don't know if they're going to mandate this here, but if they are, I'm not taking a vaccine." Actually, it's not a vaccine; that's what they call it. I said, "I'm not taking the injectable. Can I bring my guns over to your house? Because I'd rather have a gunfight with you than do it alone." He said, "Oh yeah, sure. You come over here. We're going to have a big gunfight." [Laughs.] And sure enough, they stopped. I think it was because they heard hundreds of thousands of those phone calls.

I know what the law is, and I'm prepared to defend myself. I can absolutely see many of us getting into a squabble, and we may not come out alive. But that's okay, because I've got to tell you, death is not the worst thing that can happen. If you look at what they're cooking up, it's not the worst thing that can happen. If you look at contact tracing, they are literally planning on coming into your house, faking tests, faking viruses, and kidnapping your children. And if they do, you may never see your children again. Here's the reality. A few people cannot control the many if the many are willing to stand up for their rights. But it means some of us are going to die. If you look at what they're going to do if we don't stand up and fight, it's going to be worse. So you might as well stand up early.

KS: Do you think this situation in the United States will be spread to all other countries? We have almost domestic war in Lebanon, we have Hong Kong riots, now we have riots in the U.S.

CAF: It depends on the place. Not every place. If you're in a jurisdiction that has very high debt and is basically controlled from behind the scenes by the creditors, or can be, if you have a long history of very aggressive covert operations and you haven't stopped that game locally, you're going to have problems. If you're in a jurisdiction that has low debt and has paid attention to good management and enforcement, you may not have any problems. I think it's going to be sporadic. Now, the problem is that—here's the thing; I hate to say this. I always use stories. There's a great TV series that I made Movie of the Year last year on the Solari Report called Yellowstone. You probably haven't seen Yellowstone. It's in its third season. It's Kevin Costner, who's a rancher in Montana, and there's two guys named the Beck brothers who basically see themselves as the king of the valley. Every time they want to get their way, they murder somebody, kidnap them, poison their cattle. They play dirty. They're dirty players. I told everybody the reason that I made Yellowstone Movie of the Year is the challenge before us in 2020 is: what are we going to do about the Beck brothers? There's a scene—I hate to give this away—a scene where finally, the lead rancher in the valley decides he's got to kill them. You've just got to kill them. Anyway, he tells his son, who used to be a Special Forces Ranger that he's going to have to kill him—one of the Beck Brothers. So the kid goes in to kill one of the Beck brothers, and he's holding the pistol and the guy's going to rig it to make it look like a suicide, and he says, "Why did you force us to do this?" The Beck brother looks at him and he says, "Nobody ever fights back." So my message to America is, for 70 years, nobody's fought back, and the Beck brothers have gotten worse and worse and worse and worse. So here we are.

KS: What is the long-term scenario for America? What will happen after this COVID-19 and after these riots?

CAF: I think what the syndicate would like—and there are different factions. I think it could go many different ways, but I think America is in for radical reengineering, and some of the factions would like to break it up into different pieces. The government is going to be radically reengineered, and the question is, will there be a U.S. or will they break it up? What they want to do is get seven billion chipped and hooked up to the JEDI cloud at Department of Defense and the CIA cloud for the intelligence agencies and get everybody hooked in and controlled that way. At that point, they don't need all of that governmental infrastructure and they can break up the states. And if they do, basically they can steal the pension funds and kill retirement savings. It's a much more complicated picture.

KS: Would you agree with me that we are dealing with I would say the beginning of class war on a global scale?

CAF: No, I think we're part of a war that's been going on for 10,000 years.

KS: I spoke with one American economist and he told me that probably there will be some sort of beginning of the class war.

CAF: Well, you have a group of people who've been centralizing control, and the more they centralize and now the more they audit, the more people fall out of the bottom and the social safety net falls away, and that's going to exacerbate tensions. But I think we've had—in my experience, we've had significant class warfare for a very long time. It's just now they're eating away at the broad middle class, so there's more of a basis to push back. But to me, this is part of a war that's been going on literally for thousands of years, and what's new now is you have technology that really gives them the ability to radically centralize more than they have in the past. So how much they could centralize and control is a function of technology, and every time the technology gets better, you have this period—I don't know if you've read Tim Wu's book.

KS: I haven't, no.

CAF: Very good. But basically what he describes is you get this new information technology, you get a wonderful period of innovation, and wham! Then after the prototyping, it centralizes more. And that's been going on now for centuries, and now we're just going into a whole new wave of centralization. But I see this as part of a battle that's been going on for thousands of centuries, and at the root it's a battle between good and evil.

KS: How would you describe what is happening right now in the U.S.? This is some sort of orchestrated revolution?

CAF: No. Here's the way I would describe it. Starting in the mid-'90s, a financial coup d'état was engineered. We literally had a coup d'état in '63 when Kennedy was killed, but the national security state grew and grew and grew following the assassination. Then a decision was made at the end of 1995 to radically reengineer the whole governance structure, starting by literally stealing all the money. We had a financial coup. I've documented—we had a process whereby trillions of dollars were stolen using fraudulent securities. Part of that was the bailouts, but there was something called the missing money. There's $21 trillion of undocumentable adjustments. Now that they've stolen most of the money, the reality is now you need to come back in and reengineer the government and take basically bottom-up control. What you're seeing now is that those forces are financing basically a takeover of the local cities and states. What they're trying to do is get rid of local enforcement in the police, partly by bankrupting them. And if you can get rid of the police, then you can move in on all the real estate. So I would describe this as the consolidation of the financial coup because you're exercising—before, it was done with legal and financial measures, but now you're exercising physical control of real estate and places. It's the consolidation of a coup that began in 1995.

Now, it's important to understand that a lot of those neighborhoods—and if you read the online book I sent you, *Dillon Read and the Aristocracy of Stock Profits,* if you look at those neighborhoods, here's how it worked. In 1995, an effort was made by the leadership to get a fiscally sound budget. It didn't work. You didn't get passage of a budget, so the government had to shut down. It was very messy. A decision was made then by the leadership that they give up on the current structure. Right after that, that's when you started to see, for example, all the OxyContin, the opioids started to pour into neighborhoods, the student loan debt. You changed the usury laws. So you had all these different policies change so basically you could rape and devastate neighborhoods, whether it was with debt entrapment, with usury, with drugs—both legal and illegal drugs.

At the same time, they made a decision to pull massive amounts of money out of the country and start globalization. So that money was pulled out and reinvested in a variety of places. That's what I call the financial coup d'état. In fiscal 1997, right before the beginning of fiscal 1998, I met with a group of the top pension fund leaders in the country, and we had proposed a plan—and you can read about it in the Dillon Read book—whereby you could reengineer the economy and how government money was spent and, using new technology, produce fantastic new wealth. The president of the largest pension fund, which was CalPERS, the California public pension fund, looked at me and he said, "You don't understand. It's too late. They've given up on the country. They're pulling all the money out starting in the fall." I thought he meant they were globalizing and moving pension fund money legally into the emerging markets, and what I realized later, after the $21 trillion started to go missing, was no, he meant they're pulling all the money. It was basically a criminal—if you look at what they did, they decided to reengineer the United States government on a "just do it" basis. Don't talk to anybody; just do it.

If you go to the Solari Report, I'm doing an interview next week with Richard Dolan. What we're talking about—and this is what I say in the commentary. The U.S. government does not have information sovereignty. If you're the president of the United States, you can't make a phone call without 17 intelligence agencies listening, a couple of foreign intelligence agencies, and a couple telecoms. So you have no information sovereignty. You have no financial sovereignty because all your money is run by a group of private banks that basically control your ability to finance. And everybody in America wants their check, and unless you do what the banks say, you can't give them their check. So you don't have information sovereignty, you don't have financial sovereignty. The Pentagon's budget is $738 billion a year, and if you look at the last 20 years, the average undocumentable adjustments of missing money disappearing on top of that is a trillion dollars a year on average for the last 20 years. So that's $1.7 trillion on average. They just confirmed the existence or the credibility of three videos of UFOs, and what that means is the Pentagon is saying that although we're paying them $1.7 trillion a year, they don't control airspace.

So if you don't have information sovereignty and if you don't have financial sovereignty and if you don't control your own airspace, what kind of sovereignty do you have? What I would suggest to you is that there is no U.S. government, and there hasn't been for a very long time. Why? I became Assistant Secretary of Housing in 1989, and under the law I was required to run the Single-Family Mortgage Insurance Fund, which at that point was about a $320 billion portfolio on a self-supporting basis. It took me 3 months to get the accountants to report to me so I could talk to them, which I was able to do because I'd raised a huge amount of money for George Bush during the campaign. It was only that political clout that made it possible for me to get a hold of the accountants. When I finally got them, I discovered we were losing $11 million a day, which is completely non-defiant. To fix that, I had to get a hold of data which was controlled by Lockheed Martin, which refused to give it to me. Lockheed Martin at the time was paid $150 million to run all the information and payment systems at HUD. Despite my being Assistant Secretary of Housing, they simply refused to get me the data I wanted. Finally, when I kept pushing for that and other things, I got booted out. One of the reasons I started my company was to basically figure out, let's build databases and software tools so that communities can find out how the money works and make sure that that money works in accordance with the law, because the reality is, if you were to do accounts and map out the money for 3,100 counties in America, what you would find is the money is being operated way outside the law. Of course, that "way outside the law" is not only wasting a huge amount of money, but it's helping to centralize control.

So if you think all these ding-dongs who are running around whom we're being told are geniuses are geniuses—they're not geniuses. They're fronts. They say they're billionaires, but it's not really their money. They're just part of a syndicate. One of the reasons they're billionaires is their cost of capital to the big New York banks is 0%. The cost of capital to the average American with their credit card is 15.99%. Now, if I take you and one other guy and put you on an island and I make sure that guy has a 0% cost of capital and you have a 15.99% cost of capital, how long is it going to take before everything on the island is owned by him and you have to work for him? It's very simple.

KS: So you are saying they are using this money for financing some sort of global dictatorship?

CAF: This is totally global. But for it to work globally, you've got to bring down the U.S.

KS: You have to bring down the U.S?

CAF: Right, because you have to control the federal credit mechanism. The whole globe is bubbled off of the U.S. dollar system, so you've got to control or evolve that system. And if you look at what they're proposing—and this is the whole idea of using healthcare to control—what they want to do is they want seven billion people, they want to chip us—it's all in the Bible. It's called the mark of the beast. They want to inject us with brain-machine interface and other digital technology, hook us up to the cloud databases, and basically govern the planet with AI and software managing seven billion people. Who needs federal, state, and local government if you can just hook everybody up to your cloud and manage them directly? It's very economic.

KS: I was talking with Russian neuroscientist Mikhail Lebedev and I asked him about chipping people, like putting chips in your brain, and he told me that if they will be able to do it then we won't be able to distinguish who is a zombie and who is a normal person. We cannot distinguish who is the conscious being and who is a zombie. We don't have that kind of scientific tools. He said that, for example, you can be an elderly person reading the newspapers all day, and you can behave like a normal human being for the outside world. But in reality, inside, you can be already zombie.

CAF: I don't know if you realize this—remember in January, or somewhere between January and March, when they arrested the guy from Harvard who'd been working at the Wuhan laboratory? His name is Charles Lieber. If you go to Lieber's website, Lieber Research Group, and read, he's an expert in brain-machine interface nanotechnology. So one of my questions is, was Wuhan a prototype that went bad? Trump just appointed the former head of research at GlaxoSmithKline as head of this—it's called Operation Warp Speed. You know what his expertise was? Bioelectronics. My vision of where they think they want to go is, if you look at Bill Gates, how did Bill Gates become the front man for this thing?

KS: That's the big question.

CAF: Bill Gates basically put software in everybody's computer that had a reputation of being really horrible software, but the rumor was he gave a backdoor to NSA. This was how NSA and their pals were going to get all your data. So he was the leader of surveillance capitalism, where you're not the customer, you're really the prey. He created special software for the government, who then started to lose $21 trillion by some kind of backdoor. We're still trying to figure it out. So how did he get everybody to constantly update their software? Well, suddenly there are all these viruses. You've got to have an update, and then you've got another problem and you've got to have an update. Meantime they're getting more and more access through the back door. Okay, so he did it to your computers; now he wants to do it to your body. Same thing. And you've got to keep updating because there are going to be all these viruses. [Laughs.] It's the same model. He has a business model now—you know what the JEDI contract is? Microsoft just signed a $10 billion contract with the Department of Defense (DOD) to create the biggest cloud in the world; 2 or 3 years ago, Amazon signed a huge cloud with the CIA and 17 intelligence agencies. Then just this year and last year, DOD signs a $10 billion contract with the Microsoft cloud, just at the same time that the president appoints the head of Operation Warp Speed, who was the head of research at GlaxoSmithKline, who's an expert in bioelectronics, and Bill Gates suddenly wants to inject you, and you have to do it because there are all these viruses. Connect the dots.

And in the meantime, suddenly we have professional mercenaries and paid organizers all moving in to 100–150 American cities, trying to burn the place down and doing everything they can to persuade the local officials that we have to get rid of the local police. Connect the dots. I don't know if you remember, as soon as Netanyahu—this was about a month or two ago—Netanyahu, once he'd locked up the prime minister position, he announced he wanted to chip all the kids. That's what happens when you let organized crime run things. This has nothing to do with Jews. If it did, he wouldn't be proposing to take the Jewish children and treat them like livestock. Unbelievable.

KS: Professor Yuval Noah Harari basically said that we are dealing right now with state surveillance, which is China, for example, and capital surveillance, which is for example the United States, as you mentioned. So in the nearest future, we're going to be witnessing the collapsing of the states which have very low data systems because he said that new colonialization, the states who have really good technology, will be colonizing other countries—not using force, not using military, but using data. So if you have a very bad technology base in your country, you can be very easily colonized by another country like China, for example. He said that one way he is dealing with this is using Vipassana meditation, 2 hours per day, to know himself better than these algorithms and machines who are reading his patterns. But he said this is a very short scenario. You cannot deal with that kind of stuff if you don't do it on a political level. How can you deal with China right now, with this social credit? I spoke, for example, with William Binney, an NSA former technical director, and he told me that the social credit is not only about China.

CAF: It's going on everywhere. My favorite idea was from Binney. He said we ought to teach all the kids how to build encryption systems. He said if you have thousands and millions of homegrown local encryption systems, you'll drive the systems crazy. [Laughs.] I thought that was a good idea.

KS: Harari said that in the future, we're going to be fully hacked animals.

CAF: Yes. If you allow the nanotechnology in us.

KS: Even without nanotechnology, just reading your patterns, everything which you're doing online.

CAF: Here's the thing. There are many things you can do, but one thing—this gets down to the nature of what is intelligence and what is shared intelligence, and where does intelligence come from, but if you look at all the people competing to be the winners in the system, my prediction is ultimately they will all kill each other. [Laughs.] Because the most powerful force in the universe is love, and you cannot use AI and machines to build love. That's just not what they do. They're great at speed, they're great at processing, they're great at a whole bunch of stuff, but they're not great at creating the conditions of love and intelligence. So I don't underestimate their ability to take over control and kill billions of people, but ultimately processing speed is not the basis of an intelligent system. We would have to get deeply into how intelligence works and how all the different dimensions work and what our minds are capable of. I think the biggest challenges we're dealing with are, number one, interdimensional and may even be off-planet. Because we have so little hard evidence of those two situations, trying to discuss them becomes very—it's very hard to have an organized and disciplined conversation about them because there's so much uncertainty. If you come to the Solari Report, we have a section in every wrap-up. We do wrap-ups quarterly and annually, and we have a section called "Unanswered Questions." Our number one unanswered question for 10 years has been "What is the governance structure on Planet Earth?" Because it's invisible. Every time you try and map out what you know about the governance on Planet Earth, you get into the question of, first of all, is our economy open or closed? Are we trading off-planet? That's number one. And number two, what is the interdimensional war going on? Because there's clearly something going on.

It's funny; we just published a new Solari Report on our Future Science series, and I was listening to it on Friday and then again today—I tend to listen to them a couple times—and the host was describing the fact—Neutrinos are subatomic particles. What you realize is in theory, somebody can literally map and watch across the galaxy—the communication speeds are unbelievable. There's a lot of neutrino research going on in Antarctica. But one of the things they described was that one study had shown neutrinos were emerging from Antarctica that were traveling backwards in time. [Laughs.] I said, "What?" In fact, Joseph Farrell just published an article a couple days ago, "Is there a parallel universe that you can access through Antarctica?" So if you look at what's going on in this planet in terms of our relationship with the solar system and what's going on in space around us—I mean, the Pentagon just said publicly that these UFO videos are real. So if you look at what's going on around us in space or if you look at what's going on interdimensionally—we've been trying to keep our minds in this very small, hyper-materialist, limited box, and if you look at what's really going on in this planet, there's a much more rich, complex reality. The benefit of exploring that, even though you have to deal with some of these pretty squiggly concepts, is if you look at how life works, it's so beautiful, it's so powerful. Just as an economic matter, there's so much wealth that can be created. We have been thinking so little and so small. If you open your mind to what is possible—yes, we have to go through a lot of scary stuff, but there's also unbelievable possibilities and potential.

I'm fundamentally an optimist, and I sat down in 1998 when I faced everything that was going on—and you can read about it in my book—and I said the only explanation I can come up with is they're planning on depopulating about 80% of the planet. Because nothing else makes sense. But I didn't say it to anybody. I was too overwhelmed, and I was thinking about, can I stay alive and be happy in a world where the leadership is depopulating it by 80%? There was this money manager from the city of London who called me and said, "I'm going to be in Washington. Can we have lunch?" So we went out to lunch and he said, with a whisper, "I know this sounds really strange, and I really don't want you to tell anybody, but I see this and this and this, and if you look at this change and this change..." Because we're both portfolio strategists, so we're looking at all the different dots and connecting them. He said, "The only logical explanation I can come up with is they're planning depopulating down, to a huge amount." I said, "My number is 500 million." He said, "That's what my number is." We looked at each other and said, "Oh, shit." [Laughs.] I spent a long time in 1998 thinking, do I want to stay alive through this? Do I want to live through this? Can I be happy with this? To me, it was a spiritual question. A lot of my thinking then, that's how I organized. I remember the question for me was, was I going to settle my litigation and go back inside the establishment or was I going to fight? What I realized was I have the money, I have the skills, I have the ability to win; the problem is, can I really have this fight and win and still have the ability to love? Because if I can't love when it's all over, it's not worth it. There's no point in doing any of this. So I had to organize the whole thing around what could nurture my love despite everything going on. A lot of the reason I do what I do is I just decided—I'll give you an example. I went to church one day and my co-pastor was really angry about something. I have no idea what. She stood up and she said, "Honey, you don't need a car, you don't need a man." She shook her finger at me—screaming at the whole crowd; it wasn't just me—she said, "You need to be in right relationship with the Lord."

I thought, oh, okay, that's my plan. Instead of having a plan that I'm going to build this business or I'm going to write a book, my plan is I'm going to get up every day and try and stay in right relationship. Because if we're going to build new models, they have to be in alignment with life, and there's only one way to be aligned with life and that's to do it today and then do it the next day. And life is chaotic. Life is crazy. You have to see what you can see.

It's funny because in Solari now, when we do our business plans, we do them one see at a time because we can only see as far as we can see. By the time we finish these 10 things, you know it'll all change anyway. I used to be one of those people who had a 5-year plan, a 10-year plan. Everything was perfect. Now, you have to rock and roll. It's a different world. You know the Buddhist says "with your thoughts, you create your world"? One of the interesting things I can say about my former colleagues is they were always masters at persuading everybody, "It's hopeless. You have to do what we say because it's absolutely hopeless." Secrecy and the mirage of power was their greatest power. I really believe that we have the power to invent our world with our thoughts. In fact, that's been proven. Bill Tiller went out and did the research and proved that our intention and our thoughts can change material reality at a great distance. So the critical question here is, are we going to build a human civilization and is it going to be based on love, or are we going to build a machine for a few guys to make a lot of money? It's going to come down to what you and I intend and what we work for. I think God's more powerful.

KS: Do you think we're going to be witnessing some sort of shortages of food?

CAF: Yes.

KS: There won't be enough food for everyone, or the prices will be very high?

CAF: There will not be enough real food. There'll be lots of food in the store, but whether or not you can call it food...

KS: Some artificial stuff, I guess.

CAF: That's what they want. There's no reason that I know of not to have plenty of food, but if you want to control the food supply centrally and maximize your profit off of it, then you have to have fake food. Most of the stores in America carry fake food.

KS: We have right now this digital yuan in China. Do you think they will establish in the near future some sort of international digital money?

CAF: It's not money. It's credit. If it's a currency, I can put it in my pocket, walk away, you can put it in your pocket, and your dollar is worth what my dollar is. But in a credit system, I have a credit at the company store and if I behave, they can change the value of mine versus yours. So it's not a currency. It's a credit system. If you go back and you look at why they cancelled the African slave trade, there were two reasons. One is they couldn't put down the rebellion in Haiti and they were afraid it would spread, and the second was the banks in London kept losing money because they had no way of perfecting their collateral. Once they have the brain-machine interface and once it can connect with their cloud and their mind control, they've solved those two problems. So this is not changing the currency. This is changing from freedom to slavery.

KS: I also interviewed Tim Draper, the Silicon Valley investor, and he's advocating for cryptocurrency, for bitcoin. He thinks it will be a big step to decentralization. But on the other hand, we have Jim Rogers, another investor from the U.S., and he said—we have all these brilliant people who are inventing cryptocurrencies and all this stuff, but at the end of the day, the central banks have military. So you can play with the cryptocurrencies to the extent they will allow you. If they would like to stop it, they just send in the military. He said that's why he's not investing in crypto because it will go to zero.

CAF: No, it will be whatever the central bankers want it to be. I'll give you a perfect example. In 2017, I was in a conference at the Aspen Institute with all these bitcoin developers, and they were saying, "Oh, this is the revolution. We're leading the revolution." The month before I told this story at the conference, I had been in Basel and a friend of mine dropped me off at the train station. We drive past the Bank of International Settlements, and it's 2017, and I walk up to get my ticket at the Basel train station right next to the BIS, and I put my card in and it gives me the option of paying for my Swiss Railway ticket with bitcoin or with francs or with dollars. At which point I said, "You know something? Whatever this is, I'm next to the BIS and this is not a revolution. This is a prototype." It's a prototype.

So you're right. Any system ultimately comes down to enforcement, who enforces. We live on a planet right now that is run by physical force, and that means whoever controls the physical force controls everything, ultimately. Whether your blockchain goes over satellites or it goes in the cables under the sea, whoever controls that hardware ultimately controls you. I'll never forget some reporter who'd been spiked and fired by CBS and had been impactful, had done everything right, and she said, "The military wanted me gone, and the reality is if they don't do what the military says, they lose their satellite feed. End of day, I'm gone." That's physical force. That's how it works. So to me, any currency that is 100% digital has zero integrity. None. Zip. This idea that blockchain is going to somehow give you integrity when it's the same sea cables and it's the same satellite system? If you want to chip everybody and run things with a credit system, you have to make it fashionable. I mean, you've got all these different—marketing is never one spin. You've got 57 varieties spinning to all these different groups to get them into your plan. You don't want to say, "We want to chip you and make you a slave and a zombie." They don't say that. That's not good marketing.

So they have Gates on Reddit, and he's trying to make it seem totally cool. "We have IDs, and now poor people can get access to bank accounts, and this is so heartwarmingly wonderful. Aw, shucks, gee." He's doing the Buffett spin. And then you have Tim Draper saying, "Get out of the fiat system. You can create your own money. You can finally be free." This is the 57 varieties. It's like Baskin Robbins.

KS: What about megacities and digital dissidents in these cities? I saw the Pentagon report of megacities, and they are claiming that people living in these megacities—they're living in some sort of anonymous criminal networks. And that is the biggest challenge for military. The strategies from Iraq and Afghanistan are not capable to deal with the new scenarios in these megacities.

CAF: The problem you have is if you bring everybody into the cities and cut them off from growing their own food, and you have no jobs for them, you've automated everything with robots, and you keep them away from nature and from life in an economy where they're not free to compete in the marketplace because you have technocracy and total control, then you have a lot of unhappy people. And then the question is, how do they create a healthy life for themselves if you've created conditions where that's impossible? So the question is, can they, grassroots, bottom-up, organize to manage and optimize their resources creatively and intelligently or not? I don't know.

KS: I think the only explanation is that the people who will be living in that kind of city will be genetically modified so they can adjust to that kind of environment. Like Aldous Huxley suggested in Brave New World.

CAF: If you put brain-machine interface in them and mind control them, which is basically, if you look at what Gates and Operation Warp Speed and Charles Lieber are all up to, that's what they're up to. Have you seen the Kingsman movies? Or *The Cell* with John Cusack? The Kingsman movies and *The*

Cell with John Cusack explain the idea of using very strong entrainment and subliminal programming mind control technology through cellphones. It's basically triggering a crowd to behave in different ways, including violently. So the Kingsman movie came out, and then shortly thereafter we started to see riots break out, or brawls, where people are fighting with each other, just like in Kingsman. It would happen at Chuck E Cheese, it would happen in shopping malls. And now, if you look at the riots and the protests, it looks to me like you've got major Kingsman technology at work. The rule is you have to show us what you're going to do before you do it. So in the movies, they show us what they're doing or what they're going to do. You've got major, major mind control at work. I have a very good Solari Report called "Entrainment Technology and Financial Manipulation," because one of my biggest problems over the last 10 years—I used to be an investment advisor to individuals. I don't do it anymore, but I had so many clients who were in danger of being defrauded by entrainment technology. It's used to sell people investments or sell people consumer goods or gambling or pornography. One of the reasons you have so many people in America completely addicted to pornography is thanks to entrainment. It's a beautiful entrapment tool. You can get a control file on many, many people because all you have to do is get somebody hooked on pornography, then you bring in an underage actor, and bam, you've got them on child pornography.

KS: But what about—I call them digital dissidents, the people who are against that kind of scenarios? Is there any place for those kinds of people in the future?

CAF: Absolutely. I hope the cities end up creating millions. The only way I think to see our way through freedom is to—the integrity of the digital system—the digital systems have zero integrity. They're zero integrity systems. That's the problem with doing a real financial system over them. They have no integrity. You can do a credit system because that's a zero integrity system. But if there is anybody who can bring integrity to the digital systems, it's the dissidents.

KS: Do you think that we are going into the scenario of the next big war, like the Second World War?

CAF: We are right now in the middle of World War III. COVID-19 is World War III. I bet you dimes to donuts—in the middle of March, the Chinese said "we're not taking dollars," and suddenly the dollar bubble had to bring their Chinese purchases way, way down, and we're into fast and radical reengineering. Part of this was to extend the life of the dollar, which it did, but the other was to accelerate. That's why they're calling it Operation Warp Speed. They need to get brain-machine nanotechnology into everybody and get the new credit system going because they can't keep the dollar going forever.

KS: Do you think there will be some sort of bigger military confrontation?

CAF: There could be, but the war is not between us and China. The war is between the people who want complete central control and the people who want freedom. This is a very fractured war, and there's great factionalism, everybody jockeying to defend freedom or jockeying for power.

KS: Who is China in this scenario?

CAF: That comes back to this invisible governance structure. Who's really in control? And I have news for you: our planet is run on force. If the most powerful people who control the airspace over the United States are flying UFOs around and the Pentagon doesn't control our airspace, who's that? And do they control? What you've done is you've cancelled, you've dropped income globally by 30–50%, so you shut down the economy, incomes have dropped, but the debt hasn't dropped. The more that happens, the more the creditors control. So the question is, who owns the debt? Well, I've done many studies over the last 10 years trying to figure out who owns the debt, and I can't figure it out. All I know is the people who control the airspace have the fastest ships, and they're probably the people who control the debt. Which raises the question: who's really in charge? One of the things I'll tell you is the U.S. government is not a sovereign government. It's run essentially by the central bankers, and the question is, who do they work for? My nickname for the invisible governance structure is Mr. Global, and that's the question. Who is Mr. Global, and why is Mr. Global behaving like this?

Douglas Rushkoff[*]

*"When Google says don't do evil,
they really mean, don't be human."*

KONRAD STACHNIO: How do you perceive the future role of the media in the digitizing world? Peter Sloterdijk said that in the future, only algorithms and devices would be progressive, and compared to them, humans would be conservative. Are we therefore becoming more and more the victims of technologies that render us increasingly vulnerable to manipulation? Can we survive and be safe as human beings, in the context of these advancing media?

DOUGLAS RUSHKOFF: It depends on what you mean by *media*. I look at everything as media. I look at speech as media and clothing as media. We could distinguish between natural media like water and air, and human-invented media—speech and text, radio, television, digital and all that. So, if we're talking about the future of *invented* media, then I guess it does bifurcate between media that people use to communicate with each other or with machines, and the media that machines use to communicate with one another. I guess we will be looking at that. Whether computers might be holding conversations behind our backs, I guess, is sort of the more science-fiction question you are asking. But yes—even if you look at the way computers understand the *JPEG* versus the way you or I do, it's two very different universes of comprehension and exchange. As for manipulation and all that—right now, I still feel it's less the technologies themselves that manipulate us, and more the market expressing itself through the technology. So, I don't think Facebook algorithms are that advanced. I am not worried about them so much as about the companies that

---

[*]DOUGLAS RUSHKOFF is an American writer, lecturer, columnist, media theorist, graphic novelist, and documentarian, named by MIT as one of the "World's ten most influential intellectuals."

are using them. I don't see any of these technologies as intrinsically evil or manipulative, trying to control us. I don't think they are alive. I don't believe in artificial intelligence, but I do believe there are corporations that are almost conscious, corporations that really do see human beings as resources from which to extract value…and they're using every technology at their disposal to take it from us.

KS: Corporate CEOs are more powerful right now than some governments and heads of state. Who, then, would control these emerging technologies? Will the ultimate control of them not be taken over by international corporations?

DR: Well, I don't know that it's final, but they certainly control them right now. But it depends. You could look at AI, and even the Internet itself as the body for corporations; they didn't have them before these technologies arose. In America, corporations have citizenship, they have personhood, and they have rights—but they don't have bodies. So, the Internet is sort of the first body for the corporation, and then robots and other AIs and things will be the *corpus* of the corporations. So, we'll see. I don't know who is in charge in technology. I mean, I guess finally whoever owns it, we certainly don't. So, it is corporatism itself. But corporatism is not a conscious being, it's just a force, just a kind of slavery. So, we will see. I use Bible mythology to understand what is going on now. Take the story of the Pharaoh. The Pharaoh learned about debt from Joseph and he used debt to enslave the people. The people became indentured servants because they couldn't pay him back for the grain. And then the crueller he got with his slaves—there is this section where God hardened his heart. So, basically, the Pharaoh lost free will. He lost the ability to have empathy, but he also lost ability to take an action. Even if he wanted to let the Israelites go, he no longer had the ability to make that choice, because he was now embodying the will of debt, the will of the first extractive—not a corporation, but extractive company—and I feel like that's what's happened. So, I don't look at a set of human beings as *in charge.* Even if you say, OK, Jeff Bezos is in charge or Mark Zuckerberg is in charge, I don't feel like, when they get to this level, I don't feel like they have autonomy, really, over their faculties anymore. I think that they are more the face and expression for the billions of dollars they're sitting on, than they are thinking beings. So, I don't think anyone's in charge.

KS: What would be worse for you, the fact that there's a network of people controlling the situation in the world, or at least who have a significant impact on it? Or that *nobody* is in charge, nobody controls anything now?

DR: Well, I don't know. It's the worst-case scenario for twentieth-century thinkers. People of the twentieth century would rather believe in conspiracy, would rather believe that there's someone on the top who hates them, than find out there is no one at all. That is scarier. I would rather believe that there's no one at all than there is Erdoğan or somebody at the top. If there's no one at all, then I feel like we still have some potential to steer the ship, that human beings can become autonomous and conscious and redirect this. If there really is a bad guy and he's amassed this much power—you know, a Dr. Evil on the top of the pyramid—then we are kinda fucked!

KS: The positive side of the fact there are actually people responsible and controlling the situation is that you could always reach them somehow, or somehow influence them. However, what can we do in a situation where no one controls anything anymore?

DR: Yes, if there is someone, you go there and appeal to their heart… If there is nobody, then you start to understand things more systemically and if you understand reality as some kind of dynamical system or a fractal, then even though there is no human being to go to and convince, it does mean there's high leverage points everywhere in the system, so you can change it from anywhere. So, although it's frightening, for me, it's a little bit more optimistic, 'cause it means this is not human nature, that there is no one that bad to do this to us. It is the systems we put in place that we have stopped recognizing, that we're now mistaking for conditions of nature. People think you need money in order to live, or you need the car in order to get to work—all these things that we accept as given circumstances. But they are not.

KS: One of my previous interviewees stated that people involved in technology didn't realize something else beyond their own will was driving this technological process. Something else drives it, rules the trend?

DR: Yes, but I don't think it is a *thing, outside.* I think it's more bias, a force, tendency, a leaning. The Bible blames it on agriculture. The Bible is about wandering, desert people, Bedouins trying to cope with the axial age, with the invention of text, of property, of land and agriculture from the very beginning. Abel sacrifices a goat and Cain sacrifices plants that he grew, and Cain's sacrifice is not considered a sacrifice, 'cause it's like, *you're acting like you grew that stuff—that you made it, and you make nothing. God makes everything.* So, the minute humans believe now they're "responsible" for the bounty of the earth—rather than receiving by the grace of God their lives—that's the moment we mistake our free will for creation itself and that's what led to the establishment of debt. Once again, it was about crops: now we're growing it, so we own it, we can harvest it, we can stock it, we can hoard it. And then they finally go to the desert, and over forty years, they learn—with the manna coming from the skies—that they shouldn't hoard the stuff, but just trust that it's going to keep coming the next day. That is the same lesson we're dealing with. I mean, maybe the Christians would say Satan comes in or there's some other force doing this, but in the Old Testament, Judaism, it's really not Satan making you do this. It's the system itself. It is less the entrance of evil than the incapacitation of good. When your heart gets hurt, and when you're frozen, when you can't act, I would argue in modern parlance, that is because we become parts of systems... parts of systems designed to do nasty things or very mono-cultural things like hit a particular metric. Human beings, networked and working together, being alive with each other, I don't believe would exploit each other quite the same way we do when we're just acting like gears in the system, and the central problem here is that we are applying the logic of industrial-age technology to digital technology, and they are completely different things. So, we are looking at the renaissance ideals of speed and efficiency and applying them to technologies. You don't want to just maximize speed and efficiency, or what happens to the humans?

KS: How do you perceive the future of people who will be unable to adapt to this new technological reality? It seems that some of them in this system will simply be disposable.

DR: You are talking about the latest group of people who cannot adapt. In some ways, we are only concerned about this now that it may affect us. There are millions of people who have been destroyed by capitalism over the last hundred years. So, you look at Africa or South America or India—rather, not India so much anymore—but everything around there and Southeast Asia. These are the victims of capitalism and the problem is, they've got no more left to offer us. There is really no reason to exploit the refugees of Syria. What do they have to give to Amazon at this point? So, Amazon has to look to other places to suck. So, what they have done is they have turned America and Europe into the beginnings of banana republics. It is just new colonialism—a cannibalistic form of colonialism. We run out of territory, so we eat ourselves.

KS: So, what is the long-term scenario in this context, taking into account, for example, what's currently happening in Europe?

DR: Well, it is interesting. I feel like the forces of—sort of—a monstrous dictatorship, and the bad guys if you will—let's call them the Erdoğan side or the Berlusconi side—they thrive on divisiveness. They don't like the European Union, and they don't like the United States. They like separate states, and conflict, and separate nations. I feel like the sanctity of the European Union is at risk, as is the coherence of the United States. And you can call it a Facebook plot or a Russian plot but there are definitely forces actively pursuing that agenda, real people and institutions that want to break down the global cohesion of the Rockefeller era, the Rockefellers and the CIA. Not that the globalists were above reproach, either. There was tremendous good in promoting a global community: United Nations, NATO, the International Space Station. But many of these well-meaning institutions, from the World Bank to the IMF [International Monetary Fund], also promoted economic agendas that were extractive in the longer term. Nationalism is dangerous, too, because all it does is change our focus. We act as if our problems are national and local, when the global business reality chugs along. We each get our own mob boss to run our little nation state, while the multinational corporations continue their fleecing. So even if all our nations elect Trumps and Putins, all we'd really be doing is going *nah, nah, nah—these global forces don't exist.* We have no resistance then.

People who were early on the Internet, people like me in the early 1980s, we saw the government as the enemy. They were mean, they arrested young hackers in so-called Operation Sundevil; they went to teenage hackers' homes and arrested them with machine guns and stuff, made their little sisters and families lie on the ground... All because the kid hacked into AT&T to see how the phone system worked or into the shopping mall to see how to change the temperature. These were not terrorists; these were children. Between those raids and something called the Computer Decency Act—when they were trying to censor what happened online—people came to see the government as the enemy. And what we didn't realise was getting rid of the government made the net into a free open space for corporations. And a lot of technologists happened to be Libertarians also, 'cause they saw Libertarianism as nature and everything being free. So, by delivering them the Internet, we ended up giving digital steroids, really, to corporations. That's where we've ended up. If the AI has any character to it, if there's anyone behind it, it's the embodiment of corporatism—and that is weird. So, the most powerful person on the planet is not the person but is a technological infrastructure that's been programmed to extract as much value from people as possible, by any means necessary. That's weird.

KS: Do you think the Internet and freedom of speech on the Internet can be maintained in the long run?

DR: First, I think the Internet is here to stay. I think that the underlying infrastructure of the Internet is so embedded, I don't think they can just take it away. I think too much is built on top of it now for them to change it. And the good news is that it was built with maximum openness in mind. So, even though many of the platforms that we build on top of it are closed or evil, or they're data-mining from Facebook, Twitter or whatever, the Web itself—Net and Web—can still be open. So, I am still a fan of the open Web, the open Web movement and people going back to HTML, HTML CSS and making things and interconnecting them all; the Tor, torrents are still alive, and that technology still works. So, when I think about those technologies and the teenagers of the Never Again movement from Florida and the U.S., I think, well, this could be interesting. They still have the means to create an open media society.

KS: Are technologies and social media making us more connected or rather alienating people now?

DR: Right now, more alienated, and that's because people...they are not engaging face to face. They are losing some of the evolved abilities to establish rapport with other humans. We cannot establish solidarity on the Internet; solidarity is between living people. Human beings have the home field advantage on planet earth in the real world, and we lose that advantage when we migrate into cyberspace which is the home field for the AIs. So, the more time we spend there, the more time we're away from home.

KS: Elon Musk is currently building the Neuralink company, dealing with communication between our brains. Is this a new kind of interpersonal communication between people, or rather a sign of a complete change in the definition of *human* itself? Are these maybe the last days of the old type of human being?

DR: Well, it depends. There are so many conversations you can have. You could do it from the transhumanist perspective; how is it changing? What does it mean to be human? Does the definition of the human change or are we sub-speciating? So, there is the original species and there is the new species that has all these technologies or moves to something else.

KS: I now see Silicon Valley more as a kind of religious movement than pure business oriented toward utilitarianism. Would you agree with me?

DR: They are religious, but utilitarianism is a core tenet of their religion. They believe AI will deliver them on the day of the singularity. If you look at the classes they took at Stanford, they all took philosophy with René Girard. He was their teacher and he kind of saw human beings as problematic, as evil. So, then you get that when Google says don't do evil, they really mean, don't be *human*. So, this is sort of sad. But the computer technologists also overestimate their ability and they underestimate the complexity of the human mind. You talk to any real neuroscientist and they say, *we have no idea what consciousness is,* and you talk to Elon Musk and he is, like, *of course, we know what consciousness is!* We don't even know what goes on in one cubic centimetre of soil. So, how're we going to know what goes on in the square foot of a human brain? We have no idea; we are so primitive. To me, worrying about AI replacing our minds is the equivalent of a caveman making a wheel and then saying, *so, now we lose our legs*. There's a lot going on. I am not afraid of that.

KS: I am also not afraid but rather trying to understand what's really happening here.

DR: They are crazy and that is what's going on. What's to be afraid of, though, is—if they do believe that, then they're still stuck in this Aristotelian, goal-oriented, eyes-on-the-prize, end-justifies-the-means journey to their promised land. So, if some millions of Syrian refugees have to die, does it matter, because humanity is going to get to this next stage of pure consciousness, anyway?

KS: Would you agree with the thesis that technology is not only hardware or software, but more the way we think, feel, perceive—how we react? In other words, that we're mentally becoming robots, already living in a so-called satanic Matrix as some people claim.

DR: We are human beings and it depends what you think the human is, and what you think is going on here. I think that we…the human mind reduces quantum states into realities. That is what we do and that is what we're doing all the time. Technologies both assist us with that process but then lean into it in their own way. In some ways, technologies hide from us the extent to which we are creating reality in real time. They make reality seem in some ways more real, more concrete, and less changeable. When we accept that reality is *quite* changeable, reality is up for discussion. So, we created an artificial landscape that we know we can change, and it has tremendous impact on real reality, but we sort of lost direct contact with reality as a result. I don't think it is because of Satan or stuff like that. I don't think there is something else going on. I think we forgot that *this* is going on.

KS: Will the virtual world be indistinguishable from the real one in the long run?

DR: Yes, but that's been the problem from the beginning; what is your thought and what is language? If you think about the impact of language on cognition, do you think in words, and if you think in words, then where are your thoughts? Or did words replace your thoughts? So, what's the difference really?

KS: I am asking about this in the context of an experiment conducted on a rat that can be remotely controlled externally. Slavoy Zizek quotes this experiment in one of his lectures, pointing out that the most disturbing issue is that it can be carried out on a human being and he would not be aware of external interference. And he would be reading the external manipulation as his own will. Who will control these kinds of developing technologies; the army, private corporations? Both of these alternatives, euphemistically speaking, seem disturbing.

DR: We will see. You can start thinking about the world like a zombie movie or something, and that is upsetting. But I think that the solution, if there is one, is to increase our contact with other people in the real way. Hold hands, spend time, look into people's eyes, kiss and hug and fuck if you can. Think about being kind, and if reality is a fractal—which I'm hoping it is—then, as below, so above. As in our microcosm, so too will the world change. I don't know if communicating through these corporate-owned platforms ends up serving humans. The argument... Back in the 1980s, Matt Groening's very successful comic book and cartoon characters for the Tracy Ullman show, *The Simpsons,* meant they were offered to go and have a big show on Fox, and he was concerned. *I am just going to be feeding the corporate beast with all of my great ideas and characters and things?* And Gary Panter, another artist, wrote this little manifesto that was really for Matt Groening: *Go into the belly of the beast and if you get Rupert Murdoch to promote* The Simpsons, *then you have turned the energy of this whole thing on itself.* And, of course, what happened was that *The Simpsons* became Fox's biggest money-maker and almost single-handedly funded Fox News, and Fox News brought down the republic. So, I don't think you can win that way. I think that any amount of influence we try to exert through the machine ends up feeding the machine. They wouldn't accept it if it wasn't feeding it more than undermining it. They let you poke fun at it as long as you're making good money for it. It goes back to Theodor Adorno's arguments; are you part of the culture industry or are you making culture? And if you are making culture but then surrendering it to the culture industry, you, no matter what it feels like—this is at least my experience—end up doing more bad than good, and you end up doing more harm than health. So, that is why my next book, I am doing with Norton, which is an employee-owned independent publisher. I am trying to work outside that system as much as possible. I am teaching at a public university rather than a private one, with working-class kids, 'cause to a certain point, I feel like those are the choices that matter.

KS: My last question is to refer to Bill Joy's article, "Why the Future Doesn't Need Us," when he quotes Theodor Kaczyński and his manifesto "Industrial Society and its Future." Kaczyński claims the new technological environment will be able to accept only standardized and optimized people, because the system will not be guided by ideology, but by technical necessity.

DR: The digital media environment stresses efficiency and extraction because of underlying corporate agendas and programming. Max Horkheimer wrote a book called *Eclipse of Reason.* He was one of the Frankfurt School and he talked of two different kinds of reason. There is reason with the small r, which is the reason why you do things and the reasoning behind things—utilitarian reason. And then there's reason with a capital R, which is more like your big Reasons for doing things, your values, your higher goals. And he said that "capital R Reason" has been eclipsed or overshadowed or overtaken by small reason. And digital technology has certainly amplified and extended that trend. Digital technology is really good at specific optimizations, but really bad at soul or values or genuine, platonic ideals. So, I agree with him that, as currently deployed, digital technology emphasizes our utility values as workers, as consumers—rather than our intrinsic value as spiritual, soul-whole beings—and science is not helping us in this because in science, guys like Richard Dawkins are saying there is no God, there is no meaning, there is no nothing… But from the tech side and the science side, you get the same argument that human beings are only valuable in as far as they can contribute to the expansion and growth of the market. But it is not real. It is only the way the academics talk about it or the way Silicon Valley thinks about it, but right now, it is not the felt experience of people. I don't think it is what they want. I think people do want connection and meaning, and they do want to have orgasms inside each other and that is not technological, that is not digital. They want their smartphones so they can swipe right on a hot person. I don't think they see the phone as the end in itself.

Erik Davis*

"The people who resist modernity in these extreme ways are just as modern as the techno weirdos."

KONRAD STACHNIO: Is technology becoming magic now? Thanks to technology, we're able to externalize those aspects of ourselves that—until now—we considered strictly internal. Where are the limits of the self in this context? Are there any limits, or should there be any?

ERIK DAVIS: Yeah, well, of course, when you're using big words like technology and magic, you get to sort of define them and that can be interesting to a certain degree, and then it can become a little bit tedious. I think it's important to maintain a distinction between these two but also to recognize the way they feed into each other. So, I think it's important to say, technology is still based on rational principles within a naturalistic framework of laws and technical processes. And while magic has its own technique, magic has its own kinds of laws. They are, in some ways, different laws; they refer to the night side of human consciousness or the deep archaic frames of human experience and it's important not to just meld them into one. That said, I also think technology tends to come with it, a sort of—a set of other biases towards the rational operator who's going to use technology in order to achieve certain effects that aren't necessarily those that go along with magic. While magic can be used in order to achieve concrete and specific effects to operate in the world, there's an element in which both technology users and magic users are operators who are operating in the world. Magic also opens up into a much wider frame

---

*ERIK DAVIS is an American writer, scholar, journalist, and public speaker. Best known for his book *Techgnosis: Myth, Magic, and Mysticism in the Age of Information*, he has been interviewed by CNN, NPR, the *New York Times*, and the BBC, and has had appearances in a number of documentaries.

of enchantment and other ways of interacting between the self and the world, that I think is very different.

However, I do think it's not only fair but useful—if not even necessary—to look at contemporary technology through the lens of magic. Which is to say, paying less attention to how it's working, what the rational principles are that are in the history of the particular technology, what its usefulness is in a pragmatic sense in a world where people are struggling to get by and make money, etcetera—but rather, to see the way in which technology, especially at its forward edge, blurs with magical vision, blurs with a magical sense of the world particularly in terms of being able to invoke, charge, create and craft visions. Both are literal visions, images, but also whole views of the world. So, the way that a trance state in a magical ritual will sort of shift your consciousness so that images and synchronicities and correspondences begin to take on more flesh, they become more real to you because you've sort of shifted your consciousness, we can increasingly see technology not as being directed towards the rational, but actually entering into—and tweaking and shaping—the non-rational parts of human consciousness, so that there is a magic to manipulation, there's a magic to propaganda, there's a magic to algorithms anticipating your next desire.

At this point, technology has developed in a way that is becoming, that is entering into this sort of dreamlike or "dream side" of the human mind, human personality and human consciousness in a way that blurs these distinctions between magic and technology. And that's why I think it's important to think in terms of magic because it makes you ask different questions. If you keep saying no, no! Magic is all that bullshit that comes from before people were scientific and knew how to think rationally and knew how to think pragmatically, then you tend to tell certain stories about technology that I think are no longer true and are even, in some ways, actively distorting what's happening. And what's happening is that algorithms and the invention of realities through manipulation of video and audio, the anticipation of desire, the manipulation of fear, the manipulation of hunger—not in the literal sense, but of deep desire—that these things are making technology more and more a magical tool, that's being used for certain reasons by certain powers in order to achieve certain effects. And by thinking about it as magic, it doesn't take away our capacity to criticize it but actually helps us to see even more deeply what's going on.

KS: Is transhumanism a new totalitarian utopia after Communism and Nazism? Both previous utopias only offered some kind of improvement of living conditions. The current, new utopia proposes to undermine the very foundations of the functioning of life per se, proposing—for example—immortality.

ED: Wow, that's an interesting one. That's a great question; is transhumanism a totalitarian philosophy of social organization? Well, Yeah, I would say it's an open question, right? We don't know. There are certainly a lot of visions of transhumanism that are, at least on the surface, explicitly not totalitarian. In fact, they're the opposite; they're libertarian. You know, the idea that as we understand how human biology works, how human cognitive systems work, as we get better at fusing humans with technological extension, there's one vision—or, there are visions—of a transhumanist post-human future where the individual is able to in some sense become even more singular, to become even more specific, mutating in its own self-directed way and achieving in some sense more and more capacity to make decisions, to have control over its fate... This is that kind of libertarian idea of transhumanism, that what you want to do is allow individuals to intensify their individuality in creating this kind of world of a wide variety of ways of being, as certain people augment this and other people augment that. And so, on a surface level, it doesn't really look totalitarian. But the problem is that if we look at what's actually happening, and the way people are actually using technology to change themselves—let's take, for example, Fitbit and all the self-tracking, quantified-self technologies—well, on the surface, they seem to maybe be supporting this individualistic libertarian vision well, where I can use technology to track my own body and to refine and quantitatively improve its functioning in order to achieve goals that I want. That's a very individualist way of thinking about it. But of course, what's actually happening is you're wearing surveillance devices that are piling up all of this data in somebody else's server and that can be accessed by the police, that can be accessed possibly by insurance companies, that can be accessed by employers. So increasingly, employers are demanding that people stay relatively fit and so if they have a Fitbit, it's like, we're going to check with this Fitbit to see that you're getting your twenty minutes of exercise, or otherwise, we're not going to be paying your health insurance.

So the reality of these technologies is very different than the kind of surface story and the surface story appeals to the individual; you can gain control, you're going to get stronger, you're going to become more efficient and that's kind of like baby steps towards the transhumanist future. But at the same time, it's a network effect, where you're bound up with a network that's larger than you, that's monitoring you, that's creating a database of you, that you don't have hands on, that you don't even know exists, and that other people can have access to. And so that looks a lot more like a very insidious potential form of totalitarianism and that's just sort of like an easy example of the ways in which... the fact that the future is about networks, that the internet is everywhere, the objects are speaking with each other as well as with you and there are always outside servers, there's always a kind of surveillance mechanism going on even for benign reasons that puts us out of the individualistic story. It looks much more likely that we are weaving things together more and more tightly, more and more entering a kind of hive society which in a political sense is kind of totalitarian. So, I do think there is a very much a danger there, it's already rolling forward, and we... a lot of people are plunging into that precisely because they still buy the individualist story, which I don't think is really true.

KS: Dugin said we have to prepare future generations to war with artificial intelligence—because, according to him, we don't have any other choice. There are only two choices: war, or the end.

ED: Yeah, that's extreme.

KS: And he chooses the struggle, the war and preparing for the war. And he said that even if artificial intelligence becomes far more efficient than us, way more intelligent, we still have possibilities, because if we gather all people together at a global level, then we still have chances. And also, Slavoy Zizek asked this crucial question, namely: who will be controlling all these advanced technologies? Who's going to control that?

ED: Yeah, it's a funny one. I mean, I would like to hold out that there is a possible way of imagining forms of human AI sort of pairing up, a relationship if you will, that's neither entirely manipulative or entirely violent in its resistances. And I don't know whether that's holding onto a story. But you know, I'm lucky, I happen to know some people who work in robotics and they work with actual artificial intelligence. And they've thought a lot about how do we think about things like driverless cars and how do we think about these sorts of new, increasingly "autonomous entities" in our lives? And they point out that we already have examples of human beings and artificial intelligences to a degree, operating in a variety of circumstances. If you take even... like a fighter pilot, is managing an incredibly complex system that itself has its own intelligence, its own feedback mechanisms, and there are ways to imagine hybrids of human and AI where the AI is working as a kind of amplification or a sort of, a way of managing or intensifying human capacities.

Is this going to happen? I don't know; it looks like it might be a little bit more intense than that, especially because it seems like a lot of people are willing to kind of trust the new order of artificial intelligence, the new order of the algorithmic programming of reality, which to my mind leads to a more conflictual system. But it's hard to imagine how that struggle would be waged, short of really tearing down the whole system given how much AI is being wagered or how much the system is wagering itself on the expansion of AI. But I think we always have to keep in mind that our own imaginations are not only involved in these discussions, but they're actually kind of distorting them in some way, meaning that we already know the science fiction stories. We already know the apocalyptic scenarios, the Terminator stories, the 2001 stories; there are these core myths that we have, that in a way tie up too much the older myths about our relationship with non-human powers, with golems, with gods... And there's this aspect in which we are also imagining this world and our imaginations are themselves being weaponized or being manipulated or being used in order to develop the social story about artificial intelligence. So, it's more of a complex loop. It's harder to think about what AI can actually do or what it's going to be able to do without getting, you know, kind of falling into these more apocalyptic scenarios or narratives.

So sometimes, I feel that it's just not going to be quite as extreme as we fear it might become, where we go towards that kind of science fiction scenario, that it's going to be more of a muddle, that the future is more of a complex, irritating, complicated... things not ever quite working because there's another program going on over here. And then these guys have their AI; they're doing this thing over here, and this one's amplifying this capacity but the other one's undermining it, and it's more of a kind of chaos. Which isn't necessarily a better story, but it is less—of a kind of—terrifying, you know, us against them. There's only one artificial intelligence that we're all... There's just Skynet and we're, like, trying to elude Skynet, that it might actually just be more of this immense, complicated jungle of technologies and humans and human technology couplings in a variety of ways.

KS: Well, this is the worst nightmarish scenario from Zizek's point of view. He said that the worst possible scenario right now, is that no one is controlling anything, that the better scenario would be if there were some elite controlling the population on a global level. Because in this case, you have at least some reference point. But the black scenario is where no one is controlling anything.

ED: The whole problem of control is a really, really deep issue. I mean, let's leave aside technology for the moment, you know; you get into the problem of, how do we control our lives? What are we actually doing that can control our lives even in a non-technological situation? Where does control reside? And to me, that is in a way one of the most important questions—if not the most important question—of the post-war world, let's say from 1945 when cybernetics emerge, when modern computers really emerge, when we begin to understand how ecologies of communication and control helped set in motion society. And really—in a lot of ways—our modern condition comes out of this post-war move towards a global market and then the Cold War, and all that sort of forms the matrix of these questions.

And right from the beginning, there's always been this question of: what is control? What does it mean to control? How do systems control? How do we control systems? How do we even locate where control is actually happening? So in some sense, that's why a lot of conspiracy theories are actually kind of quaint, they're kind of charming; they're like nursery tales, even if they're horrific stories of the Illuminati sitting in rooms after doing ritual sacrifices and seeding pop culture with mind-control viruses. That's pretty dark. But the idea that there's a room where these guys are all sitting with their hands on the levers, in a way is kind of an anachronistic idea. It's kind of almost a hopeful idea, the way that Zizek is talking about. Isn't it scarier, the idea which seems more likely to be, that if there are very deep conspiracies of control, that there are many of them and that they're at war with one another and so we are almost like the fodder of this war? And we can see that even in a more or less conspiratorial way just by looking at the major companies. You know, what would the world be like if it was only Facebook or only Apple or only Google—would that be a better world or worse world? Because we have a world where these monsters, these archons, these posthuman, infinite-life kind of corporate entities are waging war with one another. And so we are stuck in between with incompatible systems, and this group is taking this data and this group's taking this data and we have to move between, and real social reality is getting fractured into these different kinds of worlds, because there's not a single control on top of it all.

Is that good or bad? I mean, to my mind, it's a little better, it gives us a little more room to maneuver in the cracks and in the inconsistency between these things. I would rather live in this world than a world where Google ran the whole thing. So, that's the other side of control too, that in a way, when there are wars between the higher powers, there's more room to maneuver, even though there's also more chaos.

KS: I was talking with Sheikh Imran Hosein; he represents the Islamic eschatology. And he said that from the Islamic eschatology perspective, we are dealing with the emergence of the false Messiah, the Dajjal, who will be using technology to manipulate people and impose his own will. And Dugin said almost the same thing, that the so-called Antichrist will be the collusion between biogenetics and artificial intelligence. And according to Dugin, artificial intelligence is not a great risk to people because we are robots already. So, for robots, artificial intelligence is not a big threat.

ED: So, wait. Why are we robots already? What is the reason he was saying we're robots?

KS: Because we are being manipulated by algorithms or social engineering already, and by political engineering, like automatons. So, for automatons, artificial intelligence is not a big deal.

Wow, really?

KS: Yes, and he said we have to consider if we should go farther along this route? Because this road will lead us to clones, chimeras, artificial intelligence, mutants and all bizarre forms of life. So, maybe we should take another road and go back and think; maybe we should do something else? Maybe this is not the natural way. Maybe all of this is more some form of ideology imposed on us which we take for granted.

ED: All right. Yes, for me that's where I just see another… that just sounds like another ideology to me, because even if it would make sense in principle to go back to restore more traditional modes, that's where we start to get into nationalism.

KS: No, nationalist, not traditional. He said that we have to replace technology by metaphysics.

ED: But I don't see how that gets in. I don't see how that gets impressed without immense forms of tyranny and you could say, well, that tyranny is just as bad as the tyranny of the post-human technological sci-fi future. And you know, I could see the value of that. But whose metaphysics? Because when you start to dig down and go, okay, Dugin, what do you mean by metaphysics? He's not talking metaphysics of Islam for example, so then you get into the problem of whose metaphysics? So there's a multiplicity there in which we're back to the same problem of the global and the multi-dimensional and the multicultural, different metaphysical systems, different models.

Is there a God? Now, if you're Buddhist, there's not a God. If you are Hindu, that's many gods. Okay great, but then we're back in the same war in a sense. So, the idea that you can kind of metaphysically resolve this problem that we're in, in a simple way that doesn't reintroduce the issue, then does it really… that doesn't really jive with me. I mean, I do agree that we… if we are resistant to this order, which is coming down the pike and which some people are very enthusiastic about. They are happy to transform themselves into mutants. They're happy to see what happens; there's this kind of yen for the strange or the yen for the power, for the new powers of that zone and it's very disturbing to me, it's very creepy to me but at the same time, I can see the ways that other forms of mutating or of shifting human consciousness, human subjectivity, human collectivity could be positive. And this is where you get into, what do we do about climate change? What do we do about the earth where we're really just running it down to the edge of being able to sustain even our life, let alone all these animals that we are destroying?

So, I can see ways that they're sort of a wedding of that, and I recognize that from some perspectives, the idea of a kind of global technological green order is the worst thing imaginable. It just sounds like global totalitarianism, global tyranny against national groups or whatever, and I recognize that's part of the problem too. But I increasingly go with, if any of these conversations are going to be meaningful in 100 years and 200 years, if we're not really just talking about a tiny group of elites who are able to survive in a very degraded environmental situation, if we can imagine something that's more robust, it might involve some form of collective technological mutations, social—and I won't say engineering because everything's sort of engineered. I mean, I don't believe this necessarily but when you raise the stakes to the level that you're asking the questions at this kind of apocalyptic stage, everything looks like it's potentially a form of horrible tyranny. The traditional metaphysics, nationalism, postmodern global technology, green global response; like, it's all potentially very tyrannical because, in all of these scenarios, something about the human being is being challenged at such a fundamental level, we can almost only react with a kind of terror. And I don't know how to navigate that and still make decisions, still try to keep our eyes away and not just fall back into distraction, fall back into the little rat maze of human desires that's already kind of constructed for us so that we don't really pay attention to what's going on. But there's a passage through terror and a passage through paranoia, and I don't know what lies on the other side of that. And all I'm trying to do is just figure out how to make that passage so that I don't become overwhelmed with fear and rejection and desire, and other people's fantasies, so I can maintain some kind of sense of ground as I wrestle with these huge, huge questions.

KS: Yes. I understand perfectly. Dugin said the whole problem comes from the time when we replaced God with humans.

ED: Yes, sure. I mean that's a traditionalist argument.

KS: I asked Dugin, OK, I agree with you, but all these scientists arguing that we are going to find a cure for cancer, and we're going to make people immortal—and he said that there is nothing wrong in dying with dignity, to

die without being cured. In his opinion, this is the whole misunderstanding of our role as a human and our free will. He said that our soul is already immortal, so, we don't have to do all these things like making humans immortal. This is the way modernity understands humans in mechanistic detail. So, he said if you have cancer, if you have some sort of disease, maybe this is God trying to tell you something?

ED: Sure. Well, I mean the version of that that I would rephrase, or that I can—I don't want to say, agree with, but—resonate with, is, it's true if you just want to talk about life extension and about the way that people put their hope in the future. If they're motivated by this idea that they're going to live longer, or maybe even be able to upload themselves or at least be able to deal with cancer and things like that, that does reflect a very naive and kind of adolescent approach to the human condition. And modernity and modern medicine have erred either in tricking us to not pay attention to the fact that we're mortal, or in refusing to talk about what does it mean to die with dignity and to only look at it as a programming problem that can be solved through technology. And so you get to these horrible situations where people are basically dying and they're in the last couple of months of their life, and yet they're getting plugged into machines and it gets extended for a few more years of the kind of miserable life that sucks all their money out, all the money that their family could have used. And it's designed to do that. It's designed to deal with fear, suck all the cash out and leave you bereft with that sort of miserable last phase of your life. That's totally true.

I don't think you need to invoke God and the idea that the soul is immortal even, to resist that, and to recognize that there's a way of dealing with death and where you invite your own mortality into your life, into your mind, into your philosophy, into your politics, into your relationships with other people. Just the fact that you don't need the idea that the soul is immortal. You don't need the idea that God is giving you cancer—that those don't seem necessary to me. I think there's a harder, more honest route where it's simply the fact of it that you begin to lead in. And then, what's wonderful about taking on that fact is that it's an illusion-killer. It makes you realize, oh wait, I was clinging to this bullshit because I thought it was going to make me immortal. Oh wait, but I'm not immortal...so... Oh wait, I was just fooling myself! And so it can cleanse the thought of death and in this way, I respect traditional religion in its relationship to death. That death is very important, that it is necessary. You know, I don't have a lot of truck with immortalists who believed that it would be groovy if we could live forever, whether or not we were inside of a mainframe. I think that would drive people insane. They would either go insane or they would become something that's so different than human beings, that it doesn't really matter; it's the same problem.

What do we do with the human? And the human to me is necessarily involved with this finitude. And I also believe that it's in a context of a larger infinite that there's something in consciousness that is not limited to this one little meat sack, and there's something in our sense of awe or our sense of the Divine that is tying in with something collective or cosmic that is in us in some way. I mean, that's my personal belief, but I don't think it's necessary to argue that, in order to resist this kind of this repression of death that does drive modernity in a bullshit way. And in that way, I do resonate with some traditional critiques of the modern modes of death. But I think it's the same thing in Buddhism. Buddhism is, in a way, a practice of dying and it doesn't need the God. You don't need the God. You don't need the immortal soul. I mean there's something, maybe, that goes beyond, that carries forward, but I don't think you need that to be religious in relation to death. That's my own flavor.

KS: Thomas Metzinger, the German philosopher, said we shouldn't praise evolution because it has no purpose.

ED: It's funny if we take that as the idea that it's foolish to think there's something progressive in evolution, which from a strictly Darwinian perspective is true; from a neo-Darwinism perspective, there's no goal. There's no T loss, you know? Maybe there are certain kinds of homeostasis that mutually support the situation. So, you want to keep that going if you can and there's sort of a drive to maintain things within a certain balance. But it's interesting that precisely at the point when modern humans—because modernity is all about progress, it's a story of progress—it's just at the point where more and more intellectuals or scientist people who're really paying attention, people thinking hard, see that that progress does not exist inside of evolution necessarily, that technology tells this immense story about progress! And it still goes on! I mean people still buy new gadgets and think about the future and think about cryptocurrency or whatever, as if technology and technological modernity are forces of progress. They still are doing that even after decades of seeing all of the complexities, all of the failures, all of the new forms of domination, all of the new forms of degradation—and yet it's a myth that's so deeply woven at least into moderns, that even in the face of all this evidence, we don't believe it's true of nature anymore. But there's still this kind of idea that it's in technology, which I keep waiting for us to wake up from. But we'll see.

KS: Yes. Well, according to Dugin, progress doesn't exist at all. There is no such thing as progress because God is everywhere. He is at every point, every

time and space. So, God will come after modernists and was there before modernists and is everywhere. But according to Dugin, we are living inside of the Antichrist, right now.

> **ED:** Yes, that's an idea. That's in esotericism. You know, you could just trace it back to Steiner. For example, he was very prescient about a certain way of looking at it.

KS: Dugin said most of these scientists are brilliant guys but don't know what game they are playing. They don't know they are just a small detail in the big mechanism of Antichrist, and that right now, we're approaching the last station before our destination along this road. And we are not living outside of the Antichrist. We are living inside of the Antichrist, and technology is a new organ mediating between our outside and inside, between our inner self and the outside world. And then this reference to Sheikh Imran Hosein who said to me that from the Islamic eschatology perspective, we are living inside of the Antichrist as well—I was very astonished by these similarities.

> **ED:** You shouldn't have been astonished because even though there's all sorts of surface differences between—or your deep differences between—Islam and a certain kind of Christianity, in some ways, they're cut from the same cloth, there's a kind of dualism of dark and light so that there's an idea of a good ruler and an antichrist. There's a notion of history as something that is, if not progressive then it does have a kind of end, a kind of drive towards the final point, at which point there is a transformation like a basic sort of archetypal model that you find in lots of religions, but certainly in all of the religions of Abraham, all the religions of the book. So, in a way, you can say, I could hear Dugin saying, well, they're not aware of the game that they're playing—but he's also in a story, he's also in a myth. I mean to me, the real fear is that the assurance that kind of conviction provides is just as liable to be another story and not only just a narrative, but an actual imposed ideological framework that's being used by certain powers at this moment in history in order to control people. So, I'm like, ah sorry, as soon as you get involved with authority, as soon as you say, oh, well, we know this because of Revelation, because of the end of the last book in the Bible—which is something they put in and they didn't really want, some people didn't want that in there—they were like, that's too weird. Let's not put it in the Bible. But they did, and we're supposed to believe that the Holy Spirit made sure they made the right decision to put that in the Bible. So now we can look back and we see hundreds of years since the Middle Ages, and every ten years, somebody thinks it's happening somewhere. It's part of historical Western Christian consciousness to see the

end, and even some like to take it from Terence McKenna, who's this crazy hippie mushroom guy, not at all conventional Christian—and yet he too sees we're moving towards an eschaton where there's this transformation. It's more positive in his view. That said, I think it's really important to wrestle with the idea of the Antichrist, the idea of a Fallen World System. I mean, when I wrote Techgnosis in the early and the late '90s, (it was) sort of an interesting moment because it was the first wave of optimism—a new kind of economy is upon us, abundance everywhere! There was a real kind of craziness in the world. And I was very happy in retrospect that when I wrote my book, while I was interested in tracking the optimism and where it came from—in my mind, coming from certain religious stories and aspects of our self that take on the sort of religious or mythological framework—at the same time, I was very skeptical. And I was like, yes, but there's always a dark side and you can track it in an Evangelical Christianity in America...

You can go back and you can say, you know when they first made UPC symbols in the early 1970s, the bars on products then... there were Christians, oh this is the mark of the beast, and here's the verse in Revelation. You go back farther, satellites are there. So, there's already this idea that globalization... that the creation of a global "technium" in Kevin Kelly's phrase, is itself a kind of sign of this Antichrist system. And that paranoia is valuable to a certain extent in order to keep our eyes open, but when it gets congealed into another authority structure where this Imam or this priest or this prophet is saying, oh, this is all the Antichrist, so therefore, come to my form of anti-modern power... You know, my form of whether it's terrorism or whether it's a political movement or whether it's nationalism, or whether it's a kind of... an ethnic resurgence in traditionalism, all of those modes—once they can congeal—they're playing the same game. There's modern too; that's the thing, that the people who resist modernity in these extreme ways are just as modern as the techno weirdos. We're all part of this moment and they want to pretend that they're not, and everybody else is ideology and they're Revelation. It's like, no, man, that is not how fundamentalism works. Fundamentalism is a modern phenomenon. There were no fundamentalists in medieval Europe. There's no such thing; we only get Christian fundamentalists in a modern period, it's part of modernity. So, I just don't think you can get out of the trap that way. You can't get out of the science fiction novel that way and I also think that it becomes associated with forms of tyranny that are impossible to condone.

KS: Rabbi Joel David Bakst said if we combined the Torah and the Kabbalah with new science, then we'd be able to add a fourth dimension to our three-dimensional reality.

ED: Wow, far out. You know, I guess I would hazard… I feel like we've been speaking at a pretty apocalyptic scale and I would maybe start answering this one from a little bit more near-future kind of perspective, and arguably that itself is a problem, that we should be willing to look at the ultimate ends of the kinds of systems that we are in. But at the same time, I think that's how you get crazy. Again, if you look at the history of apocalyptic thought in the West, you see that people are doing, have been doing this for hundreds of years and on some level, they're wrong. It wasn't that bad, or it didn't happen in the way they thought it did, but it was very easy to think that way. So, I think there's a tendency, especially as things unravel as reality kind of liquifies, as we break down more and more traditional forms of authority and even of discourse, that there's more room for more of these apocalyptic scenarios to become central. So, conspiracy theories that twenty years ago were at the very fringe of consciousness are now mainstream, are now referred to in *The New York Times* and mainstream newspapers, and believed by way more people than they used to be through YouTube or whatever. So, there's always that kind of tendency and I think it's important to wrestle with those possibilities, but it's also important to have one foot a little closer to home, which is that you're still in your apartment, you're still making coffee in the morning, you've still got to make some money, there's still… you've got to deal with your mom and she's dying and it sucks, and there's still this way that we are still human. And I think, it's not quite answering your question, but I think it's a really important point.

Just a thought experiment: Imagine somebody from, let's say, someone who's already in the modern world, like you, and someone from 1700, who lives in London in 1700, a smart person, who does not understand science, thinking about what's going to happen in the future. Maybe if you transport them now to downtown whatever, to 21st-century London and that person looks around at all these people, looks at the cars, looks at the airplanes, looks at the screens, looks at the devices in people's hands and begins to understand what people are doing. What's happened with money? What's happened with pleasure? What's happened with sexuality? All of this richness and weirdness of our contemporary moment.

To that person, I believe we would look like we are already totally transformed by whatever—some post-human, demonic, or angelic, or a mixture of both. We're already in some otherworldly place. We're no longer human for that person. I mean, even if you talk to them and they seem kind of the same, we look so weird to this guy. This guy's already a modern person, let alone somebody who is living in a more medieval situation or a Paleolithic situation. So, what I draw from that—and it might be true, might not be true, probably depends on the person—but what I draw from that is that we are already in this thing. Whether you want to call it the Antichrist or whether you want to call it modernity or whether you want to call it technology, we're already in this thing and yet I believe that there are at least aspects of our lives, of our ordinary everyday, lived experience that is not simply some kind of ideological dodge. And this is what I mean by the facts of love, the facts of the body, the facts of death, the facts of... we are still in a human condition and we don't know how far the human condition can extend into what sometimes looks like an apocalyptic singularity situation. We don't know how far the human story, however it changes, nonetheless maintains a kind of continuity as we go forward. We don't know what it looks like. We don't know what it feels like.

So I think it's important to spend some of your time very much invested in our ordinary reality of lived experience and not constantly undermine everything with these bigger scenarios, these science fiction scenarios or these scientific stories, that we don't really experience anything in reality, we're just telling a story in our brain. It's just a virtual reality that's run on our meat machine. Okay, maybe that's true. It's important to wrestle with that idea and yet, my mother is still dying, and yet I still have to make a decision about what food I'm going to put in my mouth, and yet I'm still falling in love and choosing to have a child or choosing not to have a child. But that world is not just an ideological trap. There's something else in our encounter with the world, in our encounter with nature, in our encounter with other people, our encounter with our spirits, with our own energies—that continues the human story in some way.

So, when you asked about these future scenarios, I think it's important to keep that close-up perspective as well as the long perspective. Now to finally just say one thing about your question, which is that I think there is something very ominous about the way that individuals are changing their subjectivity, changing their sense of social reality, changing even their relationships to their bodies and their minds, through the logic of optimization, efficiency, productivity, and competitive advantage. That those are all elements of capital. Those are all elements of this capitalistic mega system that is also what we mean when we talk about our technological present. Our technological present is also a capitalist present, and so what happens when we give over... individuals almost willingly give over the grit and the grime of daily human life to this logic of efficiency. In that sense, I do think that something weird is happening; whether or not that's an ideology, it's an interesting question. I think you can see it as an ideology. It's an ideology of capitalism, that the point of life is to become more efficient and productive and creative, and to sacrifice yourself so that capital moving through you can manifest itself and take care of its own goals; that's sort of an ideology.

But it's also true that there's a way in which what happens as people interpolate themselves into technological systems, is that they lessen the friction between the human condition and the demands of technology. And as you lessen that friction, it may be an ideology that you can live a frictionless existence. But it's also something that is happening technically. So, you can see that human beings are changing in the way in which they give themselves over fully to these kinds of logics. And then it breaks down the difference between the human being and these larger systems more and more—I mean, if they weren't already broken down. So, in that sense, it's kind of a meta-system that's using us to extend its own logic, a logic that isn't necessary, I don't think. It's something technology necessarily has, to prioritize efficiency and productivity and competitive advantage. I think you can imagine technologies that support the flourishing of complex ecologies of beings. I can imagine an ecologically-designed technology that actually supports human flourishing in a very different way. So, I don't think it's inherent in technology, but it does seem to be inherent in the technology that we're facing now.

Can we make that whole thing change? There's the argument that the goal is to inject the highest human values or the highest capacities of visionary experience or a divine experience into this mutating machine that's in a way like, make sure the artificial intelligence is able to become enlightened or become compassionate. You know, there's a whole side of things that's doing that and more power to the bull, go forward and try to keep that kind of thing going. I don't see that so much myself. I see something more where we kind of hold onto our gritty chaos in the midst of these transformations as a way of continuing to affirm the human experience, but it's just my dice roll at this point, of a great game whose dimensions, you know, are larger than you're able to compass.

Sheikh Imran Nazar Hosein*

"The mission of the Antichrist is to transform all of mankind into automatons like himself. The Arabic word is Jasad—a being without spirit."

KONRAD STACHNIO: Could you explain the subject of the arrival of Al-Masih ad-Dajjal, which according to what you said are supposed to rule the world from Jerusalem? Are you saying that right now, we are living in a developing technological and informational meta-system, supposed to be the body of the Antichrist?

SHEIKH IMRAN NAZAR HOSEIN: There are numbers of questions already in this one question. And there is a difference in Islamic eschatology, between the release of Dajall into the world and his arrival in human form, his arrival in our world of space and time. Someone can be in this world and yet not be in our material universe. Yes, the angels are here. They don't teach this in universities, of course. But the angels are here; every Christian believes that, and every Jew, every Muslim believes that. But we cannot see the angels. No. We also have the Jinn who are beings created by the lord God from smokeless fire. And they are also here but we cannot see them. That is the difference between secular scholarship and religious scholarship. So, when Dajjal is released into this world, he is here but not in our material universe.

Our view is that Dajjal was released a long, long time ago. The first evidence we have of the release of the Dajjal is before the time of Prophet Muhammad—Allah's blessings be upon him. We have the Hadith of our prophet who spoke

---

*SHEIKH IMRAN NAZAR HOSEIN is an Islamic scholar, philosopher and author who has specialized in Islamic eschatology, world politics, economics, and modern socio-economic/political issues. He has ceaselessly and expansively travelled around the world giving Islamic lecture-tours since graduating from the Aleemiyah Institute of Islamic Studies in 1971.

about the town, one part of which was by the sea and another part by the land, and the town is a triangular town. Constantinople fits it perfectly.

And the people are ordained by the Lord God to conquer the city without a fight, only by proclaiming his name. And these are the Christian people. And so, you have got Byzantium which is the holy Christian state—this is at the time of Constantine. He first became Christian and then died. When they conquered the city and Constantinople became a Christian city, then we are told that Dajjal was released amongst them. So, from our eschatological perspective, the first evidence we have of the presence of Dajjal in this world—it could be there before, but this is *our* first knowledge that he's released among the Christians in Byzantium in Constantinople—and the consequences of Dajjal being involved there in Constantinople... Eventually, there was a split, one part of Constantinople remaining faithful to Jesus and another part splitting and coming over to the West. And this was called the Great Schism. And the remarkable difference between the two was fidelity to the law. That part remained faithful to the law, for example the law of the Sabbath, and *this* part abandoned the law. And the Lord God then cursed this part and declared them to be like apes—very powerful language in the Quran. It is *this* part of the world which gave us modern Western civilization. And it is modern Western civilization which went to Jerusalem to conquer the city. And then you have the Jews being brought back and the state of Israel there from modern Western civilization. So, there is a difference between the release of Dajjal or the Antichrist, and his appearance. His appearance is very clear in Islamic eschatology, that he will not appear in human form. You will not be able to see him ruling the world from Jerusalem until the Great War takes place. We're on the doorstep of that Great War, oh yes. And whether you are friend or whether you are foe, no one can avoid the Great War that is coming.

After the Great War takes place, very rapidly, events will unfold. This is our eschatology. One version is that these events are going to unfold within seven months and another version, seven years. So, we don't know which one it is. But immediately after the Great War, you're going to have the conquest of Constantinople. That conquest of Constantinople prophesied by Prophet Muhammad—Allah's blessing be upon him—to be understood, is meant to correct the wrongs which were committed in the previous conquest by the Ottoman Empire in 1453. After the conquest of Constantinople, then the Hagia Sophia cathedral will be returned to the Christian people. It is *their* cathedral. It was very wrong of the Ottoman Empire to convert it into a mosque. When that is returned to the Christian world, it will facilitate friendship and alliance between the world of Islam and the world of Christianity which follows Jesus. Not that part of the world of Christianity which has abandoned the law. Then after the conquest of Constantinople, the next event will be the appearance of the Antichrist in person. This is the timeline.

So, now I've explained to you the difference between the release and the appearance. To proceed further, the Antichrist has a mission, and his mission is to impersonate the true Messiah. The true Messiah, when he returns, will return to rule the world from Jerusalem and therefore from the Holy State of Israel which has to be restored. In order for the Antichrist to impersonate the Messiah successfully, he has to do a number of things. For example, he has to liberate the Holy Land for the Jews. He already has done that. He has to bring the Jews back to the Holy Land to reclaim it as their own. He's already done that. He has to restore a state of Israel in the Holy Land and get the Jews to believe that this is Holy Israel of David and Solomon. He's already done that. He has to get the state of Israel to become the ruling state in the world, and for that, he has to not only bring down the United States, but he also has to bring down the West. And that appears to be the purpose of the Great War. So, after that, Israel has a clear sail. The only fly in the ointment is Russia. That's the only fly in the ointment. But it is not possible for the Antichrist. No. Because he is not more powerful than the Lord God and the Lord God in the Quran has declared that a people who follow Jesus faithfully are going to rise to a position of dominance over those who have abandoned him.

Who are those who faithfully follow Jesus today and who still have the law, some integrity as Christians? It will be the Orthodox Christian world, not the Western Christian world. The Western Christian world is moving in a direction when a man can marry another man and get a marriage certificate. So, you have to have a PhD from Disneyland to accept these to be the true followers of Jesus. And so, the Antichrist cannot stop Russia. The Antichrist can bring down the United States and bring down the West but cannot stop Russia. Because the Lord God has ordained that those who follow Jesus faithfully are going to be raised by him to that position of dominance. When the Great War takes place, therefore, it will be a pseudo-ruling state of the world that Israel will claim to be. But that is the end of the story; when Jesus returns, he will dispose of the Antichrist. Gog and Magog will be destroyed. And that's the end of *this* state of Israel. And this makes the way now for the true ruling state to come when Jesus returns.

Now comes the part of technology. The Quran tells us something about the Antichrist which is very revealing. Our interpretation of the Quran is that the Antichrist is not fully human. He is less than human but you cannot tell by looking at him, no, that he is less than a human—because externally everything about him *will* be human. In what way does he differ from a full human being? The Lord God, having created the human being, informed us he then blew into him his spirit. That spirit, which he's blown into the human being gave to the human being some qualities of freedom. For example, freedom of will to be able to choose, to accept or to reject, freedom to think, to make mistakes. *That* freedom is a human quality. The angels don't have it. The animals don't have it. They have a spirit but not the human spirit. The human being is the only one who has the spirit in which he has the capacity to acquire knowledge independently to reach up to the stars with a human mind and to make mistakes, and the capacity to choose either to go on this path or to go on that path. This is not there in the Antichrist. In this respect, you may liken him to an automaton. He is programmed externally and so he does not think for himself—someone else thinks for him. He does not choose for himself. Someone else chooses for him and that is the Lord God. But his mission is to transform all of mankind into automatons like himself. The Arabic word is *Jasad*—a Jasad—a being without spirit. But in this case, he is a being and he has a spirit but not a human spirit. If he is to transform mankind into automatons like himself, he has to put people to sleep. So that they become the equivalent of sheep. They lose the capacity to think independently, and they lose the capacity to choose independently. And so, they become a people who will dance to any tune that he plays. He has already done that in the United States of America.

You have a whole nation of people in the United States now who are the equivalent of automatons. And the Europeans—the Europeans look across the Atlantic and they are wondering, what happened to these people? How can they not think? He has used, I believe, television as his major tool in this process of what may be described as brainwashing, the conditioning of the human mind. At the end of the road, we have instead of natural intelligence… we can actually create an artificial intelligence and use this artificial intelligence to condition the human mind. Eventually, you are not going to be thinking for yourself. I don't want to go beyond this because I will be treading in the field of the scientist who has more knowledge than I do. But it appears to me that we are now on the doorstep of an age when people are going to eventually be put to sleep in the sense that they will be acting like sheep. They will have eyes and yet cannot see; they have ears and yet cannot hear, they have hearts and yet cannot understand. And the Quran likens them to cattle, they are *just* like cattle. The Antichrist wants to reduce mankind to cattle.

How do we respond? And our response from Islamic eschatology is that the book of Allah, the Quran, the sacred scripture is the best response of all. That as you recite the Quran in Arabic, it has the capacity to heal. It has the capacity to restore. Whenever you've been brainwashed, it washes it away and as you study the scripture, the process of studying the scripture revises what may be described as internal intuitive, spiritual insight. In this way, you are able to counteract the Antichrist. This is my answer to your first question. Islamic eschatology recognizes Gog and Magog. And Gog and Magog have been endowed by the Lord God with the power which none can destroy but Him, only He can destroy. And when they are released into the world, they will spread out in all directions, when with that indestructible power, they will establish the world order of Gog and Magog. And so, when we see globalization, the emergence of the one world, global society; it is clearly the work of Gog and Magog. That one global society has to be connected or interconnected in many different ways. And here is where you have the possibility now of conducting research to find out what are the systems at work to establish and sustain a one-world society, that all be interconnected. And one very clear evidence of such is the movement towards one currency for all of mankind.

You start by removing gold and silver coins which is real money and you replace it with artificial money, paper money which has no intrinsic value. The value is assigned to it, and the value you can change. And if I don't like you, then I can bring down the value of your money and if I like you, I can allow the value of your money to remain stable. The Swiss Franc remains stable forever. The Pakistan Rupee, the Bangladeshi Taka—anyone we don't like goes down. So, you can see in the world of money, the movement from gold and silver to paper money and then to electronic money, then to crypto currencies and eventually to one currency for all of mankind which they will control. And when they have one currency for all of mankind, then all of mankind are interconnected in one global society.

We used to travel with horses and camels, donkeys and so on. And we had our autonomous means of travel, independent travel. I don't need any help from you if I want to get on my donkey and travel. All I need is to get the food to feed the donkey, that's all. But when you do away with all of this natural form of travel and now you have a new form of travel which is the motor car, you have to register the motor car. If you drive your motor car without registration, without insurance, without this and that, you will be arrested. In order to get the car registered, in order to buy the insurance and so on, you have to go through regulations, and they can then either permit you or deny you. You want to travel? They can put your name on the no-fly list. As soon as you see this movement away from the natural form of travel to a new technologically-interconnected form of travel, it is a form of control of mankind. And they can eventually put you to rest, you cannot move. You are trapped.

This is here another form of connecting the world technologically and there are many others. You can use medicine, hospitals, and so on, and the new technology that is supplied to medical science and is all patented, and so people who need this medicine have to come here to get this medicine. This is the part of the world of technology in which all of mankind is being connected to each other and it is linked to Gog and Magog.

KS: You say the Al-Masih ad-Dajjal will be blind in the right eye and he will not have inner spiritual insight. Rather, he will be a body without free will, controlled externally. Do you think the beginning of this "body" is the currently emerging external systems of artificial intelligence which can know a man better than a man knows himself?

SINH: The body of Dajjal which is what you are asking about is different from the systems which he will create in order to facilitate his mission. We must make a distinction between the two. The body of Dajjal will eventually emerge in this world as the son who is born of a mother and a father. If he is not born from a mother and father and cannot show his descent from the House of David; no Jew will accept him as the Messiah. So, he has to show his lineage to the House of David and has to be a Jew. He cannot be Christian or Hindu or Muslim. He has to be a Jew. Otherwise, they will not accept him. They did not accept Muhammad—Allah's blessings be upon him—because he's not a Jew. They did not accept Jesus because they don't know who is his father. He cannot be the Messiah. So, the body of Dajjal will emerge in the world as a baby, a human being and grow up to be a young man. And the systems of artificial intelligence, the process of transforming mankind into automatons like himself must be studied as something independent from the body of the Antichrist. Don't mix up the two. These are a means to which he seeks to transform mankind into automatons like himself. And when people are being transformed into automatons, they will lose the capacity to think independently and to act independently. And so, they become like sheep, and this becomes very easy for him now to control and rule all of mankind.

KS: What is the reason for the very fast, accelerating transformation of the world in terms of technology, genetics, socially and economically—presented as "natural" and almost irreversible?

SINH: In the Quran, there is a chapter or a *surah* entitled *Ants*. And in this surah, we have an event in the life of Solomon. He is in his kingdom of Israel in Jerusalem with the capital, and he learns of the kingdom rule by a woman in Yemen—Sheba she is called. And she has a gorgeous throne, but they worship the sun. And he sends a message to her ordering her to worship the one God. And when she receives this message, *if you do not do so, we're going to come against you with our armed forces,* she then sends a response to him by offering gifts, hoping it would calm him down. And when he receives the gifts, he says,

I don't need this, what the Lord God is giving me is far more valuable. And then he warns them: *I am coming with my armed forces.* He then asks the people in his court: who can bring me her throne?

Now, there is a distance of more than two thousand kilometres between Jerusalem and Yemen. And one of the Jinn who is in the court—this Jinn has a different category but this one is the most powerful of all—he says: *I can bring you that throne before your eyes, from your throne, from your court here.* In other words, the Jinn, these unseen beings, they have the capacity to travel from Jerusalem to Yemen at great speed and they also have the capacity to move objects through space at great speed to bring that throne here. If the Jinn can do that, they can do that with military technology. You can get a bullet to travel at great speed. You can get a missile to travel at great speed. And the Jinn is working with Dajjal. And this is the explanation of that part of the scientific and technological revolution which came to western civilization, which gave it a military ascendancy in the world. The world had never seen the gun before and the bullet travelling at that speed. Your sword in your hand has no use to you anymore. If he has a gun, then he can shoot you from a distance, before you can raise your sword.

So, new military technology is based on speed. The same thing with travel: you have camels travelling with loads on their backs and then suddenly you have the steam and the steam is used for a steam engine. And now you have a train and the train can take all the loads that one thousand camels were taking previously. And then you have a combustion engine and a motor car can travel and aircraft can travel. What we see is the movement in the direction of greater speed, constantly greater speed. However, the Quran goes on to see something more. Not only do the Jinn have this capacity to travel through space at great speed and move objects through space at great speed and have transferred this to modern Western civilization, but someone else in the court of Solomon then spoke and he is not the Jinn and he has access to a book. The Quran does not tell us anything about the book. But what we do know is that this book has in it knowledge which is more advanced than what the Jinn have access to. So, if the Jinn can allow a missile to travel at this speed, if you have access to that book, it will make the speed of the missile look like peanuts. So, there is another world of travel through space and time which is far, far more advanced than anything that modern Western civilization has access to.

Whoever accesses that book—the Lord God will choose who will access that book, but they have to be a people with faith. It cannot be the people who say a man can marry another man and get a marriage certificate. We see that already taking place now. Russia, after the collapse of communism and the Soviet Union, Russia is advancing technologically, missile technology.

And the advance that Russia has achieved has already made aircraft carriers obsolete. With Russian missile technology today, an aircraft carrier is a sitting duck, cannot be used in warfare. This appears to be the beginning of military ascendancy, which will come to one part of the world, which faithfully worships the Lord God. They will have speed that mankind has not ever witnessed before in history. This is the future that is coming. This is from the Quran. Look at the subject of speed, the accelerating transformation of the world from another perspective now. Our prophet said that in the end time, time will move faster and faster. The whole year will pass like a month. A whole month will pass like a week. A whole week will past like a day, etcetera. And the master plan that works is, as time moves faster and faster and faster, it diminishes the capacity of the human mind to think with depth.

You can see the same thing on the television screen. That is what they do, they move the images on the television screen, fast, rapidly, rapidly, rapidly. And your mind is therefore damaged when you're looking at the television and you are seeing these images on the screen changing rapidly. The end product is, you live on the surface of events; you are trapped in the here and the now. That's all. You lack the capacity to go back in history. You lack the capacity to anticipate what's coming. You are a prisoner of the here and the now. This is part of the process of brainwashing people. This is the rapidly changing world today.

KS: Islam is now almost automatically presented as associated with terrorism. How do you see the Salafi movement in this context, and the future of Islam?

SINH: I do not allow people to attach labels onto me. I have a capacity to think and a capacity to use my reasoning to understand that this is a process of character assassination, the process of trying to give Islam a bad image and this is a normal thing when people are waging war. It's been there all through history and they're only using what has already been used in the past. The enemy is always portrayed as something bad, and we are the good ones. The proper way to respond to this is to invite people to think, and that is a difficult task to do. How do we get people to think? How do we get people to try to prevent themselves from being brainwashed when they are watching television every day? And they have the internet and they have this, that and the other. Islam is being presented as terrorism because Islam stands in the way of what they want to do to rule the world from Jerusalem, that is going to be called The Holy State of Israel. Islam stands in the way, but we are not only ones who stand in the way. The Orthodox Christian world led by Russia also stands in the way. These two forces. The Orthodox Christian who sincerely follows Jesus and the Muslim who sincerely follows Muhammad—Allah's blessings be upon him—these are the two forces left in the world which are an obstacle to them. So, these two have to be presented in the worst possible light, making them look bad. That is their planning but there is a Lord God. We believe that there is a Lord God. He doesn't sleep. He's alive and they can tell as many lies as they want. They can do whatever they want to present the truth as falsehood. It cannot succeed. Because the Lord God has created this world as a moral order and the moral order is one in which truth will eventually triumph over all rivals. So, they can continue with their assassination, trying to make Islam look like a terrorist religion. It will not succeed. At the end of the road, the truth will triumph when Jesus returns. This is our belief.

The Salafi movement in Islam is comparable to the Protestant movement in Christianity. It is a religious movement without a spiritual heart; that is the Protestant movement. If you take out the spiritual heart of religion, you are left with a shell. They are like automatons and this is the danger with the Salafi movement, because they lack the spiritual heart of the religious way of life. They are incapable of internal insight and hence cannot recognize the reality of things. They are living with the world of appearances, and Dajjal is using them. Not all Salafis, but he is using them as his warriors. He has them fighting this bogus Jihad in Syria, in Iraq. He is the one who has created this ISIS. And the United States and Britain and France and the Western world is now their most powerful support. If they don't have the support of the United States and NATO, Russia and Syria—the Syrian Armed Forces can liquidate them tomorrow. They will be finished in Syria. They don't have any legs to stand on. The only reason why they are still alive and kicking in Syria is because the United States and NATO are preventing them from being eliminated. And so, the Salafi movement is comparable to the Protestant movement in Western civilization—a form of religion without the spiritual heart.

KS: What do you think about split of the Orthodox Church in Ukraine right now?

SINH: The people of Ukraine, the Orthodox Christians of Ukraine, they ought to do a little bit more thinking and not allow themselves to be passively used as passengers on the train that the Antichrist is using. All through the history of modern Western civilization, Russia has always been considered to be the enemy. Through all the history of modern Western civilization, Russia is the enemy and they have waged endless wars against Russia. The last Great War against Russia was the Crimean War in 1852 to 1855, I think, and they gave everything they could give in that war to fight Russia. The objective was to deny Russia Crimea, because if Russia does not have Crimea, Russia will not have a warm water port. Russia will be left with the Arctic when for several months of the year, it's ice. If you don't have the navy for so many months of the year, you are not the superpower. You are diminished now. So, the purpose of the Crimean War was to diminish Russia's military power by denying Russia Crimea. The Crimean War ended with an agreement that Russia would continue to maintain sovereignty over Crimea, but Crimea would be demilitarized: no naval base allowed in Crimea. That was the end of the Crimean War. Russian sovereignty over Crimea was recognized to be maintained. But you do not allow it to have a navy, a naval port. And then came the Soviet Union and Russia was part of the Soviet Union, Ukraine was part of the Soviet Union, and so on.

But now look at what happened in 1954. Nikita Khrushchev transferred Crimea from Russian sovereignty to Ukrainian sovereignty without seeking the permission of the Russian people, without seeking the permission of the people of Crimea. They did it in the middle of the night like a thief. The Russians never accepted that. The Crimea never accepted that. Why did the Soviet Union transfer Crimea to Ukraine from Russian sovereignty in 1954 in the manner in which it was done? My answer is, while the Soviet Union did many things which were good, it is very clear that the Antichrist was using the Soviet Union for its own purposes. He created the Soviet Union as an atheist state and the purpose of creating an atheist state amongst people who have the spiritual heart or religion close to them, was to destroy Christianity. Destroy Christianity. And although the Soviet Union ruled over Russia and those countries for so many years, they did not succeed. When the Soviet Union collapses, they're returning to Christianity.

If the people of Ukraine had spiritual insight, they would ask themselves the question: why was Crimea transferred to Ukraine? Why, in 1954, without Russian permission, without Crimea's permission? Russia was deprived of Crimea because the Antichrist wanted eventually that Ukraine would become an independent state when the Soviet Union collapsed, and that Ukraine would become a member of NATO. And when Ukraine becomes a member of NATO and Crimea belongs to Ukraine, Russia is finished. I mean, the plan is so plain and clear, like daylight. Why can't the people of Ukraine who are sincere Christians—they are not the people who say that a man can marry another man—if you are such a Christian and you are following Jesus, then why can't you think and understand that this is the plan of the Antichrist to ensure that when Ukraine becomes a member of NATO, Russia's goose is cooked? And Russia will be denied Crimea. And then came the coup d'état in Ukraine, and it is plain and clear who were the actors involved behind the scene. You don't need a PhD to understand that. So, the turmoil going on in the Orthodox Christian Church in Ukraine has to be understood in terms of the Dajjal's continuing effort to deny Russia the power that Russia needs to survive against the West.

If they continue with these kinds of conflict within the Church—using religion to continue your political agenda—your political agenda is anti-Russian. That's your political agenda, and you are now using the Church, using religion to pursue your political agenda. You cannot succeed. Why? Because the Lord God has said in the Quran that those who follow Jesus are going to be raised to a position of dominance in the world. And when they reach that position of dominance, it will remain until the end of the world. This is in the Quran, and the Christians of Ukraine have to ask themselves on which side of history do you want to be? Do you want to be on that side of history where the Lord God raises you to the position of dominance in the world, and you remain until the end of the world? Or do you want to be on the wrong side of history? That's my response to you.

KS: Is Islam now more a victim and a tool for achieving geopolitical goals for external forces? Islam is presented to the world almost as a Hollywood caricature.

SINH: We need to now—in answering your question—look to see what is the role of Islam at the end of history. And our answer is: it is not the destiny of the followers of Nabi Muhammad; it's not our destiny to be a dominant force in the world at the end of history. The role of being a dominant force in the world at the end of history belongs to the followers of Jesus, not to the followers of Muhammad. Our role at the end of history is to support those who are following Jesus, who when he returns, will then be the leading force in the world, ruling the world from Jerusalem.

In answer to the first question: there is a role for Islam at the end of history in conquering Constantinople. That is our important role because when once Constantinople is conquered after the Great War, Hagia Sophia will be returned to the Christian world. And the return of Hagia Sophia to the Christian world will cement a bond of friendship and brotherhood and love between these two worlds, but ours is a supporting role. So, we are not really bothered with all these people who are ruling over the world of Islam on behalf of the West. They don't represent the world of Islam. We don't have a military role to play, so it doesn't bother us. After, however, *after* the Antichrist is killed and Gog and Magog have been destroyed, at that time, said the Prophet, a Muslim army will now liberate Jerusalem. It is not the Christians who will liberate Jerusalem. The Muslims will liberate Jerusalem and at that time, these governments all will be gone; when Jesus returns, there will no longer be any Kingdom of Saudi Arabia and all of these people. They all will be gone. So, the Muslims will be liberated from the chain to which they are trapped.

Rabbi Joel David Bakst[*]

"Science fiction of the past has been surpassed by science fact of the present."

KONRAD STACHNIO: If we are entering the Messianic era, will our reality change completely? Will physical reality be changed into what it "really is"? Will the world we know disappear and will this transformation be something like "hell" and total destruction for us? Is this due to the fact that our world is now upside down and bringing it back to the right track will cause unforeseen consequences?

RABBI JOEL DAVID BAKST: What will this transformation look like? The Messianic era of the prophets and Jewish sages of the Kabbalah is not some idyllic utopian world where the wolf, allegorical or not, is laying down with the sheep. No. The wolf and the sheep, along with the entire animal kingdom, are returning to their original higher-dimensional state where they were on the level of humans today! Plants will be on the level of our current animals and the entire mineral kingdom will be on the level of our current vegetation. But don't try to envision this paradigmatic transformation. At best, we can only produce 3D anthropomorphized projections! We are talking about a phenomenon that is so alchemical that all of 3D reality is literally going to morph back into its original higher state. That is what we must be concerned about. This is not just climate change—this is atomic change!

Forget Gog and Magog and the Apocalypse and all that stuff. Yes! There is chaos and hell happening and it's going to get worse, much worse. There are, and there will be, battles and wars—physical, cyber and psychic. That, however,

---

[*]RABBI JOEL DAVID BAKST is a teaching rabbi and scholar of the Talmud and Kabbalah who studied and taught in Orthodox yeshivot while living in Jerusalem for 20 years. He has a global reach and has lectured and taught in Israel, the United States, and India.

is not the biggest problem. If I am being attacked and killed, at least I know the reality around me is still 3D, but if reality, the very atomic structure itself, starts to "pixelate" and spacetime begins to dilate, what is going to happen to my consciousness and reality? That is a death worse than death.

But this must happen in order for 3D reality to go back into its higher state that preceded its collapse. Is this a Bible story about a mythological fall of humanity? No. Rather, it is about the collapse of higher dimensionality. Prolapse is actually a more precise term because it is also an anatomical term. Because like a hernia that protrudes from the body it is, however, still attached to the body. That's why the word prolapse is important. You still have a continuity; it is contiguous. We never completely separated from out of our higher selves. It is just that we lost that 4th coordinate, the 4th direction but it is still here. We are inside of it; we are embedded in it. The language of the Kabbalah is just what allows us to see the missing coordinate now. Better yet, it is the language that allows *it* to see *us*—for the higher-dimensional Adam to communicate with us, its own micro-self. It allows the higher dimension to communicate, to transmit to its own lower self that became cut off. This is like a science fiction story, but one that is written ten-thousand years into the future. If the 4D and the 3D are perfectly aligned, then the 3D that is inside of the 4D, remains as the inner lining of the 4D. But what happens is that the inner lining gets turned inside-out. Take let's say a tennis ball. It has the outer layer that gives the ball its shape. But, on the inside there is also the layer of rubber that gives the ball its bounce.

If you have this ball without the inner rubber lining, you'll have a ball, but it is not going to have much of a bounce. On the other hand, if you only have the inner lining and no outer form to contain it, you'll only have a limp piece of rubber with no spherical shape, and certainly no bounce. This is what has happened to reality and consciousness. The inner lining of higher-dimensional consciousness got turned inside-out. It still wants to "play ball," however, by trying to mimic a real ball, but it really is only a blob. The true ball, on the other hand, has lost its bounce, its potency. Take a ball and let the inner lining of the ball represent 3D and the outer layer of the ball represent 4D. Imagine that through a small hole you put a tweezer inside the ball and pinch the inner rubber lining, and now stretch it and pull it out, while the outer surface of the ball remains. The 3D inner lining, although still attached to the outer shell of the ball, is now "inside-out." The 3D lining is now "naked" without its outer 4D covering—its garment. Humanity was originally the unified 4D-3D reality, but we lost our 4D garment. It is our consciousness that is now "naked."

This is the dimensional prolapse of 3D "falling" out of 4D. That is what it means when the verse-formula says that Adam and Eve saw that they were "naked and ashamed." What is the source of their "shame"? Not because of being naked as if we suddenly found ourselves naked in the middle of downtown Manhattan! Remember, Adam and Eve at this stage are still higher-dimensional fields of consciousness. Rather, they lost their 4D covering, their higher-dimensional clothing. Imagine a hypercube that loses all its hyper 4-dimensionality and now all that is left is a single 3D cube. Is that cube going to feel naked or what? You see, this is the source of their dimensional horror, their traumatizing shame. They know they lost their true higher consciousness. They know what has happened. The catastrophic shock is beyond the imaginable, the consequences are ineffable.

This is what it means that the Messianic era is simply the inversion of how we got into this lower dimension, lower consciousness to begin with. Remember every time you go down, you ratchet down. And lower consciousness gets locked in. It can't go back up. This is part of the problem that comes with lower dimensionality. Every time it drops one level, it totally forgets the previous level. The level itself forgets that the previous level even exists. It is worse than forgetting. It doesn't have the necessary dimensional constitution—the "brains"—to even do the processing called remembering the higher level. So, imagine, that this keeps happening, dimension after dimension. It is a runaway situation, like a nuclear meltdown, an exponential regression, but here it is a dimensional meltdown. This is the Kabbalah view of the reality that we are in right now, and this Messianic process involves none other than all of us. It is our collective consciousness, which is the Original Adam. Now here is also a controversial question: Is the Messiah an individual or not? The answer is both. The final Messiah is one individual, but the body of that one individual will be made of all the humans of humanity! We are all parts of the very body and mind of the Messiah. Every individual person and every collective nation. We are all simply different parts and aspects of the body of Adam.

KS: Should we be afraid?

RJDB: Yes. But there is something more encompassing than being afraid, it is called "holy dread." That's what we should have. Not to be afraid but to be in a state of holy dread. When you add the holy component, the Messianic element, to human fear, you get holy dread. You see the difference? When 3D consciousness encounters an "unknown" within the dimension of human 3D, we are afraid. Holy terror is when 3D encounters an unknown within the Godly 4D. You know the famous expression: "There is nothing to fear but fear itself." This means that it is just falling back on itself, i.e., 3D onto 3D. There is no holiness there. Holy dread is when you are taking two opposites and you are forcing them together. The holy component elevates the fear to a level of dread, and then you have holy dread. Now, how will it play out? No one can know. You know why? Because of the butterfly effect, discovered by the meteorologist Edward Lorenz in the 1960s, which set the stage for modern chaos theory. That is why weather is so tricky, because you can put all the facts into the computer and run a simulation. If this and this come together, what will this look like tomorrow? What will this look like in a week? But the problem is that you have the butterfly effect, which means that even the slightest change in any part of the system is so sensitive and interdependent upon every other part.

So, because of the cosmic butterfly effect, we cannot know exactly how we are going to get from point A to point B. Especially when point B is no longer in the same dimension as point A. In our case, we now stand upon the precipice of space and time. Where we are going—point B—is in the higher dimension. Going from point A in 3D to point B in 4D is not easy, because in 4D there are no longer any 3D coordinates! Although this seems counter intuitive and impossible, it becomes very possible if we use a little of higher-dimensional mathematics and 4D surface topology, upon which the Kabbalah subsumes. So, because of the butterfly chaos factor, even the Divine Mind—"God"—cannot know exactly how the minutiae of the edge of spacetime are going to play out. This phenomenon of the higher-dimensional consciousness "not knowing" Its own higher-dimensional future, however, only refers to the precise details, not to the big picture, on the macrocosmic level. The sun always sets on the 6th day of creation (Friday) before the seventh day of Shabbat comes in. The details, however—the formation and coloring of the clouds, the number and species of birds flying overhead, the exact temperature and barometer readings, etc.—cannot be known even to Its highest Self, because that's the part where It's "hiding" Itself from Itself. Since It is omnipotent, omnipresent and omniscient, concealing Itself from Itself is not an easy thing to do, in fact, it is logically impossible, because there is absolutely nothing here but Itself! But It is doing it anyway. But It cannot know the exact linear line of causality due to the cosmic chaos factor which is factored into the revelation of God's Own consciousness. This is a very deep concept. Even though initially, this sounds absurd—even if one does not believe in God—and even beyond science fiction, from the perspective of modern chaos theory, it is very logical and scientific.

Does this stretch the limits of science? Absolutely. But this, in and of itself, is not new. It is astounding that science has gone beyond what science fiction can even imagine. Science fiction of the past has been surpassed by science fact of the present. Additionally, at the rate of acceleration that we are now going, the science of the future, which, as I am saying these very words, is already becoming outdated and even obsolete. They couldn't even imagine the internet and smart phones that are now more powerful than the supercomputers and the mainframe computers of yesteryear. This is astounding. This is Messianic.

We are going where no man has gone before—except for Adam and *we* are that Adam. Adam is here, and his higher-dimensional consciousness is ultimately what is in control. In fact, although we are all deeply responsible for our actions, the direction and events of the world are virtually on Adamic autopilot. This is the important thing to know. That is why we cannot be afraid. Don't fear—Adam's here! To begin to see the signs and wonders, especially through the eyes of science and technology, that are occurring right before our eyes—that is holy dread. Think about it—Adam is more here than we are here. Because he is the programmer, we are the program. The virus got into the computer, into the program and into us. Adam is getting it out. He is almost finished. It is a matter of cosmic nanoseconds before the Adamic Messiah will turn the entirety of our current reality outside-in, and the virus will no longer have a host to cling to. This is how evil is destroyed. You don't kill the evil. In fact, it is not possible to "kill" the evil. It will keep returning—like the evil villain who dies at the end of the movie only to return in time for the sequel. Rather, we must disconnect the virus from the host and the root of the evil will be gone. Then there will be nothing there anymore because, in truth, evil does not have a separate, independent reality. Although it is very real now, and we are obligated to fight it, and even to kill it if necessary, it was never real to begin with.

Here is an example of what I mean by saying that the roots of evil have no existential reality. Imagine you have a huge balloon in the shape of a giant monster. It can be very scary, especially in the dark. It looks like it is real, but, in reality, it is just a giant balloon. You put one little needle in it and what happens? Pop and poof! It's gone. What you have left is only a limp film of innocuous rubber, that's all it was! [Laughs.] The air, in the analogy of the balloon, is representing the life force that is animating the "balloons of evil" that we appear to be embedded within and surrounded by. Really, there is nothing here outside of Itself. There is no evil, there is no Satan, there is no devil, there is no duality, there is nothing here but the higher, and even higher consciousnesses of Itself. Yet, if there is nothing here but Itself, why does evil, suffering, hell and the endless horrors of this life, whether produced by natural causes or by humans, seem so real, so ugly, and so overwhelming? The answer is: because, according to the Adamic operating system, we are inside of the equivalent of a horror science fiction story that is beyond science fiction. Once we begin to accept this, if only as a possibility, we can now begin to learn the language and code of the system behind it. I have been studying and testing out the Adamic Messiah code for over forty years. After many years of studying Jewish law and lore, Talmud and Jewish ethics, I then began to study the Kabbalah. I was learning in Jerusalem, the center of the world. I noticed that the Masters of Kabbalah had a whole secret language. I realized that they were in the 4D, working here in the 3D. As an example, take King Solomon: everything we are talking about, he knew it a million times more—he was doing it. He was stimulating, orchestrating and making the final rectification. He was Adam incarnate and he knew it. King Solomon was a fractal Adamic avatar, as many of the rabbis and Kabbalists were.

King Solomon was plugged into higher Adamic consciousness. He was the wisest man on earth, and everyone in the world, including the mysterious Queen of Sheba, heard about him. She traveled for months, from Ethiopia, with her entourage, and she checked him out and found that nobody had wisdom like he did. That is because it is all the language of the Kabbalah which King Solomon encoded into the three books of the Bible which he wrote: Ecclesiastes, Proverbs and the Song of Songs. Everyone in his tradition—and that is the tradition I am coming from—they knew the language of the Kabbalah. Yes, over the millennia, you have problems. The system breaks down a bit, Jews are persecuted and tortured, the teachers are murdered, and the Jewish people have to run from one country to another. But there is still a direct lineage, a direct transmission line, and this is what I call in my book *Beyond Kabbalah*, the "Mind of Moses." It is a living consciousness; it is an internet that stretches across space and time. It is always peer reviewed. For example, everything I am sharing with you here, is not my speculation, or my theories—it is simply the ancient, futuristic language of the Kabbalah.

KS: You said that science is a projection of a higher dimension and science currently stands on its head. Therefore, all science and technology will be changed. How would this be done?

RJDB: What, in their essence, is science and technology? Why is it evolving exponentially, and yet no single person or company or government oversees it, and no one knows where it's going? There are symposiums, interviews, books and innumerable websites about our future. What the Kabbalah of the Adamic Messiah says about the future of science and technology is totally unexpected and counter intuitive. Technology is not only coming from the scientist and the technologists. Yes, technology is being discovered here in 3D, but it is also being revealed from 4D. By whom or by what? Is it being seeded by a benevolent alien civilization? No. It is being orchestrated by the higher-dimensional consciousness of the Original Adam who is now "finishing his work" in the Garden of Higher Consciousness.

As Arthur C. Clarke famously said, "Any sufficiently advanced technology is indistinguishable from magic." If we understand "magic" as also inclusive of "miracles," then technology is also much more than what we think it is.

Technology is nothing less than techno-miracles. Science and technology are fractals of the light of Adam's own parallel consciousness, that are penetrating and interfacing with our present 3D reality in our here and now, *right now.* We are not only rushing forward into the future, but we are also being pulled and sucked back into the future *through* the higher-dimensional Tree of Knowledge. The branches, twigs and thicket of the inter-dimensional "Data Tree of Knowledge" that leads us all back into the Tree of Life, which is at the very center of the consciousness of Adam Kadmon.

It is intriguing to note that the Hebrew word for knowledge is *da'at*—as in the English "data." What is all this *da'at* data based upon? What is running the Adamic operating system? It starts with divine energies, something like the dynamic of the Oriental yin and yang. In the Kabbalah, it is the dance of God's straight, expanding light creating interference patterns with His contracting, curved light. The straight, expanding light is the masculine energy, and the curved, contracting light is the feminine energy.

It is like two beams of light that are split and then reunited to produce the effect of a hologram. Even though I have spoken mostly about the higher source being Adam Kadmon, what the Kabbalists refer to as the *Ain Sof* is the "true" God of Israel. The Ain Sof also has the Ohr Ain Sof, the *Light* of the Ain Sof. It is an eternal ratio. As the Light of the Ain Sof is to the Ain Sof, creation is to the Creator, just as human is to God, and, as "He" is to His Name. Even when we say only "Ain Sof," it is shorthand for the "Light of Ain Sof." This is because the Ain Sof is always going to be beyond our vanishing point. Like in art or photography, you have a horizon point that you can see up to. Then right behind that, you have the vanishing point. The vanishing point is the Ain Sof. The horizon point is the Light. That is the Light of the Ain Sof. The ratio is eternal. It is only a question of whether the Light is on the inside, or on the outside of the Ain Sof—that is the only difference. The Light is never separate from the Ain Sof. In fact, the Light is really the inner lining of the Ain Sof that gets turned inside-out.

We are the inner lining of our own higher consciousness, but when the inner lining gets exposed, it stimulates the virus. The virus clings to it and takes over. It is like a Petri dish where you germinate and grow bacteria or viruses. The virus is not evil in itself. But evil is also not an illusion. Rather, it is real, as real as a virus, but as I explained, a virus is not a true-life form, it can only mimic the "consciousness" of its host. So, what is the truth about evil? Is it real or isn't it?

What Kabbalah does is that it takes all the opposites, e.g., the Western concepts of God and the Oriental concepts of *not*-God and synthesizes them together to create a new middle. This is a tool from quantum physics called a coherent superposition—one thing superimposed upon another. What you are looking at, trying to grasp is never this thing or that thing. It is never a "this" or a "that," but something new in the middle. It follows a pattern similar to Hegel's thesis, antithesis and synthesis, except in Kabbalah consciousness, you have to stay in the tension of all three together, at the same time. How do you do this? You take the *this* and you negate it. Then you take the *that* and negate it. Then you include the *this* that you originally removed, and you also include the *that* that you also originally removed. Meaning, you create something that is more than both. It is suspended in the middle. True consciousness is when your consciousness is suspended in-between while giving birth to the new middle.

The new middle, the coherent superposition, in the moment is like a hologram. It's being projected and suspended in space. It needs at least two cameras, i.e., two projectors, projecting two images, one upon the other into the center, and then it comes alive. This maneuver is crucial because this is how we get around the virus, even though we are embedded in it, including how we process our thought. But this exercise of consciousness can prevent the virus getting what it wants—our consciousness, a juicy host indeed. With this consciousness tool, we never assume anything is what it appears to be. Only, we don't say it is an illusion, but at the same time we don't give it hardcore reality. It is rather, a type of virtual reality. Now, "one man's virtual reality is another man's primary reality." But that man's reality can be a virtual reality to another man's higher reality. Over a hundred years' ago Georg Cantor, the German Mathematician, developed the idea of an "infinity of infinities," i.e., that there were levels of infinity. He created a mathematical system where you can now have infinity to the first power, infinity to the second power and so on. Such a framework is subsumed in the Kabbalah. When you apply this to the Kabbalah of consciousness, you have the Divine Pleroma, i.e., levels and gradations within God's endless dimensions of the Light of His consciousness.

As the Divine Wisdom iterates replicas of Itself, it descends and cascades down the pleroma of consciousness into lower dimensionality, and then concretizes, assuming lower forms. The Kabbalah teaches that Divine Wisdom iterates into the wisdom of the Torah; and the wisdom of the Torah, in turn, iterates into the code of the Seven Sciences. This is what is happening with what we call science and technology. You know why it is moving so fast and that no one can stay on top of it all? It's because we are not discovering it here in this dimension, rather it is coming from the Messianic Era. It is coming from the higher dimension itself. If we can begin to understand this, it turns everything on its head. Everything. This is the science of the future—I wrote a chapter about this in one of my books. When we follow the roots of science, surprisingly, it takes us back into the higher dimension. It is part of the higher dimension that has fallen out. That is why it is so miraculous and techno-magical. It is evolving every day beyond anyone's imagination, because it is not only coming from here. It is dripping down, as it were, raining down from "heaven"! It is coming through, seeping through from the other side, because we are right up next to it and interfacing with its other side. The Messianic Era is all here, right now.

KS: Could you explain the subject of the liquid light radiating from the center of Jerusalem from the so-called Foundation Stone, which is supposed to change all humanity?

RJDB: In the center of Jerusalem, adjacent to the Western Wall, and underneath the golden Dome of the Rock, lies the Foundation Stone. Externally, it is not very impressive—just an outcrop of rock atop Mount Moriah, where King Solomon's Temple stood 3,000 years' ago. It is also where Jacob had his dream-vision of angelic entities ascending and descending upon a celestial stairway to heaven. Yet, its secret is the key to Adamic consciousness, and thus, it is the key to everything. Its purpose and destiny are to change all humanity.

From the perspective of the Kabbalah, the responses to the grand, puzzling questions of life are unexpected. Yet, they are not based simply on faith or religious thinking. Rather, Kabbalah is the Wisdom, or the Science of Truth, which is also the science of the future. According to the Adamic Messiah operating system, the Foundation Stone is the equivalent of the collective pineal gland, which is the toroidal center of global Adamic consciousness. A toroidal center is very different from a point in the middle of a circle, drawn on a flat piece of paper. It is also very different to the center of a sphere. A toroidal center is the vortex at the bottom of the funnel of a giant, cosmic, torus-shaped, interdimensional vortex, a tunnel between dimensions, a literal "stargate." That is the secret of the over 3,000-year history of Kabbalah-based Judaism. Three thousand years' ago, King David made Jerusalem the capital of ancient Judea, and his son King Solomon built the Holy of Holies on top of this very Foundation Stone. It is upon the top of this Mount Moriah that the well-known Ark of the Covenant was housed. The Jewish priests were the guardians of the collective pineal gland of humanity. That is the secret of the Temple of Jerusalem. That is the secret of the Foundation Stone. This is the secret of the living enigma of the nation and people of Israel. It is the collective pineal gland of humanity in real time, right here, right now. This is not limited to a religious belief. Rather, it is simply a micro-macro relationship.

Let me explain this micro-macro relationship. On the micro-level, located in the center of the brain is an enigmatic little organ called the pineal gland, that is the subject of remarkable new scientific exploration. Likewise, on the macro-level, located in a world center, is an enigmatic rock known as the Foundation Stone, that is the subject of remarkable ancient Jewish traditions (as well as having some of these traditions adopted into Christianity and Islam). On the micro-level, the pineal body has historically been associated, both in the Orient and in the Occident, with different functions of consciousness, including being the seat of the human soul through which the spirit enters and leaves. On the macro-level historically, the Foundation Stone has been associated in the Bible, Talmud and Kabbalah traditions with different functions of global consciousness, including being the "seat" of the world's collective soul, and through which, the world's spirit enters and leaves. On the micro-level until now, however, there has been no mechanistic model or physiological explanation as to how the pineal gland functions, and why the human body even needs such an organ centered in the brain, the consciousness center of the body. On the macro-level until now, however, there has been no mechanistic model or metaphysical explanation as to how the ancient traditions of the Foundation Stone actually function, and why the collective world body needs a Foundation Stone centered in Jerusalem, the consciousness center of the world. On the micro-level, it has very recently been medically proven that the pineal gland is capable of generating a natural substance known as Dimethyltryptamine (DMT), an extraordinarily powerful essence that is able to alter one's personal consciousness, transport a person's mind into an inner metaphysical dimension, and imprint one with a radical life-changing spiritual experience. On the macro-level, it has long been known that the Foundation Stone has been prophesied, that at the inauguration of the Messianic Era, it will generate a universal substance known as *Mayim Chayim*—"Living Liquid," an extraordinarily powerful liquid-light essence that is able to alter our collective consciousness, transport humanity's mind into an inner metaphysical dimension, and imprint all of us with a radical, world-changing, Godly experience.

The Foundation Stone in Jerusalem that is currently under the Golden Dome—an Islamic shrine—built upon the spot where the Second Temple stood, and also where the First Temple, Solomon's Temple stood, is where the Holy of Holies was located. That is the collective pineal gland, and that is why, for 3,000 years, competing nations wanted to conquer it, possess it or to destroy it. Why has that one spot on this entire planet been crisscrossed and conquered more than any other piece of property in the world? Why? What is going on there?

You have seen pictures that show what the planet earth looks like at nighttime, where you see the concentration of electrical lights where major cities are located. Or, you have seen the flight patterns of airplanes on a map. You see the concentrations of the crisscrossing. Some cities are very concentrated, and others are sparse, and some are almost barren. You can clearly see the major hubs because they have got many more lines going through them. There are more planes that are arriving there and taking off from there. So, you've got hubs and super-hubs and mega super-hubs. By analogy, Jerusalem is the mega super-hub of Adam's consciousness. If you were to look at all the crisscrossing of all the empires of the Western world, there is no other geographic center that is crisscrossed more than the Temple Mount of Jerusalem. It is undeniable. If you don't know history, then it can be denied, but for those with their eyes open, there is something very suspicious going on throughout human history. Why? Jerusalem is the gateway, the vortex and the stargate back into the fourth dimension, the original higher-dimensional Garden of Eden.

Following the collapse of higher-dimensional consciousness into this lower dimension, only the Foundation Stone remains. Due to the holographic nature of reality, there are micro foundation stones everywhere in the world. This is what accounts for all the holy places on the globe. But all the meridians meet at one vortex—the Jerusalem Foundation Stone. The Foundation Stone is like a vestigial organ that is all that remains of the higher-dimensional pineal gland, which is also known as the Tree of Life. The Foundation Stone is the principal and central magnet of attraction to the Western world. That is what is driving everybody crazy, because it is all about Adam and the cosmic DMT—the Living Liquid that is about to flow. This is also the Kabbalah explanation as to why there is now this phenomenon of the popularity and growing interest in the world about DMT and ayahuasca. By the way, when the word "pineal" is transliterated into Hebrew it is virtually identical in sound with *"peniel,"* which literally means, "Face of God." A profound and life changing truth is staring us right in our face.

DMT and ayahuasca are revealing models to understand something profound about global consciousness associated with the new Messianic paradigm. Pineal-generated DMT is a profound and unexpected model for what is known in the Torah Kabbalah tradition as *Mayim Chayim,* the Living Liquid. This higher-dimensional, hormonal-like liquid is prophesied to be secreted from the Foundation Stone by the prophets Zachariah, Ezekiel and Joel. A watery substance is going to begin to trickle out, continuing to increase until it turns into a river of light of pure Messianic consciousness. This is what ultimately will flood the world and fundamentally transform human consciousness.

KS: What is the relationship between the restoring of Jerusalem and the writings of the Gaon of Vilna? What role does Jerusalem and the State of Israel play in the arrival of the Messianic Era? Could you explain the subject of the arrival of the Messiah as consciousness in this context?

RJDB: The Kabbalah school of the Gaon of Vilna, together with the entire spectrum of Torah and Kabbalah, also places an emphasis on the role and mission of what is known in rabbinic tradition, and especially in Kabbalah literature, as the Twin Messiahs—the Josephic Messiah and the Davidic Messiah. Although it is shocking—and even disturbing—to many people, the saga of the Twin Messiahs is the standard model in classical Judaism. Utilizing this doctrine, the Gaon of Vilna and his disciples were spearheading a covert movement to return and begin rebuilding the Land of Israel. This was at the end of the 18th and the beginning of the 19th centuries. They were attempting to consciously stimulate and trigger the beginning of the final redemption process by emigrating to Israel when it was still called Palestine, and by resurrecting the barren land that had been laid waste for 1,800 years. This is the thread that binds together the Gaon of Vilna, the restoration of Jerusalem, the Messianic Era and Adamic consciousness.

The Twin Messiahs are two forces within the super-soul of the people of Israel. This is an extremely complex and esoteric field of study. Simply put, however, the Twin Messiahs are, on a national level, the inner mechanics that drive the process of exile and redemption through the almost 4,000 years of Jewish history, going back to Father Abraham. Both of the two Messiahs are the central players in the cosmic tikkun-rectification of the collapse of Adamic Consciousness and Adamic reality. These forces can manifest within individuals within any given generation, as well as manifesting within collective processes. Anyone or anything involved with exile and suffering is an aspect of the Josephic Messiah, and anyone or anything involved with the Davidic Messiah is an aspect of redemption, bliss and ecstasy. The final and completed 4D Davidic Messiah is none other than the Adamic Messiah. The process that leads up to that point is the collective process of the 3D Josephic Messiah. The rebirth of the State of Israel in 1948 is a manifestation of the Josephic Messiah. The State was founded by mostly secular Jews who had rejected Torah and Kabbalah, and to this day, it is primarily run by a secular government. Consequently, it is not yet completed—this will only occur when Israel and the world fully enter into the Messianic Era.

KS: Do you think that with this coronavirus, we can avoid the scenario of Gog and Magog? This virus is an aspect of the mercy of God, as you pointed out. Am I right, or did I misunderstand something?

RJDB: Yes, based upon the current evidence, I believe this is the case. However, because of the cosmic butterfly effect, even if we know the correct trajectory, the smallest amount of anything can have radical consequences on how it all plays out, how it changes. But based now upon everything, it appears that the coronavirus is an aspect, or stage of the prophesied "battles" of Gog and Magog. Now, there are always two ways in which something spiritual can reveal itself: through the "left side" which would be constriction and judgment, or through the right side which would be more mitigated with compassion and kindness. But even in this latter case, through compassion and kindness, the "battles" of Gog and Magog would be a disaster and a severe crisis. It is like someone who needs to have an operation. In the end, the operation is successful and the person gets healed. But a person can have a horrendous experience before, during, and after the actual operation. Or, a person can have the best and easiest experience of the operation where everything goes well and there are no complications. It used to be that before they had drugs and anesthetics, people were operated on while they were fully conscious or semi-conscious.

Something radical has to happen. That is what we have to understand. In order to go from 3D to 4D, which is what the entire concept of the Messianic Era is about, a radical paradigmatic "tipping point" must be reached. Unfortunately, when there is an over-emphasis on the Messiah part—even though I myself use that term, "Adamic Messiah" is the preferred term—it can take away from the actual transformation of reality, which is the Messianic Era. Regarding the Messianic Era itself—the dimension which I refer to as 4D in contrast to 3D—for us to return back to that 4D state, it has to occur regardless, but there will be some discomfort and pain. So, we have the left-hand way and the right-hand way. The right-hand way is what appears to be occurring, because Gog and Magog is primarily about a global concept. Forget about the battles, the wars and the "apocalypse." All of that may, in part, happen, but it doesn't have to. We have to first understand, what are the principles of Gog and Magog? Gog and Magog represent the *klipah*-crust—*klipah* means a shell—that is what is surrounding this dimension that we are in. Literally, everything here—down to the very molecules and every atom—is surrounded by an invisible membrane. Every thought, every word, every action, every event, all of this is surrounded by this membrane. Collectively, that membrane is called Gog and Magog. The prophesized victory over Gog and Magog is when all the membranes covering 3D reality and consciousness will be removed simultaneously. So, Gog and Magog is totally global and it involves everybody and everything. There are three accounts of Gog and Magog in Scripture: in the Books of Ezekiel, Zechariah, and the Book of Joel. According to the simple reading of the Scripture, it looks horrendous—absolute apocalypse.

However, I believe—based on, again, all of the evidence—and when I say evidence, I mean taking the formulas of the sages, i.e., the kabbalah formulas from the Talmud, the Midrash, the Zohar and the Kabbalist, and plugging them into what is happening and thereby staying away from biblical prophecy. It is very easy to read a verse and it will appear to line up, even uncannily, with current events. However, if one is going to do that—I don't care whether he is a Christian or an Orthodox rabbi—you have to be prepared to do the same with all the verses that are surrounding that verse in Scripture. You cannot just take one verse because it fits in. And even though there may be truth in that verse, it is still being taken out of context—and the primary purpose of prophecy, ironically, is not "prophecy" i.e., seeing into the "future." It is not about a prophet who had a vision 4,000 years ago, 3,000 years ago or 2,500 years ago peeking into our current generation—this is not Nostradamus. They are describing formulas, configurations. They are describing the equivalent of a chemical chart. And then, depending upon all the other factors in any given generation—in our generation—how will it manifest? How will it play out? There are always the two ways that it can play out: the rough way or the soft way. Remember, even with the soft way, there is still an operation—something has to be cut and removed. The question is, do we want just a few drops of blood, whatever that may represent, or a bloodbath?

It appears that the coronavirus itself is a great act of loving-kindness, compared to the alternative apocalyptic nightmare of a bloodbath. The former is God's compassion because God, a.k.a. Adam, the Adamic Messiah, which is the consciousness that is really orchestrating all of this, is doing this to achieve the same goal. This goal is to cause separation between people and families, parents, children, community, sports and entertainment, i.e., everything that is done, including politics and the nations—the nations are all being separated from each other. Everything is closing down, shutting down. No one knows what is going to happen, even after the curve flattens, as they say. There are so many unknowns. But the one thing that is most crucial is that it is global. Everything that the United Nations aspired to and attempted to achieve, together with diverse governments, and people on a community level and on a therapeutic level—it has all been turned upside down. Now, as I pointed out, on the other hand, we have got more global transmission through the internet going on than ever before on this planet. It was already growing exponentially during the last 10 years, 5 years, and this last year, but this has put it into hyperdrive. Zoom must be making a lot of money [Laughs.]. But this is good. Again, this is what I see—this is what Adam is doing himself and herself—Adam and Eve together. (Actually, there are two Eves—the two female energy centers of Adamic consciousness.) We are now on the threshold of literally returning to the original higher-dimensional Garden of Eden. We are going back into the roots of the Tree of Life. We are passing through the thicket of the branches of the Tree of Knowledge of Duality. Because we are in the middle of it, we cannot even see that we are in a forest because we are so deep in it.

We hope and pray continually, as again, this is all based upon the math, the logic—nobody wants to believe what is about to happen is going to happen. It does not matter if it doesn't happen tomorrow, or if it doesn't even happen in a few years, or even if you want to say in theory 10 years, or whatever. Because, once space-time starts dilating or contracting, what you thought was a long period will be experienced as a very short period. Similarly, when you are far away and you are looking at all the events going on here, it is just a matter of moments that is taking place. This is the essence of Gog and Magog and this is the good news. All the Hebrew letters also have a numerical value. Together, the two terms "Gog and Magog," in Hebrew equal the number 70. The Hebrew letter *ayin* also equals 70 which is also the first letter of the word *o'hr* which means skin, animal hide or leather. Now, the first letter of the Hebrew alphabet is *aleph* which equals number 1. The letter *aleph* also begins the word *ohr*, which sounds identical to the word for skin which is spelled with the letter *ayin*. But when spelled with the letter *aleph,* which equals the number 1, this word means light or illumination. Thus, in ratio, as skin is to light, the letter *ayin,* which equals 70, is to the letter *aleph* which equals 1. Gog and Magog, which equals 70, is the "skin" or the membrane of lower 3D reality, but it is about to be transformed back into the light of the number 1, the unity of the higher 4D reality. The word in Hebrew for "secret" (*sod*) also equals exactly 70. "Gog and Magog" is the "secret" of the re-inversion of the 70 archetypal nations of the world back into a singular unified humanity. (This ratio is also the relationship between the numbers 1 and 7, which is at the root of the secret of the number 7. The six days of the week are followed by the seventh day, the Sabbath, and the six millennia are followed by a seventh millennium, known as the "Great Sabbath.)

KS: You said that we are approaching the number 999, and then we will go into the 1,000 and everything will be changed from that moment. As we approach the singularity moment, we reach the tipping point first, where we are going to have a quantum-like jump, or something similar which occurs, and then everything will change. Would you explain a little bit on this?

RJDB: You said it correctly. We are about to hit the tipping point. We are about to make that quantum jump, a quantum leap, back into our original higher-dimensional consciousness and reality. Yet, this concept is nothing new. This is what the whole purpose of the Jewish people was about from the beginning, going back to Abraham, in truth going back to Noah and Enoch and Adam—it is all one story. As I explained, you have to start with this assumption, even if it sounds too bizarre or radical. It doesn't matter, because initially, we only have to consider it as a model. Then we do the math and see how it plays out and if it answers more questions than other systems do. That is the sign of a true system—if it can resolve the apparent inconsistencies and contradictions, apparent problems, and yet still function under the same operating system. The starting point is that our entire reality and consciousness is inside of a greater all-encompassing consciousness. Initially, we can forget our concept of God, forget Jew, non-Jew, Torah, Bible, Christianity, Hinduism, science, atheism, and virtually anything you can think of. We begin by letting go of everything. We start with an assumption that we are inside of a greater consciousness. That is what is called Adam. There are different layers, levels and aspects to this "Adam": there is Adam Kadmon (Primordial Adam), Adam HaRishon (Original Adam) and Adam homo sapiens, as we are currently now. An aspect of this Adamic consciousness collapsed and part of the inner lining of this super-consciousness got turned inside out. But there is a consistent ratio, of inner to outer. Anytime, anywhere that life turns inside out, it goes from 1 to 70. Seventy, again, is the secret of the skin, of the flesh. The number one is the secret of the same flesh and skin on the inside. You have to simply use a topological model ("spherical geometry"). You have to envision this. You have to use the surface of a toroidal shape to envision what our minds alone cannot yet grasp. Start with a circle. You put Jerusalem in the middle of that circle and let that circle represent all of the world. Now you cut it up into 70 slices, like 70 slices in the pie.

Now, that is only a two-dimensional surface. Even if you now take that into a sphere and make Jerusalem the middle of a sphere, that is also only a partial model. Rather, imagine this on a rim—you have got a 360-degree circle, that is the rim, and now imagine that is a funnel, and it is creating a tunnel going through itself, like a cosmic wormhole. This is the torus model. On the edge is the crust. When consciousness falls out into the cosmic graveyard of dark matter, what happens is that the dark matter clings to it. It is now subject to the gravitational pull of the dark matter. Of course, it is not a gravitational pull; we know gravity is not really pulling. It has to do with structure and shape and how heavy or dense things are.

Your question that you mentioned, how do we defeat the virus? You have to approach it on its most basic, fundamental level, and that is topology. It is surface structure. The virus wants us to think in terms of lines and squares and cubes and circles. That is Euclidian. That is Greek. That is 3D. Instead, imagine the curvature of space, like a portal into a giant cosmic torus that takes you through and into the 4D. But the most important thing is that the upper funnel, which represents the higher consciousness, turned inside-out and it fell into a lower dimension. That is us. (How and why it happened is another story.) But now we are going back in. That is the Messianic Era. Actually, the Messianic

Era is only the nexus between the lower funnel and the upper funnel. There is a little canal there, a "worm hole" that takes us from "here" to "there." That short period is the Messianic Era. When we go back up into the higher dimension, the other side of the cosmic torus, the upper funnel, this is what is referred to as *Olam HaBah,* the world or dimension to come.

I am laying out the big picture, which is really important, because we have to see the forest here. We are going back into the higher dimension through a type of toroidal structure. It is energy, it is consciousness. Coming back to your question of how do you defeat the virus? By, ironically, staying on the surface. Always stay envisioned—*in* the vision. The virus likes corners. It likes edges. That is what it clings to. When you stay in a rotating, toroidal flow, the virus has nothing to cling to because it is constantly moving. What was on the inside is on the outside and vice versa. There is no duality. The cosmic virus hates that. This is also what I refer to as "Möbius strip consciousness"—only one surface but with two "sides." The torus and Möbius strip are consciousness tools that can be used as instruments to identify the consciousness virus and to shake it off, because it cannot cling. It needs three-dimensionality. When I say three-dimensional, I am including duality in that. In the higher dimension, there is no duality. It works with the whole system. So, the tipping point is absolutely the Messianic Era. That is why terms like "tipping point," and "the singularity" have been part of the language of our times for the last 50 years.

KS: But how can we know that we are really into this Messianic Era right now?

RJDB: That is why we can be somewhat thankful that we have this phenomenon of the coronavirus as opposed to an apocalyptic bloodbath scenario. It has brought the world to its feet. It is so global, it is so radical, no one alive today can fully contain the impact of its effects and consequences. It brings with it all the inconvenience, all the isolation, and yet the psychological effect this is having is profound. So here is a sign that is so blatant, so explicit, that no one can deny—no historian can come along and say, "Something like this happened once before in Ancient Rome or in Egypt or China or World War I." No. Everyone's jaw is hanging open. That is the proof.

Again, this is not proof based upon simple belief or dogmatic faith—there is no faith here. That is important. We don't want faith. We want science. We are making calculations based upon this—it is a reset. It is a cosmic reset. Sooner or later—even according to the secular view of the field of consciousness, people have been talking about the tipping point forever. But it seems like it is never tipping. In fact, things are getting worse and worse, even with all of the good that is being done on the global, universal consciousness level and so forth, like people getting together and meditating at the same time around the world and all these types of things. But the tipping point seems to be more elusive all the time. People fundamentally have not changed. Leaders have not changed—and not just leaders in the political world—leaders in the religious world and leaders in the secular, New Age world. We have this crust of jealousy, envy, power and control. And it is not because people are bad; it is because we are in the dark matter itself. We have all been commandeered by the same dimensionality virus.

I am trying to show you how, from a non-religious perspective, just how the science of kabbalah looks at the facts in front of us. Something has occurred that is not only other-worldly, but outright "alien." Yes, we have had these dystopian movies and books, i.e., *Andromeda Strain* and *Planet of the Apes* where humanity is almost completely killed off, or humanity actually dies. Till now I have been referring mainly to the *medium* of the virus and the reaction it is generating in us. The other purpose of the coronavirus is the message behind it: what in the world is a virus? It is right in our face. A virus is the most bizarre thing in all of creation, especially when the theory now is that all human life, from an evolutionary perspective, is coming directly from a virus. With no viruses, there would never be evolution because there would never be any change in any genetic structure. So, this is also very suspicious. What is the message? The name of the game is that, as the corona virus is to us, in turn we are to Adam. This is absolutely shocking, but when everyone wakes up to that realization, the awareness itself will begin to dissolve the virus. It won't have an unconscious host to hang onto.

Now, it's not that humanity itself is evil. Yes, we are a type of virus, yet we are also a mixture of the Adamic good that has been hijacked by the viral evil. We have the host within us—that is Adam. That is pure consciousness. That is pure God and pure light. But there is something clinging to it that animates us and gives us our 3D consciousness because everything has its backside, and the backside is really the inner lining that gets turned inside out, as I explained, and now the virus is king. It is an invisible enemy. It is a war that is worse than a war because you don't even know where your enemy is. We have a model now with the plague of the corona virus. The virus is not a true-life form. That is exactly what Adam is saying to us. Adam is the higher consciousness that has been trying to deliver that message to us ever since the collapse and "hijacking" of his own consciousness. Part of his higher-dimensional self collapsed into time. We fell into this thing called time and history. It is not that it is not real, but it is not what it appears to be because it is cut off from its own true 4D consciousness. You are looking at a cube out of the context of a hypercube, and by definition it is going to be a very limited and a warped view of reality. All the nations of the world are the cubes, as it were, that fell out of the Adamic hypercube, and they all have to go back in. And where are they going back in? That is Jerusalem, that is Israel, that is the Torah, that is the Kabbalah, that is King Solomon's wisdom. It is simply the point of indentation, of the hollow in the middle of the funnel that we are going through.

How can we know that Israel, as a holy nation, is approaching this Messianic Era right now?

RJDB: Israel is a microcosm of the world. Everything that is going on in the world is going on to some degree, greater or lesser, in Israel as well. Everyone is in the same boat now, quite literally, and this is a sign that was previously unimaginable. For example, the Vatican is locked up, the great Jewish religious centers are locked up and all the synagogues are locked up, and many leaders from all affiliations have died from the coronavirus, including religious rabbis. So, it is affecting everybody across the board. This itself is reason to be suspiciously wise. There are no good guys and there are no bad guys anymore, because that which is about to happen is Adamic. And Adam contains everything in humanity, Jew and non-Jew. The center of the vortex is the Foundation Stone, so it will center around the Dome of the Rock because that is the pineal gland of the world. If someone cannot relate to the central role of the pineal gland on the micro-level or to the central role of the Foundation Stone on the macro-level, then really, we have nothing to talk about. Anyone who is not fascinated with the pineal gland and what it is doing in the human body, and why it produces dimethyltryptamine, is plugged into a very different platform. That means that we are working with completely different operating systems and there is no common language.

KS: So how do we give the signal to Adam? By just intention?

RJDB: Science, nuclear physics, medicine and technology are not coming only from us. All this advancement in science and technology is mainly coming from the fourth dimension. We are just seeing it manifest in 3D. How is that for a science fiction story, right? [Laughs.] This makes for such good science fiction—only that it is for real. Elijah the Prophet, which is simply the lowest aspect of Adamic consciousness, is so transcendent from our own collapsed consciousness. There is the impossibility of communication between a higher consciousness, i.e., a civilization that is so far advanced, that there is no mode of communication, there is no interface. So, Elijah is the collective term that is used. That is what Adam sends first. Elijah is the one who "announces" the holy face of the "transformation of consciousness" which is nothing more than the Messianic Era.

What is he announcing? He is announcing that we need to start learning the language of consciousness, because when he comes and brings universal peace, the tsunami of viscous light will be so beyond anything we can imagine that we will be like a billion lightbulbs that are all going to pop. That is destruction, but destruction from a good reason, because if we don't have the vessels and we don't have the language, then we cannot go into the Messianic Era. How can you go into 4D? An analogy is that it is like a really bad trip on LSD, were you don't know that you are in another dimension, so you are trying to hold onto 3D, and that is hell. That is what is about to happen. So, what can you do? Once someone can entertain this as a possibility—that is all we need. Can we simply entertain this as a possibility of what is happening, to explain all these bizarre things that are now happening in the world simultaneously? Now what if this consciousness needs us also to become the docking station? Adam's consciousness has to dock somewhere to begin the process of the great cosmic interfacing between his 4D and our 3D. He needs humans to do that—which is only his own lower-dimensional self. Everybody has their own concerns and fears. You can only dig as deep as your soul goes. In the end it is a soul problem, meaning, whether or not your higher-dimensional soul is connected to the Adamic pineal body, which is the global Foundation Stone. This is also the portal and "star gate" back into the Garden of Eden and the Tree of Life.

Jack Rasmus*

"The central banks and the governments will not allow cryptocurrencies to supplant the regular monetary system."

KONRAD STACHNIO: I would like to speak with you about this pandemic and the long-term scenario for Europe and United States, China. What will happen? Because we are facing a really serious situation.

JACK RASMUS: Yeah. Well, let me take that question on. What will it look like after, or what will happen between now and after? There's really a couple phases here. We're right in the middle of it right now, in its more intense contraction phase, and we see the real economy everywhere virtually shutting down except for basic necessities. That's true in Europe, that's true here in the U.S. It looks like same for much of Asia, although it looks like Asia may be coming back in terms of activity a little bit. Although it's not clear whether that will be temporary too. There are reports of a second wave of infection beginning to occur in Asia. It's not verified yet, but there's some indication of that. Of course, the big risk is that if you go back to work too soon and more people get infected, then you do have a second wave. There are forces in the U.S., I'm sure in Europe and especially in the U.S., that want us to go back to work because they don't like the fact they're not making any money, and they really don't care about how many workers get sick and die because they're just, like good capitalists, thinking of their own bottom line here. I've heard

---

*JACK RASMUS studied economics at Berkeley and took his doctorate at the University of Toronto (1977). He is Associate Adjunct Professor of Economics at St. Mary's College in California. A Chinese edition of his latest book, *The Scourge of Neoliberalism*, is forthcoming in 2021. His work focuses on economic inequities and regularly appears in *The European Financial Review, World Review of Political Economy, World Financial Review,* and *Z Magazine.*

there are thousands of workers in the U.S. meatpacking industry that are now being infected. It appears these business forces have had some influence with Trump for a while now, and Trump was talking about "We're going to be back by Easter," but then the reality and the science overwhelmed the ideology and the pursuit of profit and he said no by Easter, admitting "we're going to lose hundreds of thousands of people here, even if we do the best possible." All we can do is mitigate, not stop the virus at this point. In other words slow down the process. But Trump will change his mind again about opening the economy. He constantly flip flops. I don't think there'll be any real solution to this health crisis, and thus to the disruption of the economy, until they get a vaccine or some sort of treatment that clearly cures people functionally so that they could go back to work. Until you see the medical scientific solution, the pressure on the economy is going to continue. Maybe not as severe as the initial effects that we're seeing now, in especially Europe and the U.S., but it will continue even after that. And the economy will not really fully recover, I believe, until you really have the medical solution.

I strongly disagree with all those Pollyannas who say that it's going to be V-shaped recovery. There's not going to be V-shaped recovery here by any means. Why? Because there's been great psychological wounds inflicted on both the psychology and expectations of consumers and businesses. That's not going to go away very quickly. You can provide income protection to some extent; that's going on now. But the $2.2 trillion U.S. "CARES" bill just passed by Congress is just a mitigation, as even they're now admitting, just putting a floor under the economic collapse to some extent. But they're going to need an even bigger stimulus bill by May/June if they want to get through the rest of the summer. Whether that happens is going to be determined by a political fight in the U.S. because, again, business interests, capitalists, do not want to drag out the economic crisis as much as we'll probably have to in order to save lives. So there'll be a big fight over that next stimulus bill coming in May or June.

I've written on my blog several articles in February–March that said, look, if there is truly a war with the virus going on—and there is—then we're going to have to go to a war budget in the U.S. similar to what we did in 1942. If you look at 1940–41, the U.S. Government spending before World War II was about 10% of total GDP. In one year, 1942, that rose to 40% by the end of that year. And at one point in '44, was 70% GDP. That was a war mobilization in '42, and I'm arguing that we have to go to 40% of GDP again. If the government spending before this crisis in 2019 was roughly $4.5 trillion and that was 21% of GDP, we're going to have to add another $4 trillion in direct government spending—not in business loan bailouts of bankers or investors. That's done by the central bank, the Federal Reserve and not part of direct government spending. And not in the form of more corporate tax cuts, either, because that's also not going to have much effect stimulating the economy in present conditions of severe contraction. It has to be direct government spending to households and small businesses. We have some of that direct spending started but it's not sufficient. The CARES ACT's $500 billion to workers in the form of extended employment benefits and an initial round of household cash injection and checks, plus $367 billion to small businesses in grants, and loans that will probably convert to cash anyway. But all that's just a 6- to 8-week solution. We're going to have to have an even more massive stimulus, direct stimulus by the government, equal to 40% of GDP. And that has to come soon this year. Whether that happens is a political question. We'll see.

But that's what I believe has to happen. We have to go on a true war mobilization footing with government spending taking the lead because the psychology of investors and businesses has been so hammered—and consumers too—that even under the best of circumstances—let's assume the very unlikely scenario that by June this health crisis element is over—the economy will still be wounded and businesses will not invest. They will be very, very cautious. They will not bring everybody back to work. Banks will not lend their own money very readily either.

Look, after the last crisis in 2008–09, we had a decline in bank lending and real investment for years after that, continually. So the banks will not lend except to the very safest, biggest customers. You're not going to get investment snapping back. And in fact, investment wasn't doing so good in the U.S. before the virus hit anyway. For 9 months in the last year, 2019, we had a contraction in real capital spending going on. We had a 6-month manufacturing recession. We had consumers that were showing signs that they were tapped out on credit and debt. And we had a trade war that was holding back growth as well. The real economy was therefore quite weak in 2019, not robust and strong, as Trump likes to say. And all that was happening on the eve of this. It was not a strong economy, and this crisis has simply precipitated and accelerated the collapse. It was already slowly slowing down. And in Europe, the same scenario. But now the virus effect has exacerbated and accelerated it all. It's telescoped it, and now we're in a deep, deep downturn.

The deep and rapid contraction of the real economy is going to affect the psychology of investors and businesses and the spending by consumers and households. Some of the money by the stimulus bills to date will be hoarded, because both businesses or consumers don't know if this thing's coming back, how long it's going to go on. Households will buy necessities, but that's it. They're not going to go out and buy new homes, cars and all the rest at levels they had before. They're going to sit on much of the bailout money they're going to hoard it. They'll use some of it to pay down some of the debt they've accumulated to date, and businesses will spend it on stocks & bond investments, but they'll mostly hoard it. Same for many households that will still have jobs,

As economists like to say, the multiplier effect from the CARES Act bill is going to be very, very low here for government spending. Businesses, what are they going to do? They're going to hoard it. Banks are going to hoard it. They're going to keep it for future debt payments, maybe, because they've also borrowing big time, drawing down their available bank loan credit lines and issuing record corporate bond debt. Businesses were drawing down their credit lines by hundreds of billions in February and March, as this thing began to unfold. And issuing hundreds of billions of dollars in new corporate bonds. Record levels of corporate debt occurred in February because corporations and businesses are gathering in all the cash they can, in this dash for cash. In economist terms, it's the return of what's called liquidity preference by businesses, investors and households. It's also what's called a liquidity trap. Giving businesses more money doesn't result in more investment, hiring, and growth in a severe and deep economic contraction. We're in a liquidity trap with a vengeance. Monetary solutions don't work in the current scenario. If anyone doubted John Maynard Keynes' explanation of why business investment did not, would not, could not lead a recovery from the '30s Depression despite near zero interest rates and free money, this is a repeat event today revealing the same. This is a massive liquidity preference, liquidity trap going on.

Until the psychology changes, businesses are not going to open up their wallets and invest and expand production or hire everyone back tomorrow. They're not going to expand because people aren't going to be buying things at prior levels as well. That's another reason. In certain industries like the oil industry, you have a total true collapse of capital expenditures going on. That's not going to come out of it. The same is true with large sections of retail, of leisure, hospitality, travel and mass entertainment industries. They're just not going to come "back to normal," even under the best of assumptions. Not in the short term and likely not in the longer as well. The economy is now severely wounded, and ending the virus effect—even if quickly—is not going to change the economic crisis fundamentals very much. The contraction now has an economic dynamic of its own.

You've got to remember that every time there's a deep recession, business looks for ways to cut costs. They focus on ways to become more efficient in using their employment. They replace jobs more with new technology and automation. That's what they're going to do coming out of this, too. They're not going to hire these people back in droves, I don't believe. As long as this virus isn't resolved with the vaccine, the uncertainty is going to hang over everybody, business and consumer alike, and the hangover is going to keep the recovery very, very slow. And businesses will look for new ways to cut jobs, not rehire, or rehire those laid off as part-time or temp workers.

Now, the big wild card with this very slow recovery, if it comes, when it comes, the big wild card is the credit system, the banking system, and by that I mean the shadow banking system as well as the commercial banking system. They're about the same size. But the shadow banking system is far more unstable and fragile. If there's a credit crunch, at least I'd say in financial system terms, there will be defaults and bankruptcies that will cause a major crisis in the credit system. Credit will freeze up. When that happens what you've got is the overlay of a financial crash on top of this already real economy collapsing.

You see, in 2008, it was different. It was the financial side that crashed that dragged down the real economy, and it was only halted when the Federal Reserve dumped $5 trillion into the banks and then engineered low interest rates for 6 years after that. The Fed at the time said, "We're going to take the money back when we get recovery. We'll sell off our $4.5T balance sheet." I said at the time in my 2017 book, *Central Bankers at the End of Their Ropes,* it would not happen. Central bankers were at the end of their rope and would never retract the excess liquidity injected to save the banking system. And I predicted all of this in my 2016 book, *Systemic Fragility in the Global Economy* as well. In fact, my central bankers book is subtitled *Monetary Policy in the Coming Depression.* We are certainly, certainly in a great recession here right now. The question today is will the nonfinancial corporate sector default on the massive debt they accumulate the past ten years that is now coming due? And will deflation in financial markets spill over to exacerbate deflation as well in real goods and services? The longer that we have this contraction in the real economy, the more fragile the financial system will become and the more susceptible it will be to a crash itself. When that might happen, I don't know for certain, but the odds are increasing it could within the next six to twelve months.

But right now we have the Federal Reserve bailing out the banks even more than in 2008–09, spending even more, injecting even more liquidity to bail out the banks even before they fail this time. In 2008, they were failing and we spent $4–5 trillion to bail them out after the fact, and of course central banks globally did the same. Globally, it was a $20 trillion bailout by liquidity injection. The problem with injecting so much liquidity is that you might save the banking system from collapsing, but you inject so much liquidity in the global economy, after it's all over it ends up in fueling financial speculation and growing financial bubbles and fragility even further again. This is one of the great contradictions of capitalism right now. They generate banking crises caused by too much excess liquidity over decades, too much investment going into financial markets. It causes these bubbles and crashes, and then they have to bail it out with—guess what? More liquidity. So the solution to the problem becomes the problem once again.

That will be the inevitable consequence once again of the Federal Reserve now injecting trillions of dollars into the banking system. Already it's promised $6 trillion. Even before the crash came, in early 2019 the Fed had abandoned raising interest rates and started cutting rates again, providing more cheap money. And then it started its QE once again, although it didn't call it that, last September by pumping $500 billion into repo market to keep that market from going under. And then when this virus thing started, the Fed announced still another $2.2 trillion—i.e. $1.5 for repos and $700 billion once again for buying mortgages and mortgage bonds and treasuries, call it QE, QE5, whatever. So going into this virus crisis in February 2020 the Fed had spent $2.7 trillion over the prior 6 months, and now it's another $4 trillion at least promised by the Fed in March, and it may be open-ended. And right now the Fed is not only pre-bailing out the banks and the shadow banks, it's setting up once again facilities to deal with the worst fractures in the financial system that are appearing, for example right now in the municipal bond market. We also are seeing problems in the money market funds and commercial property and commercial paper markets, in the repo markets, and now they're pre-bailing out the consumer credit sector. Credit cards, auto finance firms, and whatever.

The fed is becoming a garbage can for assuming corporate debt everywhere. It's original mandate from its formation in 1913 up to 2008 was to bail out only the commercial banking system. In 2008–09 that was expanded to bailing out the shadow banking system as well—i.e. insurance companies, hedge funds, finance companies, and all the rest of the high risk taking and speculating financial system that had grown as large as the commercial banks. But now it's every private financial institution and sector that holds debt. And nonfinancial corporations at all levels as well. They're prepared to bail the whole thing out. And the Fed's doing it even before the banks and non-banks default or go bankrupt. It's a general pre-bailing out of the entire capitalist system. Read the Fed's original mandate. It says nothing of that. Well, they may bail it out in the short run, though even that's not guaranteed—we'll see whether we have a credit crisis nevertheless within the next 12 months or so—but even if they do bail it out in the short run, what the Fed's doing today is such a massive injection of liquidity that for the next decade we will have nothing but financial instability occurring on a repetitive basis. Essentially, you could say this: fiscal and monetary tools that mainstream economics says are used to stabilize the economy no longer function that way. These are tools being used to subsidize capital incomes across the board. That's subsidization's been going on for two decades now. So the capitalist state is so integrated now with maintaining values and maintaining capitalist incomes that it's a total different animal in the 21st century. It's become one with capital.

If you look just at tax cuts in this country since 2001, George W. Bush gave $4 trillion to corporations and investors, with some tax crumbs thrown to consumers. About 80% of the $4T went to businesses & investors; about 20% to consumers. Then we get Obama, and Obama gives $288 billion in tax cuts to business in his 2009 bailout. Then he extends Bush's tax cuts for another two years to 2010 and passes another $800 billion in business tax cuts in 2010. And then he takes $1.5 trillion out of government spending on social programs to pay for it in 2011, and then in 2013 he makes Bush's tax cuts permanent at the cost of another $5 trillion. So we had over $10 trillion in tax cuts mostly going to investors and businesses under Bush and Obama, and then we get Trump, who has already passed $5 trillion in tax cuts, most of it, again, for businesses, multinational businesses, corporations, and all the rest. $4.5 trillion in January 2018 over the next decade and another $429B in 2019 in tax loopholes. It's massive tax cuts. $15 trillion and rising. And on top of that, we fight these wars in the Middle East that cost $7 trillion. That brings us to the Cares Act passed this March 2020, which according to reports amounts to more than another $600 billion. Well, no wonder. Add it up. $15 trillion in tax cuts, $7 trillion in wars, that's $22 trillion. That's the U.S. national debt last year, 2019. Of course, that national debt now is going to go to $27–28 trillion by 2022. Meanwhile, the financial side of the capitalist state is getting very unstable, and the system itself is getting very unstable.

Systems and empires crash most often because of financial instability internally. That's what causes them to go under when they cannot continue economic growth and continue the standard of living for the people inside it. You can go back to ancient Rome. Let me go off on a historical tangent here. Why did Rome collapse? Because it lost its agricultural base. It lost the economic surplus that it used to finance its armies with when the barbarian so-called invaders took over Spain, Sicily and North Africa, where its agriculture was located, its agricultural economy. It lost it. That was the fifth century. It had already lost its eastern agricultural base and surplus when Egypt went to the Eastern Roman Empire early in the 4th century.

So Rome could not afford to field the army to protect its borders and it crashed. The same thing happens to all empires. Look at the British Empire. It loses its colonies after World War II and it becomes just a shadow, a shell of former self dependent on the rest of Europe and the United States to stay alive and dependent on the rest of them allowing it to become a financial center. But of course, with Brexit on the horizon, Britain will no longer be that financial center. Britain is going to be an economy about the size of Northern Italy within the next decade. It'll be totally irrelevant. The same thing is happening within the United States now. The same thing. We have this fiscal crisis, we have a monetary crisis, and both monetary policy and fiscal policy are just conduits for the subsidization of capital incomes. It's undercutting the standard of living for the rest of the country. At some point, people were fooled thinking that Trump was going to do something about it—and of course, the Democrats ran a stupid campaign by incompetent candidates and they lost to Trump, and now they're trying to get back in the game. But they're having a hard time, mostly due to incompetent leadership and continued dumb strategies. But it's a 50-50 question of whether Trump might not win again because of Democratic incompetence, electoral incompetence. In fact, Trump has taken control of the Republican Party. He has control of the "red states" and therefore control of the Electoral College and the Senate, and the Supreme Court now. Don't forget, in 2000 the Supreme Court gave the presidency to George W. Bush by stopping the vote in Florida. Something like that could happen again in another close election.

So all these institutions of government are working together to support capital in this country, and the most extreme and rapacious forms of finance capital in particular. Former bankers from Goldman Sachs investment bank are running the economic policies of the U.S. since Trump came into office. They're everywhere in high positions in his administration. Don't count out the possibility that Trump may even, if this thing continues, call a national emergency and suspend the November election if this virus thing gets worse. That's quite possible. Then we're in a de facto political civil war in the United States, and much more disruption, and therefore much more uncertainty in the economy. Now, that's an extreme possibility, I admit, and I don't want to be alarmist, but you've got to look forward and ask yourself what's the worst case scenario? What's the best case scenario? What's the likely scenario, what's in between the extremes? The most likely scenario, to get back to the original question, is that we're going to have, at best, a very, very slow, rocky recovery here for the rest of this year and a very slow recovery at best for years to come. It's going to change the consciousness of people in this country and it's going to change the politics in this country like we've never seen before. It could go further right and it can go in the direction of progressive politics. But that's something no one can predict yet.

KS: What do you think about China? Do you think China will be the biggest winner in this whole scenario here? For example, in terms of economy?

JR: In terms of its economy, China has the ability to redirect investment into public investment a lot quicker and with less internal political opposition than the United States does. We'll see whether it can do that. But China is very much an export-oriented economy, and the global economy has nearly collapsed. Global GDP is not coming back quickly. The supply chains are really broken, and it's going to take quite a while to reestablish those supply chains. So globally, there's no global V shape recovery in this scenario either. Both Europe and Japan, the other two advanced capitalist economies, were already in trouble economically in 2019, were stagnating or in recession, largely because they too, like the U.S., relied primarily on monetary policy as the main stimulus after the 2008–09 crash and eschewed fiscal policy. They all engaged in austerity fiscal policy. Again, that's because the bankers were in control of the politics and the policy since 2008–09.

Monetary policy means "give the money to the bankers first, and then we'll decide how much we want to dribble down to the rest"; whereas fiscal policy means "give it to the household, the consumer, and they will then recover the banking system by spending." Bankers and their bought for politicians don't like fiscal policy because its bottom-up. They like top-down monetary policy. Europe and all the advanced capitalist countries were following this sort of policy after 2009, but now that policy has come to a dead-end. In Europe and Japan and the U.S., it was all the same but it just couldn't be taken any further by 2019. As I say in my book about central banking, monetary policy was at a dead end and the central banks at the end of their policy rope.

It couldn't be taken any further in the U.S. either when Trump came into office. Trump artificially pumped up the economy with his massive 2018 tax cut, but only artificially. Most of that $4.5 trillion (over a decade 2018–27) tax cut went into the financial markets and we had this big bubble, a 25–30% rise in the stock market, $3.4 trillion in stock buybacks and dividend payouts under Trump, and trillions more in corporate debt issuance due to low interest rates. And that bubble collapsed in a matter of weeks in 2020. That collapse, by the way, stabilized recently, but it's going to go down again. This is a dead cat bounce, a classic bear market rally, as they call it in the financial markets.

So monetary policy is the primary lead policy for capitalism in the 21st century, and it has failed. It couldn't go any further, and finance capitalists running the policy show don't like fiscal policy. But now they've got to engage in fiscal policy. And now they're going to pay a price with these massive deficits and debts they've run up in recent decades due to trillions of dollars in business-investor tax cuts and war spending, and no one knows how much that's going to cause an even greater overhang and a drag on the economy after this whole virus thing runs its course. But Europe is worse off than the U.S.

Same with Japan. And now emerging markets are going to really take it in the ear, as they say, particularly countries whose currencies depend on global trade in commodities and oil. They're already in a deep crisis, and the IMF lending a trillion dollars is not going to cover defaults in sovereign debt that are coming You can see the dimensions of the coming crisis in emerging market economies in Argentina and places in Latin America.

So the global economy is going to be very, very weak in the months and years immediately ahead. If China depends on sales into the global economy, that's not going to recovery very fast for China. In summary, how much is that lack of export production going to play on China's economy? China can probably make it up in other ways, but there are limits to that too. We're going to see. China's probably better off than the other emerging economies but its economy is not immune from broader global developments by any means. But if there's another wave of problems with the virus in China, then all bets are off for China recovering too. And you've got to remember, China engaged in massive fiscal spending after 2009. 15% of GDP, which pulled up the emerging markets selling commodities to China as well after 2012. Emerging markets in China did not suffer as much as Europe and North America and Japan after the last crisis. But that's not going to happen this time. If China cannot sell more goods into the global economy and trade. It's not going to buy us much commodities from the emerging market economies, and therefore you're not going to get that recovery in emerging market commodities or in China as sharply as occurred after the 2008–09 great recession. I think there'll be some recovery in China, but it won't be very robust. It won't be enough to pull up the EMEs, and it certainly won't be enough to pull up the Western advanced economies.

KS: Do you think that we are going in the direction of some sort of class war in Europe, or maybe even in the U.S., some sort of revolution?

JR: Yeah, I think the leadership of the western capitalist countries is grossly underestimating the discontent that's going to occur in the working classes at the median income levels and below, in particular. They're really going to be left behind this time. How long can they go on getting partial income support? Or those who are working under really terrible conditions, very unsafe, unhealthy, dangerous conditions out there during this virus crisis and collapsing economy. It's not just doctors, nurses, and first responders. The people who keep the utilities going, the people who keep the trucking and the delivery of food and necessities going, the people who keep running the warehouses and so forth—if that food delivery system breaks down, you're going to see something very apocalyptic, I think, very dangerous.

To people who are working overtime and and under hazardous conditions the politicians are saying, "You're our heroes." Yeah, well, that's not enough. That's not going to cut it. Why aren't they getting hazard pay? Why aren't they getting adjustments on their mortgages, rents, and so forth? We need to reward those people with extra compensation, who still have to work to keep society from collapsing. At a certain point people are going to realize, "Hey, we're on the shitty end of this stick. They're taking care of themselves, the bankers and so forth; what about us?" You'll start seeing a lot of wildcat strikes in protest. Workers are going to start getting angry about having to choose between their lives, the lives of their families, and their livelihoods and jobs. I'll tell you one thing. Revolution isn't around the corner for one very important reason. People engage in revolution when they have an organization that leads the way. Just having discontent over conditions is not enough. That will erupt in discontent like the Yellow Jackets or Occupy Movement and so forth. That dissipates. You need an organization. You need a political party that will really represent them.

The problem is, you've got Social Democratic parties, whether they're in Europe or the Democratic Party in the U.S. or whatever, who don't really represent the working classes anymore. They threw a few crumbs their way, but they don't rely on the working classes. They compete for the middle class, the professionals, and so forth, and the business class and small business and so forth. I don't believe they will come up with a program and a solution that people will be able to get behind. Already, most working class folks distrust all the political parties. Certainly in the U.S., they distrust the Democrats almost as much as the Republicans. But until you get a real organization that people feel that they can get behind, that has the answers to the crisis, you won't really have a political revolution, I believe. It takes organization. That's the number one question before us today. The unions don't seem to be that aggressive in moving in that direction. They're tied to the Social Democratic parties and they do whatever the Social Democratic parties tell them to do. So I don't see them leading it. I don't see a new kind of resurrected Labor Party here or anywhere really doing it.

What will? I don't have the answer to that. But I do know that that's what must happen. I'm not advocating any particular organization out there. I don't see anything that fulfills that task. But it will come. People will demand it when they see that the ruling class here has no solution to the crisis except to lower their standards of living even more to protect those who have the money. That's the only solution that appears to be occurring. People will at some point say, "That's not good enough."

KS: But would you agree with the statement of Gerald Celente, who said that we are going into not a recession, but a Great Depression? This scenario like before the Second World War—we have trade wars, we have currency wars, we have Great Depression, and then you know the end of the story. What do you think about this?

JR: Back in 2010, in my first book on the crisis in 2010 called *Epic Recession: Prelude to the Global Depression,* I said you've got to distinguish between what's called "normal" recessions and great recessions (or what I called epic recessions). I didn't like the word "great" because that term is being thrown around without a definition. Economists like Paul Krugman were saying "Oh, great recession. It's worse than normal but not as bad as the 1930s." That's just economic analysis by adverbs. It doesn't tell you anything.

So in my book in 2010, I distinguished between what's a normal recession, what's a great or epic recession, and what's a depression, both quantitatively and qualitatively. I pick up that theme again in my latest book, *The Scourge of Neoliberalism,* published just a couple months ago.

What's the difference? Normal recessions are recessions that aren't associated with a financial crash. They're just a short contraction of the real economy. You get overproduction in one area, or maybe you have a policy error like occurred in 1981 where Reagan purposely slowed down the economy to make the average household pay for the cost push inflation from oil and the embargos. Those are normal recessions.

2008 was not normal in that you had a banking crash. A banking crash will make the real economy contract faster and deeper, and then that faster and deeper contraction will feed back onto financial instability and exacerbate that in turn still further. So you got the financial and the real economy both following each other down deeper, which means it takes longer to recover from it. That's a great recession, where the banking crash is stopped at one event. Subsequent banking or financial crashes are prevented. The banks are quickly bailed out and the real economy and jobs slowly, very slowly recover over the course of years.

Now, take the Great Depression in the 1930s, is still different from a normal recession and a great recession. What causes a depression is a series of financial banking crashes that come one after the other in a relatively short time frame. That drives the economy down and ratchet deeper, deeper, every time you have a financial crash. And that's what happened in the 1930s. The Great Depression of the 1930s, as I pointed out, was not just one precipitous falling off a cliff. It was a series of stabilizations and contractions that went deeper and deeper as the banking system got worse and worse, and series of banking crashes in turn fed back on the real economy that got worse and worse, and defaults in the real economy caused even further crashes on the banking side, and you have a mutual, negative interaction between financial cycles and real cycles.

Mainstream economists don't understand financial cycles, and they don't understand how financial cycles interact in a mutually amplifying way with real contraction in the real economy and vice versa. In my 2016 book, *Systemic Fragility in a Global Economy,* I presented in the final chapter a theoretical proposal and hypothesis of how those two cycles interact with each other and exacerbate each other in a great recession downturn and even worse in a great depression. So whether we're going to get into a great depression after 2020 will depend on whether we have a bona fide banking financial system crash that occurs later this year or after, and whether they can stop that banking-financial crash. The Fed and other central banks are already putting out trillions of dollars to prevent that now. To pre-emptively bail out the banks and the financial system. But if those trillions don't work and we have a crash anyway, then what the hell are they going to do? Then they'll really be at the "end of their ropes." Can they stop it? It's a 50-50 proposition and we'll see if we have subsequent rolling financial banking crashes. Then you will have your great depression.

KS: What about digital money? Do you think that we're going to have a scenario where the central banks will introduce some sort of digital money instead of paper money?

JR: Yes, they will. Central banks will introduce digital currency—if anything to hold off the private sector from creating a money supply by creating their own private digital currency. The central banks and the governments will not allow cryptocurrencies to supplant the regular monetary system. They'll prevent it. They've already taken steps to do that in terms of regulation and taxation and so forth. But they'll allow cryptocurrencies, bitcoins and everything, as a kind of speculative play, kind of like gold futures or valuable paintings or something like that. It's a pure speculative play. They'll allow that. And the banks will play a role in collecting fees on all that. But they won't allow it to be a true digital currency out of the control of the state capitalist government. So central banks eventually will introduce their own digital currencies, and it will be very slowly and very controlled. But being electronic and digital, whether they can really control that in the long term remains to be seen. I'm not so sure.

KS: But what about China? They're introducing their own digital currency. What do you think about this?

JR: All the major monetary countries are going to be dabbling and experimenting in this. But the Chinese and the Russians have another motive here, and that is to get out from under the dollar and the U.S. dominated international payment system. It's that payment system and the dollar that are the crux of the U.S. economic empire. The U.S. global economic empire cannot function unless the dollar is the dominant reserve trading currency and unless the U.S. banking system is able to control it all and is at the center of international payments system. Because it's the international payment system that is dominated and controlled by the U.S., it allows the U.S. to see who's violating the sanctions. That's why this move by Europe to establish INSTEX, it's called, to trade with Iran, is so important. If that takes off and establishes itself, then of course the Russians and the Chinese may join it. Or the Chinese and the Russians may establish their own INSTEX-like payment system and bring other emerging markets into it. This is all a fundamental challenge to the U.S. global empire, and the U.S. throwing sanctions at everybody has just accelerated the whole process of moving toward an alternative. It's one of the most damaging aspects of Trump's trade and sanctions policies.

KS: Do you think that we are facing the last days of globalism and the neoliberal system right now?

JR: I just finished a book on neoliberalism, *The Scourge of Neoliberalism, U.S. neoliberalism from Reagan to Trump*. One of my conclusions was that what you see with Trump is neoliberalism on steroids, neoliberalism 2.0. I define what neoliberalism is in terms of policies and in terms of structural change in Capitalism; it's, a very materialist kind of explanation. I think there's a lot of ideological fluffy notions floating around about what neoliberalism is, and only partial explanations. Austerity is not just neoliberalism. Neither is deregulation and privatization. Neoliberalism is a lot more. Neoliberalism is those sets of policies in four distinct areas—fiscal policy, monetary policy, industrial policy, external policy, trade, currency exchange rates and so forth—that was developed in the late '70s, early '80s, by Britain and the United States as a response to the crisis of the 1970s. Neoliberalism is what the U.S. instituted to buy itself decades more of economic dominance, economic hegemony. It was the American-Anglo solution to do that, to extend hegemony. USA as the dominant partner; UK as the junior partner.

And neoliberalism has always meant globalization and financialization. Without the financialization of the U.S. and the global economy, you would not have globalization in other ways because that financialization had to occur in order to allow the globalization in other dimensions. So the two are both sides of one coin. I define financialization quite different than most others have, whether left economists and others. I'm not going to go into that definition or review that book. I went into it in depth in my *Systemic Fragility in the Global Economy* book published in 2016.

But basically, one of my conclusions was neoliberalism grew and expanded very aggressively in the U.S., through Bill Clinton and George W. Bush, but it hit a wall in the 2008–09 crisis. Obama could not put it back together again fully because of the crisis. Those neoliberal policies were undermined by the natural evolution and change of capitalism itself from the late 1970s through the present. Neoliberalism served to help restructure capitalism in the '80s and '90s very successfully in response to the 1970s crisis decade, but then these same neoliberal policies created after 1980 have become a drag on the further development of capitalism in the 21st century. Neoliberalism no longer works, so capitalists will replace it with some other policy mix that better suits its needs in the 2020s decade and beyond. So the contradiction between neoliberal policies and capitalist structure began to emerge, and with 2008–09, the contradictions revealed themselves more fully. Trump represents a futile attempt to restore, neoliberalism, in a new virulent, aggressive form. The trade wars, for example, or what he's doing on the external policy side. The massive tax cuts on the fiscal side. The massive deficits created by war and tax cuts. Going after the industrial side with more privatizatons, deregulations and destroying unions and so forth.

But I predict Trump won't succeed. I predicted in one of my chapters at the close of my 2020 book on Neoliberalism that changes that are coming within the structure of capitalism and at the material base of capitalism are undermining neoliberalism and that it will fail early in the 2020s decade. It may be failing now right before our very eyes in the wake of this virus thing. The question then becomes, what's going to replace it? That will either be, in my view, a move to a more progressive kind of economic capitalism, more like the New Deal of the '30s, or it may evolve into a more neofascist corporatist kind of economy in the next decade. It could go either way. But it's not going to be neoliberalism as we've known it from Reagan through Trump. It's going to be something else, either much worse or better. That's a political solution question.

KS: Slovenian philosopher Slavoj Žižek said that normality will never return. Do you think that we're going to face the collapse of the European Union soon? For example Žižek and others proposing some sort of communism for the economy as a solution for a crisis.

JR: All right. Normality. What's normal? Nothing is normal under capitalism. Capitalism is always dramatically changing. You would say in 1980–82, "Are we going back to the '60s and '70s? That's what was normal." No. Neoliberalism was not the normality of the preceding decades. So the decade that's coming and after is not going to be normal in the sense of returning to neoliberal economy and political institutions as a reflection of that. No, it's going to be a new normal, whatever that is. Because capitalism is always changing, and it's changing at a more rapid pace here in the 21st century than ever before. In the Neoliberalism book just published a few months ago, I point out the evolution in labor relations and markets and in the character of exploitation that's coming with artificial intelligence. It's going to destroy 30% of the occupations, and already we have a third or more of the people working in contingent jobs, part-time, temp jobs, gig work where they can hardly survive. Well, it's going to get even worse with AI. All these simple decision-making jobs in services and manufacturing are going to go away, and it's only going to be highly professional technical jobs that are going to be able to maintain a standard of living. Professional jobs and jobs that are oriented towards making profits and generating greater productivity for capital. The rest are going to be even worse off than they are today. So the new normal is going to be very difficult next decade, you might say.

KS: I asked Tim Draper, what about these people who cannot adapt to this new AI system where there is no job for them? He said that they will adjust themselves to the new economic system and that's all. Like all the times in history.

JR: A very callous response.

KS: But maybe it is that simple?

JR: Well, I'm not so sure the young people and millennials, Gen Zers coming behind the millennials, are going to accept that. Already, a majority of the United States say they're socialist. They don't know what that means, but to them it means "not the above." They're becoming very anti-capitalist. People like Draper and others better watch out with that kind of an attitude because people just aren't going to accept that kind of an attitude. In other words, "I've got to lower my standard of living? Instead of working a part-time job at minimum wage, I've got to work three part-time jobs, or I've got to live with five other people instead of one other person in an apartment, or I can't afford to have a family or afford to have kids?"

Young people see their whole life before them, and that scenario is not going to be acceptable to them. At some point they're going to really be upset, and we're getting closer to that point. I'm not saying it's around the corner, but that's unacceptable to say "I'm condemned to a life of a kind of indentureship, of low pay, no benefits, whatever." Others are saying people have to have some kind of universal basic income. Well, something like that might happen here when people start rebelling. I don't know. It's going to take something like that, because the capitalists simply aren't going to give it to you. Whether that happens remains to be seen. But I think that's a very arrogant, elitist, egotist answer, condemning millions and millions of people to a very unsatisfactory life. I don't think they're going to accept it. I think he's playing with fire with that. But that's how they feel. In the U.S. here, an expression of that is what's going on now with "Maybe we should accept more deaths. It would get the economy going. That's more important." In other words, "My revenues are more important than Grandma and Grandpa and your Uncle Ralph dying. That's more important." That's a capitalist attitude. It's them and us.

The rest of us aren't really considered full human beings by these people. You've got to understand how they think. I worked in their ranks for 19 years. I know how they think. Before that, for 13 years, I was a union organizer and a local president and a strike leader and everything. So I've seen from both class sides how people think. Their different sets of values, about life and other people. Capitalists think different, very different. Draper is a good example of the way these guys think. If you can't make them money, then you're less human.

And what about Europe and the European Union? Well, that's a 50/50 proposition. I thought it was going to unravel in the last 2011–13 crisis there, and I saw this new internal imperialism emerging where Northern Europe was exploiting the hell out of the Southern Periphery and a new kind of extraction of value was going on at the state to state level. Greece, of course, was the most extreme expression of that, and I wrote this book, *Looting Greece: The New Financial Imperialism Emerges,* published in 2016. They stabilized that by beating down the Greek opposition in the Syriza party and making it capitulate. I thought it would result in Greece and others splitting from the Eurozone monetary union and currency, and I still think that's a possibility. Unless the leadership of the European Union realizes it's going to have to spend more of its wealth in maintaining stability and raising the standard of living on the Southern Periphery as well a split is inevitable from it. Maybe Italy instead of Greece. If it doesn't adjust its policies, and, it has to do that fiscally, then the Eurozone is doomed eventually. A union based on a currency and single monetary policy cannot prevail. But a greater emphasis on fiscal policy and sharing the wealth in the Eurozone will never happen. German banks won't allow it to happen. Then that's the future of Europe, one way or the other. We'll see.

As far as Žižek and communes and so forth are concerned, you've got to beware of intellectuals. Left intellectuals not just those on the right. They create all these fantasies off the top of their head because they aren't rooted in the reality of average working people. He has a lot of good ideas; I've read some of them, ideology and so forth, but some of the stuff they come up with is really crackpot. It comes off the top of their head. It doesn't come from the real experience of real people. But you can't blame them because all they've got in their ivory towers is the top of their head.

John Perkins*

"We can take the approach that we're going to go into collapse, or we can take the approach that we're going to be smart enough to figure our way out of this."

KONRAD STACHNIO: In previous interviews, you talked about Latin American countries—saying that they would be the leaders of what you called the life economy. Can you elaborate?

JOHN PERKINS: First, I want to say that the coronavirus pandemic, climate change, income inequality, species extinctions and so many of the crises we face today are symptoms of global social-governmental-economic systems that are failing us, what we can refer to in general as a death economy. Latin America has been hard hit by these crises. Since the time of the Spanish Conquest its people and resources have been terribly exploited. Beginning about the time I was an Economic Hit Man in the 1970s, Latin Americans came to understand this and have struggled to make changes. In a way, Latin America is a microcosm for the world's efforts to transform the death economy to a live economy. At the same time, it is also an example of how the anti-progressive elements, those who represent the status quo, the death economy, are striking back. The life economy is based on cleaning up pollution, regenerating destroyed environments, and developing life-style and business approaches that do not ravage our planet. The death economic system is one based on conflict, warfare, the threat of war, and on destroying the Earth, tearing up the resources upon which our corporations depend. So, in the death economy, people are ultimately destroying themselves. And we need to replace that with a system that cleans up pollution and pays corporations to mine all the glass and plastic floating around

---

*JOHN PERKINS is an American author best known for his book *Confessions of an Economic Hit Man* (2004). His book spent over 70 weeks on the *New York Times* bestseller list and has been published in at least 32 languages worldwide.

in the oceans, to clean up all the oil spills everywhere, to regenerate destroyed environments, and to develop new technologies that recycle and that don't dig up the earth anymore. We really need to move into a whole new economic system, recognizing that the system we have right now is failing us. Some of the countries in Latin America are taking a lead in that. The indigenous people have always understood the importance of long-term sustainability and they have been successfully practising it for thousands of years.

KS: You are saying the biggest global revolution will take place soon. What do you mean by that?

JP: It's a consciousness revolution. I've spent most of my life traveling around the world and was recently in Russia and Kazakhstan. I travel a lot, and what I experience is that people truly are waking up. There is a new consciousness that we are destroying life as we know it on this planet; a pandemic has hit us, the glaciers are melting, the oceans are rising, the Earth is speaking loudly—and people are listening. Now, there is also a reaction against that. So, what we're seeing in the United States with Trump, or what we're seeing to a certain degree in Poland with your government there, and then what we're seeing with people in Hungary, or around Brexit in England—in many parts of the world, there's a reaction against this awakening. Whenever you start to move in the direction of change, there is always a reaction against it. But I think, overall, people around the world are understanding that this system is not working. It's a system that's given us tremendous benefits, amazing technology, science, medicine, and art and so forth. It's been very, very successful but it's come to an end. It's gone out of balance. We know there's a pandemic, and climate change, and we know that species are going extinct at a very rapid rate. We know that fewer than fifty individuals own as much wealth as half of the world's population, and that half of the world's population is basically starving or on the verge of starvation. So, that's a failed system. That's not a system of being human that works. So, we can take the approach that we're going to go into collapse, or we can take the approach that we're going to be smart enough to figure our way out of this. Throughout history, human beings have done pretty well at getting through crises. Look at World War I, the Great Depression, World War II, and the Cold War; those were times when people were convinced we were done for. As a kid growing up in the Cold War, I was convinced that the Soviet Union was going to take us over. That didn't happen. You in Poland probably know that better than anybody. So, where are the crises? How do we react to the problems? I think we'll solve the problems. But there's always a possibility that we won't, and that we go extinct like the dinosaurs.

KS: In one interview, you said that we were dealing with the emergence of the first global corporate empire.

JP: Yes. We have a truly global empire, a corporate empire. It's not really an American empire, though the U.S. government certainly supports it. Our military too often steps in to support it. But it's a corporate empire and it is global.

KS: You said that this empire must collapse. Do you see any signs of this right now?

JP: All empires collapse and this one is in the throes of collapsing. But I think there's another possibility, and that is that we'll transform—and that, I think, is the hope that we have. I know a lot of corporate executives who are very smart people; they know that this system isn't working. They don't know quite how to transform it because they're afraid that if they lose market share, they'll get fired, replaced by someone who again only cares about market share. So, I tell audiences that I speak to around the world, that everybody needs to form a consumer movement and pick a corporation—Monsanto or Chevron or Nike, or pick another choice—and send them emails. Then, get all your social networks to send emails too, and get everybody out there sending emails to say, "Hey, I love your products, Nike! I want you to be successful, but I'm not going to buy your goods anymore until you pay your workers fair wages." And I know the executives of corporations, including Nike, want to hear that. I know some of them. They want to get those emails so they can take them to their main stockholders and say, "Wake up, we've got to listen to our customers." Every corporate executive knows about Woolworths, Eastern Airways, Sharper Image, Kodak and Polaroid, huge corporations that failed. They no longer exist. And executives are very aware that they are very vulnerable, and have to listen to their customers. So, it is up to us, the customers, to really move this forward, this consciousness revolution. I think we are in the process of doing it. I am very hopeful that we will do it. There is always that possibility we won't, and we'll go extinct like the dinosaurs. And the Earth will be better off when that happens since it will mean that we haven't acted as good stewards.

KS: I am still thinking about technological unemployment. Bill Gates said that software substitutes will replace most of the people in the job market. Of course, we can send emails to the CEOs of the biggest corporations—but what will happen to the masses who are unemployed because of robotics?

JP: I spent a lot of time with a top advisor to Vladimir Putin—Sergey Glazyev. We hung out together in St. Petersburg and then in Astana, Kazakhstan. We were both there speaking at two conferences and we've been communicating since. He thinks that the world needs to move into something more spiritual and compassionate, that the whole economic system needs to revolve around basically what I call the life economy. He is very much in agreement with that and thinks we have this possibility; he has also written about it in his brilliant books. Yes, artificial intelligence is on the way, and one thing that people don't seem to take into account is that artificial intelligence certainly won't be able to do everything we do, because it won't have the emotions. That means it won't have love, and it won't have compassion. It also means that it won't have jealousy and anger, and it means it'll be able to look at the world's situation, the crises, and come up with real solutions not based on politics, not based on anger or selfishness, but based on objective solutions. Will we accept them? I don't know. I think we very well might. There is a real hope in artificial intelligence that it will be able to analyse all the crises we're currently facing and recognize that each of those is a symptom, not the problem. Climate change is not the problem. World hunger is not the problem. Nuclear holocaust is not the problem. Those are all symptoms of the failed economic, global, political, social system that I call the death economy. Artificial intelligence should see that and say, "here's the solution: build a life economy." Will the leaders of Russia and Poland and the United States and China accept this? I don't know, but I hope that they will and if you talk about putting people out of work, what you're really talking about is putting people out of drudgery-type jobs and giving us the opportunity to spend more time hanging out with our children, making art and music, writing books and making love! Let's face it, robots aren't going to need good housing, or good hospitals. They're going to need technicians working for them, but the robots don't need to be paid. So, we could go two ways here. If you figure that the oligarchs, the corporatocracy, are totally ruthless and that they're going to enslave the rest of us, make us all live very poor lives and live in slums, well, that's one possible scenario. The other possible scenario is that robots will free the rest of us to do things that human beings perhaps were meant to do on this planet. We weren't necessarily meant to clean toilets, pick up rubbish on the streets or even to do a lot of the calculations done by people working for banks and such things. We can do more things like I do, such as sitting around all day writing books and talking to people like you. Isn't that wonderful? I'm freed up to do that because I am a writer. You have the opportunity to do that too, because of your profession. Wouldn't it be nice if everybody had that opportunity to do what they love? How many people go to college so that they can clean toilets in a hotel?

KS: I agree, but can this plan be real—not just for a few people, but also for the global masses? It's simple to apply it to small societies but on a global scale, it's a totally different scenario. Slavoj Žižek, a Slovenian philosopher, said that young people are currently in advanced unemployment and that there's no place for them in society, and they know that. I am just wondering whether all these people who will be without work will arm themselves and form a revolutionary movement, or terrorist groups?

JP: That's a possibility. But there's also a possibility that the people in charge will get the message that ultimately, that's not going to work, and that they're going to have to take care of people. We're certainly seeing the bad side, the one you describe, in countries that're going right wing, such as Hungary, the U.S., and during the 2017 coalition in Austria. We are also seeing it in Brazil and other Latin American countries. In those places, this movement is certainly very disturbing, very concerning. We have a very strong right-wing movement here in the U.S., and it's happening all over. I want to believe that's a reaction. So, there is consciousness, an awakening to these serious problems on this planet, and there is a real definite movement toward making a more sustainable planet, more compassionate planet. But every time you have a revolution—and we're at the beginning of a revolution—there's always a strong reaction against it. People don't want change. People are afraid of change. And what we're saying here is that we *must* change the system radically. We have to move from a death economy to a life economy. That requires change. People are very afraid of that as you expressed, fear of robots and of AI. As I said earlier, I would like to think that there is hope in AI, that it can help solve our problems and teach us something, and can free us up to have more conversations like this, so that nobody has to clean toilets, nobody has to push numbers, nobody has to do those menial tasks. But it could go either way. I think when we start to look at these kinds of changes, it's a typical human reaction to be afraid and say, "Oh no, I don't want robots, I don't want AI; it's going to change everything. I'm used to the system the way it is now. Let's keep it this way." And so, the right wing steps in, basically a conservative movement that says, "let's go back to the way it used to be, let's go back to the old systems, let's look to our father figure, an authoritarian figure who can tell us what to do." They know what to do; they are smart, and they make a lot of money. Let's just turn ourselves over to them. And that's, in a way, what this whole right-wing movement is about, turning authority over to people they think they can trust. We see this in the United States very strongly with Trump, who is out of control. Let's face it: Trump's crazy. He's a narcissist. It's pretty obvious he is a psychopath. People in the United States and many other people around the world say, "Oh! He's decisive, he can make decisions. He's right at the top." The truth is, he's like a puppet manager. We are just puppets.

KS: Do you think Obama was better than Trump?

JP: I have no doubt that Obama is a much smarter human being, a much more rational human being, a much more compassionate human being. I don't think he was a narcissist. However, the system was bad then too. He was working under a system that was basically dysfunctional. The one great thing about Trump is that he is giving us the gift of showing the whole world the shadow side of the United States, if the world's willing to look at it. We have a very strong shadow side and that is huge corporate control, mostly by a relatively, few mostly White men. So, corporations were in control under Obama, they were in control under the Bushes, and under Clinton. They've had control for a long time. But it wasn't quite as obvious. Under Trump, it's become very, very obvious. So, Trump has exposed this deep shadow side. On top of all of that, I have no question that Trump is a very disturbed individual emotionally. You know the word: narcissist or sociopath? Well, Trump meets all the criteria for those things and incidentally, that's not uncommon for people who lead big corporations. They rise to the top because they don't care what anybody thinks or does. Trump has some very, very deep psychological problems. You asked about Obama. Obama had a lot of flaws, there's no question. He didn't do a good job with running the government partly because the United States government was dysfunctional. Republicans controlled the Congress, during most of his presidency. He couldn't get much done as the system was rotten. But, under Trump, we are seeing a man who has a Republican majority right now in the Senate, so he has passed outrageous legislation, including a tax bill that is going to go through and which is a terrible piece of policy, horrible. But the heads of big corporations like many of those policies, and the wealthy people also like them; so, they're supporting Trump, and the Republicans are supporting him.

KS: Do you think that radical Islam could pose a danger to this corporate empire in the future?

JP: I don't like radicalism on any front. I don't like radical Islam. I don't like radical Christianity. I think radicalism is dangerous under any circumstances, yet I also understand that a lot of radical Islam has happened because people are very dissatisfied. Frankly, if I were a fourteen-year-old boy growing up in Palestine or Iraq, and U.S. drones killed my family members, and if I were being told that I'd experience an eternity of beautiful women and paradise by strapping bombs to my body and blowing myself up, I'd probably do it.

KS: But do you think that radical Islam can be a threat to this corporate agenda globally?

JP: The House of Saud, the royal family in Saudi Arabia, is Islamic and they're certainly not against big corporations. As a pure religion, Christianity is against big corporations and against usury. Christ knocked over the tables of the money lenders. But, in practice, the Catholic Church and Christians in general are not opposed to usury or banking. So, I think we have to make a distinction—whether it's Hinduism, Buddhism, Islam or Christianity—between the principles of religion and the way that religion is used to justify gaining material success.

KS: What do you think about the privatization of everything right now, of health care, public space, public service, police, army, etc? Is it some kind of end game for the global corporate agenda?

JP: Absolutely. It is a robbery, a crime; it's terrible. Privatization of public resources is despicable and yet it is happening on a big scale, but it's very, very destructive. It is creating what I call "predatory capitalism." I'm not opposed to capitalism at all; I am a capitalist myself, but this form of capitalism, predatory capitalism, is the exact thing that's creating the death economy and that's in the process of destroying the planet as we know it. It's something we really have to turn around. And privatization is very, very dangerous at the levels at which it's happening.

KS: Is it true that from the economic perspective, Europe is dealing with the same scenario that third-world countries have previously?

JP: Well, I wrote about that in *The New Confessions of an Economic Hit Man*. One of the reasons I wrote that book twelve years after the original was published was because I thought the system of the Economic Hit Man, perfected in developing countries, had now basically invaded Europe and the United States. So, this whole system that was so successful in Africa, Asia and Latin America has now come home to roost in the United States and Europe.

KS: What do you think about the mass migration taking place right now in Europe? What will be the outcome of it?

JP: I don't know how people will react to this. Mass migration is just another symptom of a system that's totally broken. Mass migration is because of wars and climate change, and both of those are the result of this very, very broken system that I call the death economy. They are indications of so much that is going wrong. How are we going to deal with that? The only rational way, ultimately, is to change the whole system and that's a big job. But we have to look at all of these things—whether it's the pandemic, climate change or mass migration—as symptoms of the much bigger problem, which is the death economy. I think nations are becoming increasingly irrelevant. The corporations control the world now. Take a look at the Chinese economy; it is built on international corporations, global corporations. Without global corporations, the Chinese economy could not have taken off the way it did. The Russian economy, the Brazilian economy, the Indian economy, the American economy—they are also all built on huge corporatism. So, corporations are what's really running the planet right now and they're doing a bad job. But we have to understand that they're totally dependent on us, the consumer, the investor, the worker, the manager, the owners. Corporations are dependent on you and me and all of us for their existence. They cannot survive, cannot thrive, without our participation. The good news is that, ultimately, we have the power to control these corporations.

Mikhail A. Lebedev[*]

"Why not have a God that is a robot?"

KONRAD STACHNIO: Google's Ray Kurzweil said that in approximately fifteen years, artificial intelligence and biotechnology will able to fix our immune systems to the degree that we become immortal. What would you say to that?

MIKHAIL A. LEBEDEV: Was he basing his predictions on some good science? I mean about the immune system. I know his predictions about computers getting smarter than humans. This I can trust. Computers definitely will be smarter than humans and more intelligent, etcetera. About the immune system, I'm not completely sure because when you deal with the actual biology of humans, there are so many problems, so it may not be so easy to fix the immune system. But we can imagine that theoretically, we could become immortal. So, yes with this I can agree; this is not impossible to become immortal. There is no principal limitation.

KS: So, what would be the consequences of us becoming immortal? Because in that particular moment, everything would change dramatically. The whole structure of life would be changed.

MAL: Yes, I said theoretically this was possible. So, there is no critical limitation. Practically, it will probably be impossible. Maybe the duration of life will be

---

[*]MIKHAIL A. LEBEDEV, PhD is an award-winning scientist in the fields of Neurophysiology and Brain-Computer Interfaces. Having earned his PhD at the University of Memphis, he currently holds the positions of Scientific Head and Chief Research Scientist for the Centre for Bioelectric Interfaces at the Institute of Cognitive Neuroscience for National Research, University Higher School of Economics, in Moscow, Russia, and Senior Research Scientist at Duke Medical Centre.

extended, but in the end, something will ruin the person's life. So basically, this is not like a real problem, but yes, let's imagine. So, everyone became immortal... Yes, I can imagine that. [Laughs.] I will make one prediction. Right now, people care very much about losing their memories. People are really afraid of losing memory, but immortal people will probably work on deleting some of their memories so they do not feel that they've lived forever. They will probably get some sort of refresh, to feel new, fresh and born again. [Laughs.]

KS: Thomas Metzinger the German philosopher said that in the near future, we are going to be able to delete and download memories and cancel them out. Do you really think we're going in this direction? Is it just science fiction to erase memories or to even purchase new ones?

MAL: Again, in principle, it is possible. Practically—probably in the nearest one hundred years—we will not be able to do this, because nobody knows how memory works. But what will be possible is that probably, we will be developing more and more advanced tools to modulate memories for certain things. Maybe for certain things improve memory, and in some situations maybe make use of forgetting. But those methods still will be kind of crude and it will not be like writing a vivid memory so that you are altered. So, the major problem is that we do not know much about memory. Even the predominant theories of memory may turn out to be completely wrong. For example, right now there is a predominant theory that the hippocampus is the side where memory starts to form, but the hippocampus is such a small structure of the brain, an old, archaic cortex. So, I can't imagine that this is the principal structure for remembering. Probably, like twenty years from now, the explanation of how memory works will be very different—but to be able to download memory, at least you need to know where it is started, how it is started. This is still not very well understood. There are crude methods, pharmacological, electrical stimulation, that could modulate the process of remembering, retrieving memory, etcetera.

KS: I was talking as well with one Russian philosopher and he said that our goal is to prepare future generations to fight with—to war—with artificial intelligence. How would you comment on his statement?

MAL: He said that because he is a philosopher, and philosophers—like, for example, experts in ethics, they need all means to justify their own existence. So this is why he said this, he is making up this problem so philosophers can work on this. Soon, we will have bureaucrats, administrators working on this because since this is the "problem," then we need some government department working on this, some regulations, restrictions, etcetera. [Laughs.] I think this problem is far-fetched. If there is a real war, there is no way humans can win because we are specialized, biological objects, we live as biological organisms. You cannot compete with computers already; computers defeat us in chess or in reading encyclopaedias. A computer can read one hundred volumes of an encyclopaedia in five seconds. I would think about artificial intelligence just as a useful tool for us. I think it will continue to be this way.

KS: I am just wondering from what perspective all these statements come? For example, Elon Musk is constantly talking about artificial intelligence and how great a danger this poses to us, that we'll have to connect our cortex to Neuralink just to survive in the new artificial environment. A very similar statement was made by Kurzweil. So, when ordinary people listen to statements like that, they think "Oh, my God! We really have to prepare ourselves for a war against AI." That's why I would like to know your point of view as a scientist.

MAL: I think they have a picture of these anthropomorphic robots with artificial intelligence—and these anthropomorphic robots are evil and they fight us. But remember, that we also have the same tools, like computers, etc. There is no real problem. Okay, so there is an evil robot that has artificial intelligence, but I have the same helpful artificial intelligence in my computer, so I can use it to fight this robot. So, there is no need for me to fight with this robot—I don't know, with the sword or something like that, guns. I can develop the same tools. If we are talking about being smart, smarter than a computer, we are already lost, just in certain ways—but soon there will be many more levels. Because I remember thirty years ago when they discussed this…'would computers at some point be able to play chess like humans'… and they said *no, no, there are too many combinations, the computer will never figure this out, only humans. It's intuition and understanding.* But now, the computers win at playing chess. So, the same will happen with face recognition, analysis of visual pictures etc. I don't agree there are any principal limitations for computers.

KS: However, all the time, we talk about artificial intelligence as something a bit mechanical, based on logic and algorithms. And yet we know man isn't very logical. So, will AI be able to compete with us in other areas reserved so far for humans, such as the soul, deep biology or intuition and consciousness?

MAL: So, it *used* to be that artificial intelligence was algorithm-based but now with all these deep-learning improved neural networks, nobody even knows how these networks learn. So, it just learns, and does very well. So basically, it performs almost like a human brain; it has a lot of neurons, connections.

They modify through learning algorithms, and it learns, so this will definitely improve in the future. I think artificial intelligence in the end will perform almost like humans, even (with) emotions you can model. This artificial brain can behave emotionally, but the subjectivity and soul will always remain the problem. It will be very hard to resolve. Some people would argue that since this robot is so smart, maybe it is conscious—but intuitively, we understand it's not conscious, right? Because it is made just of materials, but still we cannot *prove* much. So, I even doubt we can resolve the problem of consciousness, the hard problem of consciousness that is subjectivity. Because whatever you do, you'll always get perfect, materialistic explanation like, the light comes to the eyes, I see this... This gets analyzed, goes to my speech centre and I produce words. So, whatever you do, you will never resolve it, whatever methods you use. But all of us understand we have subjective feelings, etcetera.

KS: Geordie Rose, the founder of the D-Wave computer systems company—and his second company is A.I. Sanctuary—said in a lecture that in the near future, they'll be able to create such advanced artificial intelligence that it will be like an alien god among people—free of any connection to us because it will be so advanced. We'd be like worms to it. Is this scenario real or more a hoax?

MAL: Yes, I think it sounds like a hoax. His logical flaw is that this *something* will be on its own, that we somehow do not have the same tools as this creation. But we will always have the same tools.

KS: Really? So, this creation won't be able to just deal with reality on its own?

MAL: It may, but it will be still easily controllable, I think.

KS: Oh my God! You are giving us some hope. Thank you! [Laughs.]

MAL: [Laughs.] For example, I'm not an expert in computer viruses, but someone told me all those viruses already infected all the computers in the world, and they are just waiting to show themselves. But I hope that computer scientists have a way to control this. [Laughs.]

KS: Hopefully. I saw one of your interesting statements quoted by the British *Daily Mail*. Namely, that brain implants—chips—will copy our consciousness and we could become some kind of zombie population. Is it even possible that "humanity" will evolve into a community of zombies?

MAL: Yes, absolutely. Imagine you start to fill your brain with this stuff and then at some point, maybe you are becoming a zombie. It is absolutely real, I think, because actually there is no way to distinguish a zombie from the conscious person. There is no way to determine consciousness. So indeed, imagine you start implanting stuff in your brain and you behave more or less okay, but you already are a zombie—but for external observers, you are like a normal-behaving human, especially as some humans have very limited behaviours. Just imagine some old, old grandfather just reading the newspaper and saying a few words. If he became a zombie, then nobody would even notice. [Laughs.]

KS: Maybe from the beginning he was pure zombie, but we didn't notice that?

MAL: Exactly (laugh).

KS: As Professor Catherine Malabou pointed out in a lecture, one of the biggest challenges in the world of robotics is that robots remind us of dead people. Hence the concept of making them more similar to the so-called ancient Gods or Buddha figures, and not to humans. Do you think our fears of robots reminding us of the dead can be overcome? Or maybe humans—by absorbing NBIC in the body and copying the behaviour of machines to such a degree—we will be like them? Could we become so dead inside that robots' necrosis won't be a problem anymore?

MAL: Yes absolutely. But I guess that's okay—why not have a God that is a robot? Actually, this may be the perfect solution. First of all, this creature will be different, right? Then very smart because it has a good computer inside and the problem it is not human is solved already, because he's not supposed to be human because he is God. So, yes, this looks like a good idea. I am very sceptical about ethics like "Oh! You're not becoming a human anymore," but to me what's the problem? You can try whatever you want.

KS: In one of his lectures, Slavoy Zizek said that his friends—scientists—sent him a video in which they were able to remotely manipulate a rat, externally. The animal walks left or right, controlled externally by scientists. Zizek asked them if they could do something like this with a man? They replied that, of course, the man would not be conscious of outside interference, just like a rat.

MAL: Absolutely. In fact, this is the real problem because all these stimulation methods… they are getting advanced. Soon, you may get a stimulator in your pleasure area or motivation area. First of all, you will be able to motivate yourself but also somebody else could control you. If you want complex actions from me, then you will have to invest in my training but to *encourage* me to do something, maybe it's just a press of the button. Then I will have no doubt that this is really what I want to do. In fact, this is not far from reality because of these deep-brain stimulators many people are getting for Parkinson's disease. So, if a neurosurgeon implants a slightly different area, then you will get a person whom you could control by stimulation.

KS: It is hard even to think about the consequences of that kind of technology in the hands of the military, for example.

MAL: For the military it will be perfect.

KS: We already have groups of people in Europe who organize themselves in foundations and associations. They send petitions, letters to governments claiming they are being remotely manipulated. They're in every country.

MAL: Yes, but this is schizophrenia. This actually makes sense. When you want something, you understand that this is what *you* want. "I want to do this"—and it is obvious for me but maybe for them, it is not obvious. They feel the desire but maybe they do not understand that it comes from them, and they attribute it to somebody else? But curiously, I work a lot with monkeys and some of them look like schizophrenics and I was thinking, what if the monkey is schizophrenic? Maybe a monkey thinks it's being controlled by aliens for example? But if it doesn't prevent it from a normal life like getting a banana, eating, that's okay. So, whatever, if it doesn't contradict survival and evolution.

KS: So how to distinguish someone who really has schizophrenia from someone who has been subject to such technology? If we're really going in that direction, we don't know who's who. Am I right?

MAL: Exactly. All these methods of stimulation are very crude but they work. As opposed to brain-machine interfaces, they're the ones that try to extract something from the brain and decode it—this is hard because we do not know the code that the brain uses. So, it is hard to decode, but *sending* stimulation to the brain, although it's crude, it works because the brain starts to try to interpret the stimulation and then adjust, plastically adapts. So, yes, it may easily become a control signal. I've seen a scientific meeting when they stimulated the brain from the surface, and they noticed that the person liked it and got addicted to the stimulation.

KS: So, is there any possibility of people defending themselves against that kind of advanced technology, or are people already totally defenceless?

MAL: The same way we try to defend ourselves from drugs, yes, it's the same. That's another method of interfering with the electrical circuit of the brain.

KS: Would you agree with this statement made by Theodore Kaczynski in his *Industrial Society and Its Future*, namely "the concept of 'mental health' in the technological society is determined mainly by the degree to which the individual behaves according to the needs of the system without showing signs of stress."

MAL: Okay, yes, I think it makes sense. It looks like, I guess, an optimization problem or something, regulation.

KS: So, basically, you can be mentally healthy being psychopathic?

MAL: Yes, exactly, I think it makes sense. Yes, look at different societies, look at Japan for example where they work—I don't know—for sixteen hours per day, but at some point, they start to show signs of stress. So, maybe only this limits their hours of work?

KS: Ray Kurzweil claims that being a human does not mean being a biological organism but "constant change." Do you think that in the future, we'll not be able to distinguish even who's a human and who is not? Currently, we still rely on biological appearance. What would happen if you were a hologram with artificial intelligence and other advanced technology? I'm unsure I could call you a human. According to Kurzweil's statement, it's not a problem because being human means constant change. Who would you call a human?

MAL: So, probably we just need new definition of human. That's the only thing. So, I agree that we may change and become holograms, why not? Of course, this is not a real possibility for tomorrow but in principle, this is possible. It's again just a playing with words—like, you say "human" but don't define what it is. So, if you say a human is strictly a person with a biological body and two arms and two legs, then of course, a hologram is not human. But if you use a different definition, then it's fine. We can definitely change.

KS: So, if I call my chair or my table "human" it will be human, by just changing the definition?

MAL: ... No ...

KS: There's a core element in the definition of "human"—a basic correlation between us. I talk to you, you talk to me—and somehow, we can communicate with each other. At some deep level, I know you're human, not artificial intelligence. But who knows, maybe you're AI already?

Could be. [Laughs.]

KS: But somehow, I feel you are a still real human. So, something else must change, not just the definition.

MAL: Okay, imagine you're an experimental subject and placed in a room where there are only chairs, and all you see are chairs. Then you can develop a special relationship with the chairs. You can even communicate with them [Laughs.] By the way, this can be done. This can be a very cruel experiment, but the human brain is very plastic. I will give you an example: they may put you in the body of Einstein, for example, in virtual reality; you look at the mirror and you see Einstein. Imagine how your IQ improves just from that. So, if you're put in the virtual environment and you are the chair, then you will adapt to be the chair, just with VR methods.

KS: So, it depends on your identification?

MAL: Yes, identification and statistics, basically. You deal with the statistics of this world and these forms your perception.

KS: You can do it just by training, or chemicals, or maybe by mind engineering? Is it possible right now?

MAL: I think with virtual reality, you can already modify your perception of the world significantly. You want to be a hologram? Just go to the VR and convince yourself you are a hologram. Just imagine you're in this virtual reality only for one year and then your perception of the world will be significantly disturbed.

KS: So, should we have any limitation, in the definition of human being—or should we be anything what we want?

MAL: I do not like limitations. So, yes. It will actually be useful to be anything you want.

Paul Craig Roberts*

"Digital money is a means of police state control."

KONRAD STACHNIO: Does our future mean an even greater social stratification into the so-called "ultra-rich" on the one hand, and those almost entirely excluded from the jobs market—the so-called "disposable people"—on the other? Will these "disposables" desperately fuel new criminal organizations to survive in a world that offers no place for them? What will happen to the masses of people deprived of their jobs by robotics, artificial intelligence, and state-of-the-art manufacturing processes? Will there be a place for them in other economic sectors?

PAUL CRAIG ROBERTS: The extreme distribution of income and wealth that currently exists in the U.S. is not sustainable. It deprives the mass of the people of purchasing power with which to purchase the products of the businesses owned by the wealthy. Preventing the growth of income on the part of the mass of the people curtails the flow of profits to those who own the businesses. The offshoring of middle-class jobs is turning the U.S. into a third-world workforce employed in lowly-paid, domestic non-tradable services, such as waitresses, bartenders, hospital orderlies, and retail clerks. Just as—despite promises to the contrary by neoliberal economists, there were no jobs, much less the better ones promised for those Americans whose manufacturing jobs were moved offshore—there are no jobs to take the place of those eliminated by robots. The only way for societies to survive robotic employment is through socialization of the means of production. Assuming AI doesn't eliminate the human race, socialization of robotic industry would produce enormous leisure for humans. What they would do with it is unknown.

*PAUL CRAIG ROBERTS is an American economist, author, and former associate editor at *The Wall Street Journal*. Roberts also held the position of the United States Assistant Secretary of the Treasury for Economic Policy under President Ronald Reagan.

KS: How to sell more to consumers who earn less? Isn't continuous expansion the guarantee of capitalism? What will happen to the economy if we are replaced by robots? Robots do not buy and do not spend, and that is what drives the economy. How can there be a "consumer economy" if there is no employment?

PCR: There cannot be. This question is not asked by robotics' proponents, and it is not part of the discussion.

KS: Does educating oneself in some cases make sense—if you are bound to become unemployed?

PCR: The education that still works is education in personal skills that cannot be offshored. For example, hairstylists, heavy equipment operators, doctors, dentists, electricians, home repairs, skills that require on-site performance. Possibly, in the future, robotics will take over many of these skills, but for now they are safe from offshoring.

KS: What scenario do you foresee for Europe in the context of mass migration? Is the refugee crisis merely that, or rather, a symptom of Europe's crisis as such, Europe being unable to feed and receive such a number of people—people who come there just for a better life, which is more and more lacking in Europe?

PCR: The refugees overrunning Europe are the consequence of Europe's support for Washington's wars of aggression in the Middle East and North Africa. In the 21st century, Washington has destroyed in whole or in part seven countries, killing, maiming, and displacing millions of peoples. Washington now requires its servile European vassals to accept the refuse from its wars of aggression.

KS: The rescue offered to respond to the phenomenon of the robotics of jobs is "guaranteed income" and the transfer of people to other sectors of the economy that are not robotized. Is that just wishful thinking?

PCR: It is the propaganda of the ruling oligarchy. They are unable to identify what the other sectors of the economy are that can absorb workers displaced by robots.

KS: Is the current crisis—and are other series of crises—not the best and fastest way (according to some publications) to force whole populations to move into the new order and post-industrial society?

PCR: These terms, "the new order," "post-industrial society," "globalism," and so forth are all made-up nonsense terms to confuse people about what is really happening to them. As people do not know what the terms mean, they assume something is happening that is ordained and that requires their "adjustment." In this way, they accept their own destruction.

KS: What will happen to the middle class in your opinion? Will it become a revolutionary class by playing the role foreseen by Marx for the proletariat?

PCR: In the U.S., the middle class is being eliminated and compressed into the lower economic class. There is no revolutionary spirit, so far.

KS: Do you think the private sector will finally take over the government and TTIP will be the final end of the process? Is there still a chance to reverse this trend?

PCR: In the U.S., U.K. and elsewhere in the Western world, many aspects of government have been turned over to private profit-making businesses. For example, in the U.S., prisons are privatized, the inmates' labor sold to private corporations such as Apple. As prison labor is paid almost nothing, their wages are a huge subsidy to private businesses. Many aspects of the U.S. military have been privatized. Politicians have given lucrative contracts to their friends to feed and supply the military, to transport it, and to provide security forces to protect military positions. Everything the military formerly did for itself is now done at far higher costs by private companies. In the U.K., the postal service has been privatized. In the U.S., public education is being privatized via charter schools and student loans. There are many examples of government functions being turned over to private companies. In Florida, the Division of Motor Vehicles no longer sends out notices for vehicle license renewals; it has been contracted out to a private firm.

KS: In the future, will we have to deal with a new social division into castes like in—for example—India? On the one hand, you would have the privileged castes like programmers, engineers and so on, all serving the technological system, while on the other hand, there'd be the "disposable people." Will the initially "privileged" ones—with the development of artificial intelligence and robotics taking over their jobs—not eventually become "disposable people" themselves?

PCR: There is no privileged job caste. In the U.S., engineers and programmers, especially software engineers and IT professionals, have seen their jobs offshored to Asia. Americans graduating from universities expecting to find jobs to pay off their student loans find instead that the jobs have been sent to India and China.

KS: What will be the new business model? At present, it is moving away from the industrial model, i.e. production for the purpose of earning, into—for example—privatization of public space. What Bill Gates did, will this be a future economic model with such companies as Uber or Airbnb and the so-called sharing economy? Is this the real answer to shrinking employment?

PCR: There has never been anything but one "business model" and that is (the model of) exploitation. Exploitation will continue; it is all capitalism knows.

KS: Do you think there are still secure investments in the world where people's cash can be safe? What do you think about cryptocurrencies in this context?

PCR: Governments can do whatever they want. They can ban cryptocurrencies. They can confiscate gold and silver. They can force the use only of digital money which provides the government control over your bank account.

KS: In some circles, there is a conviction that there will never be a lack of jobs because there will also be human needs to satisfy. Machines will replace us in simple work and then the demand for other things will increase. This way, a big market segment to be filled up will appear in the world. Do you agree with this?

PCR: This is nonsense. Consider, for example, allegedly, the U.S. has been in an economic expansion since June 2009, yet the participation rate in the U.S. labor force continues to decline. This is unprecedented. When the economy is expanding, the labor force participation rate rises to take advantage of the job opportunities. The low U.S. unemployment rate is achieved by not counting the unemployed. If an unemployed person has not searched for a job in the past four weeks, the person is not counted as unemployed. People search for jobs for months and years and become discouraged. The discouraged are not counted as unemployed. In the U.S., the real unemployment rate is about 23%.

KS: What country would you choose for the best economy in the 21st century?

PCR: The countries on the rise are Russia and China. The Western world is locked into decline.

KS: Does peace for America mean the death of its economy? What would happen to the economy of the United States if the "war against terror" ended?

PCR: What would end the war? President Eisenhower warned the American people about the undemocratic character of the military/industrial complex in 1971. Imagine how much more powerful this interest group is today. The American economy is harmed by war as war wastes resources. What also harms the U.S. economy is monetary policy that favors a few large banks and financial speculators, and the offshoring of U.S. manufacturing and professional skilled jobs.

KS: Is it possible today to achieve freedom by people, in a peaceful and democratic way? Can an individual still find some security in a present and future society where more and more key decisions are made without him?

PCR: Freedom has never been achieved or maintained in a peaceful way. Freedom requires killing oppressors.

KS: Do you think America still has a chance to stand on its feet economically? Or as is predicted by some, will it become a third world country, one big Detroit?

PCR: America is already a Third World country. The only jobs available are in lowly paid domestic services.

KS: Would a society dependent on government through guaranteed or social income not be a psychological catastrophe for people, for as long as the scenario of guaranteed income and social life is possible on such a large scale?

PCR: A social safety net is only a minimum guarantee for those who experience adverse results. Therefore, it does not threaten people or society.

KS: In mental health terms, depression now frequently results from people believing changes are imposed upon them, that they are not the ones making them. Do you agree?

PCR: The powerlessness of people because decisions are made for, and about, them by ruling oligarchs causes frustration, but only for those sufficiently awake to be aware. People who live in The Matrix have no awareness.

KS: Can China and Russia still model themselves on the neo-liberal American economy if we know it has failed?

PCR: If China, Russia, and Iran follow neoliberal economics, they will fail along with the failing Western world.

KS: What do you think of the "austerity measures" policy as a practice for saving the economy?

PCR: Austerity measures have never saved any economy. Austerity destroys family income and, thereby, financial security and purchasing power. It harms society and destroys trust in government. Austerity imposed by the E.C. on Greece and Portugal forced a significant percentage of the women of those societies into prostitution.

KS: How do you view the neoconservative policy of the United States in the context of maintaining the hegemony of the United States?

PCR: It is a prescription for nuclear Armageddon.

KS: Do you think the dollar will be replaced with another currency?

PCR: All of the main currencies have been subjected to massive creation by QE programs. It is the same in the U.S., E.U., U.K., Switzerland, Japan, China. All the currencies are inflated, so why would one—or some combination such as the IMF SDR [International Monetary Fund Special Drawing Right]—replace the dollar?

KS: If money becomes fully electronic and eventually becomes an equivalent of energy (according to technocratic demands), what will be the consequences?

PCR: If money is digital, no one has financial privacy, and governments can force compliance by cutting off a person's access to his money. Digital money is a means of police state control.

KS: John Perkins, author of *Confessions of an Economic Hit Man*, says we are living in an unprecedented time of great crisis, presenting an opportunity for us to build a new, better world. He said we are living in a time of an

upcoming revolution since we've never before had so much global contact with each other through the Internet. Do you agree?

PCR: John Perkins might know this, and I might know this, and a few others, but how many of mankind know this? And if they do, have they any idea what to do about it other than to submit, which historically is what they have done? People need information to wake them up and possibly move them to action. But given the presstitute nature of the entirety of the Western media and the controlling influence of oligarchs, wresting control of the explanations from the ruling class is a difficult undertaking. In the dystopian novels that portray the future of mankind, the oligarchs win. Considering the defeat Marx's revolution has suffered, and considering the powerlessness of the working class—now branded "the Trump deplorables"—it seems unlikely that with the mass of humanity powerless, poor, and without any influence whatsoever, we will "build a new, better world."

Richard Falk[*]

"If a digital Fukuyama tells the world that 'the end of history' has been reached, he should be scorned this time around."

KONRAD STACHNIO: Do you know what is the role of the so-called Black Budget in building the power of the USA as a global security state?

RICHARD FALK: It is not possible for someone without access to highly classified materials to assess accurately the policy significance and content of the Black Budget in the years since 1945, including the financing of a range of intelligence activities and a variety of covert intervention projects. It is possible to put forward the view that the CIA and special operations forces are both partially financed by the Black Budget that has been integral to the formation and execution of American grand strategy since the end of World War II, building its unaccountable claims on government spending for global security as a byproduct of Cold War imperatives. The Black Budget has, above all, provided a cover for unlawful encroachments on the sovereign rights of foreign countries, mainly those of adversaries, but also extending to thwarting leftist political movements from controlling governments in countries whose foreign policy was under the tutelage of the United States. The Black Budget has also evidently been used to keep secret the financing of the research and development of new weapons and surveillance technologies. As with other bureaucratic innovations, the removal of an original justification for an undertaking does not easily lead to its abandonment or even downgrading, especially if shielded from

---

[*] **RICHARD FALK** is an international law and international relations scholar and Professor Emeritus at Princeton University. He served as UN Special Rapporteur for Occupied Palestine, and has annually been nominated for the Nobel Peace Prize since 2008. His recent books include *Power Shift: On the New Global Order*, and *Palestine Horizon: Toward a Just Peace*.

scrutiny by its secrecy and related non-accountability. In this respect, although the size of the Black Budget steadily grew as one side effect of the Cold War, its ending in the 1990s did not lead to reduced appropriations.

Most modern states finance their secretive activities through some form of "Black Budget." What distinguishes the U.S. Black Budget is its scale, global projection dimensions, and integration into an overarching design for establishing and maintaining a global state, and its ties to unlawful policies and practices outside the domain of territorial sovereignty, and most of all, its linkages to sustaining the United States as the first "global state" in history. It is not just a matter of its planetary interpretation of American security, but of its subsuming under the banner of security a wider hegemonic agenda of economic dominance, cultural hegemony, and ideological influence. There is no serious pretension that after the Cold War the U.S. Government was taking over responsibility for *global* peace and security as envisioned in the Charter of the United Nations, although there was a brief claim to this effect in 1990–91 when the American president, George H.W. Bush, proclaimed "a new world order" based on UN authority and international law in response to defending Kuwait against Iraqi aggression. Such a claim was never subsequently repeated.

The idea of the U.S. as a global state is a geopolitical endeavor related to power and wealth rather than on any normative (based on law and morality) or cosmopolitan (meta-nationalist) conceptions of security. It is rationalized and justified by reference to national interests as measured by military superiority, economic advantage, alliance cohesion, and by the exercise of global leadership supposedly for the benefit of all humanity. The substantive priorities of the Black Budget are designed by American political realists who are by training and disposition distrustful of any loss of sovereign control over national policies and practices, are suspicious of the UN and international law, and seek to validate foreign commitments by reference to the promotion of national interests.

There is every indication that the Black Budget has been over the years "bipartisan" in the sense that it receives equal support from the U.S. Congress whether the occupant of the White House is a Democrat of a Republican. This bipartisanship extends to overall support for the defense budget and for a capitalist approach toward financial and labor markets, environmental protection, and corporate regulation. Donald Trump was opposed by part of the national security establishment when he sought the presidency in 2016 because he was perceived as a threat to this bipartisan consensus, and especially the commitment to maintaining control over a global security system. Trump did challenge aspects of the consensus, but when it came to militarism there has been no rupture since he entered the White House. The Black Budget has been rising during his presidency, reaching $81.1 billion in the last fiscal year, suggesting that Trump, despite withdrawing from economic, humanitarian, and environmental internationalism and asserting a belligerent brand of chauvinistic nationalism, is not willing to dismantle the American state apparatus of global surveillance, secrecy, and control, and even more tellingly, to abandon the network of overseas military bases, the far flung naval presence in the world's oceans, and even the militarization of space.

Underlying questions arise as to whether the Black Budget of the United States and others is an inevitable implication of the military technology now available to many states, its range and accuracy that overcomes distance and time, precluding targeted states from defensive responses to threats. These conditions create multiple vulnerabilities of societies throughout the world, however powerful, to subversive violence from within and transnational violence from without, making readiness for war a permanent feature of political life. The global security state is reinforced by a trend toward autocratic national leadership throughout the world. It is important to associate the Black Budget with both innovative military software and hardware as well as with the surveillance/secrecy impulses of governance at the national, regional, and global levels of political organization. More concretely, the threats of terrorism and more recently, of contagious disease, give surface rationalizations for security capabilities that penetrate the most private activities of citizens as well as the secret undertakings of foreign governments, whether friendly or not. Such technologically driven circumstances bearing on the shrinking of time and space, if correctly and humanely interpreted, would encourage rapid shifts in emphasis and ideology from *national* and *militarized* security to *human* and *ecological* security. There are no signs that this desirable shift is happening, and so the roots of militarism grow deeper into the soil of political life in all its operational contexts.

KS: Are we currently entering the era of global digital dictatorship? Over those who colonize other countries technologically as well as on those that are colonized?

RF: I am not convinced that the core reality of this epoch will be shaped by "digital dictatorship," and I am not entirely sure what is meant by the term. There seem to be contradictory tendencies arising from digitization, providing pathways to both domination and autonomy. It is true that vulnerability to cyber-attacks will give potential dictatorial control to the more technologically sophisticated political actors, but to what ends is impossible to anticipate, as well as what counter-moves might be taken by less digitally sophisticated states. There are also possibilities of non-state actors acquiring control or neutralizing capabilities with respect to such technologies.

I suspect that the greatest dangers will arise at the interface between artificial intelligence (AI) and robotics, with drones already prefiguring such militarized applications of digital technology. As with other weapons innovations, it is not at all clear that political outcomes will be determined by military superiority. The historical novelty of the anti-colonial wars of the last century was that they were won by the side that possessed *inferior* military capabilities. There is as yet no evidence that digital technologies will be able to impose stable dictatorial governance at home or compliant colonies abroad. The dynamics of national resistance must be taken into account. What could happen is a weakening of the legitimacy and effectiveness of the state-centric world order, which has dominated the international scene since the Peace of Westphalia in 1648. Digitization could result in new configurations of authority and power, mergers of weaker and more vulnerable states to augment postures of digital anti-colonialism.

The near future of geopolitics may be shaped by the agendas and undertakings of the two global states, U.S. and China, the former declining, the latter ascending, and poised for rivalry, if not confrontation. The dynamics of their interaction is likely to shape the geopolitical structure of world order, at least for the remainder of the first half of the 21st century. Which of these two global states comes to possess superior mastery of digitization may give a clue as to how this rivalry will play out historically, but still may not reveal whether digital dominance will be translated into usable forms of geopolitical leverage or transnational structures of political dictatorship both within sovereign territory and within the sovereign domains of foreign countries or regions. For the foreseeable future there will be a variety of intensifying tensions between the territorial dimensions of *authority* and the non-territoriality of *influence* and *behavior*. At present, autocratic nationalism is obstructing transnational flows of people (walls at militarized borders, anti-immigration policies and practices), capital (retreat from neoliberal globalization), and goods and services (trade wars, sanctions). What the prospects are for digital internationalism, especially if hegemonically motivated, remains obscure.

KS: Will the new apartheid of our time be division into people who are "technologically enriched" (through, for example, embedded microchips or gene editing, thus being more adapted to the technological environment) and those who do not have these embedded enrichments?

RF: At present, the clearest historical examples of apartheid involve race and nuclear weaponry, although the structures of domination and victimization are specific to each instance in both categories. The idea of apartheid derives from South Africa's racist political regime of a white minority imposing its exploitative will on a large black majority. It has been applied in two different ways to Israel's control over Palestine: *territorially* by reference to Israel's occupation policy as implemented in the West Bank since 1967 exemplified by applying Israeli law to Jewish settlers and military administration to the Palestinians; *ethnically* by reference to Palestinian people whether living in refugee camps in neighboring countries or as involuntary exiles, or in pre-1967 Israel as a minority in East Jerusalem, or in Gaza under occupation. This is a dynamic of ethnic domination that generates structures designed to subjugate the Palestinian people as a whole, however dispersed, and not as in South Africa under the territorial control of the Afrikaner government.

Nuclear apartheid relates to the Nonproliferation Treaty and its implementing geopolitical regime. Despite treaty provisions calling for nuclear disarmament as urgent priority, the existing nuclear weapons states retain possession, development, and deployment options while other states are prohibited from acquiring the weaponry even if possessing convincing security reasons for gaining a deterrent capability (as could be argued on behalf of Iran), and risk an aggressive regime-changing intervention if perceived as seeking to cross the nuclear threshold. This provided the rationale for attacking Iraq in 2003. In effect, the five permanent members of the UN Security Council are the self-appointed custodians of the weaponry, and all others are subject to an unconditional prohibition relating to their acquisition and possession, and selectively subject to geopolitical enforcement. Various exceptions to the prohibitions exist, including Israel, India and Pakistan, and more ambiguously for North Korea.

The prospect of a technological apartheid is situated somewhere between envisioned scientific capabilities and science fictional fears (e.g. of designer genetics; mass produced clones or warrior robots) and dreams (e.g. of eternal life, perfect health, and supplanting God as the master of the universe). There is a great deal of uncertainty as to whether countries that are geopolitically dominant in the world will also be able to control the frontiers of technological innovation in a number of areas. Religious scruples and legal prohibitions might also dissuade a political actor from acquiring those technological capabilities that are premised on hegemonic control, exploitation, and victimization. Unlike apartheid as an international crime, the metaphoric suggestion of a technologically based apartheid, is not based on race or religion, and therefore the emotive relevance of the allegation of apartheid seems less justifiable. Nuclear apartheid is metaphorical but it is premised on clear demarcation lines between having and not having the weaponry, although the distinction is blurry with respect to countries such as Japan and Germany that have the technological capabilities to become a nuclear weapons state in a matter of months. Unlike the racial and religious forms of apartheid, its metaphorical extensions do not have clearly identifiable boundaries of inclusion and exclusion. Despite its lesser technological capability to cross the nuclear threshold, Iran is treated as a greater threat to the nonproliferation regime than is Germany or Japan.

Against this background, I am not sure that "technological apartheid" is a helpful way of distinguishing between beneficiaries and victims of various technological innovations. Class may be the biggest divider as it has been for many devices associated with the digital age. The impact of technology on state/society relations via face recognition surveillance is another dimension of hegemonic control, but again a thin application of the apartheid metaphor as the markers of differentiation are unclear and contested. Unlike "nuclear apartheid," which considers a single menacing technological sector, the projection of "technological apartheid" projects technological domination across the spectrum of human concerns, which somewhat characterized the colonizing period following the Industrial Revolution, which gave Europe control over both military hardware and navigational maneuverability.

It may be timely to worry about "digital dictatorship," and I am sure its attainment is on the secret long-range operational investigations of geopolitical actors, both to avoid being left behind and potentially subjugated, as well as to achieve a controlling upper hand.

KS: How do you perceive the future of Fatah and Hamas?

RF: It is a difficult time of challenge for the Palestinian struggle, which casts a dark cloud of uncertainty over the future of both Fatah and Hamas. This uncertainty pertains, especially, to Fatah, which provides the main organizational underpinning for the Palestinian Authority that has represented the Palestinian people on an international level ever since the Oslo Framework of Principles was agreed upon in 1993. This framework presupposed a negotiating process that was widely expected by the UN, governments, and the general public to be committed to the establishment of an independent Palestinian sovereign state on the territory occupied by Israel since the 1967 War. This solution was accepted internationally, giving rise to the two-state consensus on how the conflict between Jews and Palestinian Arabs could be resolved and the competing claims of self-determination accommodated.

If the formal annexation of a substantial part of the West Bank takes place in coming months it will not only be the final nail in the two-state coffin, but also draw into question the viability of the Palestinian Authority as the voice of the State of Palestine. There are other relevant arenas that give the PA a rationale for a continuing existence, especially if it can find alternate funding for its rather elaborate governmental structures, including the pursuit of its grievances in the International Criminal Court, but most of all, by taking advantage of the situation to seek joint and unified leadership of the Palestinian struggle and arrange more authentic representation in international arenas, which would involve bringing Hamas in from the cold. The representation of the Palestinian people has been weakened by the persisting inability to obtain sufficient political unity to establish legitimate leadership of the Palestinian struggle for rights. Israel has contributed to this Palestinian diplomatic weakness by its continuous efforts over the years to keep the Palestinian movement factionalized and the Palestinian people ideologically, geographically, and diplomatically fragmented.

Hamas, in contrast to Fatah, and the PLO, has never endorsed the two-state approach as a tenable basis for reaching a sustainable peace between the two peoples. Hamas has challenged the underlying legitimacy of the Israeli State, and its exclusivist claims to be the State of the Jewish people. In recent years, following the electoral successes of Hamas in Gaza in 2006 and its takeover of governance from Fatah in 2007, it has claimed and controversially exercised a right of resistance, but most characteristically in defensive and retaliatory modes, and not as a strategy of liberation through armed struggle. Hamas has also negotiated, usually by way of Egypt, several short-term ceasefires with Israel, and in recent years, has proposed publicly and by back channels long-term ceasefires, including in a proposal for a 50 year ceasefire, although conditional on Israel lifting the blockade on Gaza and withdrawing to 1967 borders, an action long ago unanimously prescribed in UN Security Council Resolution 242.

Hamas also apparently reached out by discreet diplomacy to the Bush presidency in the years after its electoral successes in 2006 to exert pressure on Israel to agree upon some kind of long-term pause in hostilities with respect to Gaza. Yet neither Israel nor the United States, nor the PA, seemed at all interested in any kind of accommodation with Hamas if it did not include a recognition of the legitimacy of the Israeli State and a renunciation of any Palestinian right of resistance. It should be remembered that the U.S. Government had encouraged Hamas to participate in the 2006 elections, to shift their behavior from a reliance on armed struggle to the pursuit of its goals on a so-called "political track." It was believed at the time that Washington assumed that the people of Gaza would repudiate Hamas, and this would solidify the political control of Occupied Palestine under Fatah influence and control, which was viewed as more moderate in relation to both means and ends. When these expectations were frustrated, the U.S., together with Israel, refused to treat Hamas as a legitimate political actor. Hamas was blacklisted as a terrorist organization that engaged in unlawful violence, pointing to the rocket attacks directed at Israel following the Israeli "disengagement" from Gaza in 2005, which involved withdrawing IDF troops across the border and dismantling the Israeli settlements. The time line between Israeli provocation and Hamas retaliation remains contested, and hard to unravel and. resolve, but what seems evident is that the Hamas provocations were indiscriminate, yet doing far less damage and being much less intrusive with respect to the Israeli civilian population than did the Israeli attacks and indirect control mechanisms continuously imposed on the people of Gaza often in the form of harsh collective punishment prohibited by Article 33 of the Fourth Geneva Convention.

It is now difficult to tell whether various developments in the present context will bring about any changes relevant to Fatah and Hamas. It is possible that Israeli annexation of large portions of the West Bank will give rise to renewed and more successful efforts at achieving political unity among Palestinian political factions. Given the failure of several past attempts, it would be irresponsible to predict success for such an effort, although a sustainable achievement of political unity with respect to representation, leadership, and the tactics of struggle would be a very favorable development from a Palestinian perspective, improving prospects for some sort of eventual political compromise. The issues facing the Palestinians have taken several turns for the worse in the last few years, principally due to overt and unconditional support given to unlawful Israeli expansionism by the presidency of Donald Trump and shifts in the regional balance as a result of Arab priorities now emphasizing the rivalry with Iran as to regional supremacy and an accompanying willingness to abandon support for the Palestinian struggle. For Israeli politicians, there is present the window of opportunity provided by Trump's unconditional support of Israeli ambitions, but this window could close, at least part way, if Trump loses to Biden in November. Similarly, unrest in the Arab World could at any point lead to a second phase of the Arab Spring, possibly bringing to power a leadership in either Egypt or Saudi Arabia more responsive to renewed solidarity with the Palestinian struggle. How Fatah and Hamas will relate to such future developments remains a black box at present. Also, whether the experience of the COVID-19 health crisis alters Palestinian priorities relating to their political alignments, agenda, and tactics is impossible to discern at this stage as is its impact on the regional and global play of relevant geopolitical play of forces.

KS: Will Hezbollah become the biggest threat to Israel in the future? Because of military training in Syria and the weakening role of the U.S.?

RF: My understanding of these issues is limited. Although Hezbollah has had the benefit of battlefield experience in Syria, I think this enhanced capability would be relevant more to discourage Israel from repeating its 1982 ground attack and subsequent occupation of southern Lebanon that became untenable inducing Israel to withdraw in 2000. I believe that Israel is mostly concerned at present about Hezbollah's augmented defensive and retaliatory capabilities if Israel were to launch the kind of land invasion that culminated in the siege of Beirut that occurred almost 40 years ago. It is my understanding that Hezbollah has acquired accurate long-range missile capabilities that could cause heavy damage to Israeli cities, but if used offensively, it would likely bring about a disproportionate Israeli response with ruinous consequences for Lebanon. Hezbollah has demonstrated its capabilities to maintain a sustained campaign of territorial resistance, and possibly possesses a sufficient deterrent capability to discourage Israel from mounting an aggressive military campaign even from the air and sea. Overall, with the internal strife and tensions experienced by Lebanon in recent months, and still unresolved, Hezbollah seems to have become a weaker political actor in the internal Lebanese balance of forces, and highly unlikely to take any initiative that would provoke Israel to take major military action. An aspect of Hezbollah's apparent political decline in Lebanon is the perception among the Lebanese people that Hezbollah became too close to Iran, which funded its activities and was a principal supplier of its advanced weaponry.

KS: How do you see Europe's future in the context of Islamic fundamentalists returning to their home countries in Europe after the defeat of ISIS?

RF: Much depends on whether the "victory" over ISIS as projected is seen as the end of the story. If perceived as only a pause in violent challenges directed at Europe, or even with uncertainty as to the future, there will be public hostility to readmitting such individuals, especially former ISIS fighters. ISIS was itself a reaction to the U.S./UK occupation of Iraq after 2003, suggesting that such fundamentalist responses can arise whenever civilizations clash, and particularly when the West seeks to assert control over the political life of a non-Western society in the post-colonial era.

Against this background, the repatriation of ISIS fundamentalists is a very difficult issue to speculate about, and is likely to reflect diverse national policies that are put in practice rather than a common European Union approach. The treatment of ISIS applicants for reentry will likely depend on whether the vetting process will be willing and able to draw reliable distinctions between hardened militants and disillusioned recruits, and how families of ISIS fighters will be viewed in the overall context. It is likely that most European governments will be reluctant to issue visas to those ISIS families who are without valid passports, yet seek to return to their native countries. There are issues associated with uncertainty as to how particular individuals participated in ISIS, what sorts of connections they have with their families in Europe, what job opportunities would await them, what effects their repatriation would have on domestic political tensions. Some of these issues are explored fictionally, with great intelligence, by Kamila Shamsie, in *Home Fire* (2017). My guess is that there will be a great reluctance by most European governments to permit the return of anyone closely associated with ISIS, and over the age of 18. A problem of their statelessness is likely to emerge.

KS: Would you agree with the statement of Chris Hedges that currently the only way to survive as human beings is disobedience to the elites?

RF: I think there is provocative value in taking seriously this injunction from a commentator on the current scene who is as thoughtful and justice-oriented as is Chris Hedges, and yet to serve as any guide to action, or even as a source of reflection, there is a need for greater particularity. Such a general call for disobedience is vague, and dependent on interpretation within a great variety of contexts. We need to know far more clearly what Hedges means by "survive as human beings" and by "disobedience to the elites." Is it a call for the defense of human dignity against the state by establishing appropriate and effective forms of resistance? Is resistance limited to nonviolent tactics or does it depend on the context? Is the primary concern here with the word "human" (as in the quality of life) or with "survival" (as "bare life" in terms of subsistence)? Above all, is it a clarion call for the transformation or abolition of predatory capitalism and global militarism?

If we try to respond more concretely to Hedges based on personal perceptions and circumstances we will end up with a wide array of responses. From my perspective, I think Hedges is speaking within an American context, and delivering a central message that our constitutional democracy is faltering, and needs renewal by way of a movement of radical reform, possibly in imitation of the civil rights movement of the 1960s as guided by Martin Luther King, Jr.. In my darker moods I think even this degree of reformism is not sufficient, and that the challenges faced need to be conceived in the more activist framework of radical social action associated with the thinking and tactics of Malcolm X. Even in the somewhat less polarized times of the 1960s both of these charismatic leaders were assassinated, although King's demands for access and equality became more fully realized and endorsed by elites than were the economic and social demands of Malcolm. Many might have thought that King's vision was fully realized by the election of Barack Obama to the presidency in 2008, but such an assessment overlooked King's anti-militarism and planetary humanism. These earlier expressions of semi-authorized "disobedience to the elites," even when seemingly effective, can be reversed. The very success of anti-racism occasioned racist reactions, exemplified by the Trump presidency and the accompanying revival of a white supremacy movement to previously unimagined heights of influence.

If the idea of disobedience and resistance is directed at American militarism and foreign policy via a renewed peace movement, it evokes memories of the anti-war movement that became influential in the final years of the Vietnam War and in reaction to fears of nuclear war that emerged at various stages of the Cold War. Again, as with civil rights, short-term policy modifications were achieved, but the structures of militarism adapted, and regained control over policy and behavior in ways that resumed the old patterns only recently deemed unacceptable. Adjustments were made to remove the triggers that arouse popular opposition and unrest, but the structures of abuse are resilient, and can be imaginative in evading mandates for change. Militarists reestablished their influence after the Soviet collapse by exaggerating a range of security threats and identifying new enemies, exerting greater control over media coverage of war zones, and by professionalizing the armed forces and modernizing its tactics so that the politically sensitive draft could be ended. The justifications for inflated military budgets gained political support, and the former patterns of military intervention, thought to be discredited after the Vietnam experience, were re-stabilized.

Underlying Hedges' call to action by citizens is his acute distrust of and opposition to the status quo, and his lack of confidence that political elites can be persuaded to adopt policies and programs that benefit the majority of American citizens, let alone humanity in general. National challenges, whether climate change, pandemics, or social justice, are not being properly addressed, and reliance on the traditional constitutional correctives of electoral politics seems to lack the vision and leadership needed. The critique of "choiceless democracy" strikes many of us as convincing given the absence of proposals for structural change by the major political parties. In this respect, an "extraordinary" politics of a people's *movement* needs to challenge the established order of elites by embracing a transformative vision that transcends the "legal" channels of Congress and electoral politics to win its mandate for revolutionary change. Arguably, Bernie Sanders was somewhat animated by such an assessment of the political situation and recognized the need for movement politics more than trusting traditional electoral politics to get desired results. His goal of gaining the presidential nomination of the Democratic Party in 2016 and again in 2020 was fueled by the hope that the imbalances of society, dramatized by gross inequalities, would lead the DNC gatekeepers to permit entry to a candidate advocating the necessity of a certain amount of structural change. Despite his popularity as a candidate, Sanders' defeat was a recognition that he posed too great a threat to the established order regarded as beneficial to the political and economic elites of both political parties to permit his candidacy. Sanders was seen as posing a structural threat, whereas Obama was not, despite the color of his skin. In this sense, race is less structural than capitalism, militarism, or even support for Israel in the current American scheme of things.

Keeping the focus on the American setting, the central force of Hedges' outlook is to remind the citizenry that the party system will not generate the leaders or policies required to achieve necessary and desirable change. And feasible change is not enough, nor even durable, as Obama's presidency confirmed. My own way of interpreting this condition of political closure at the policy levels of governance is to make reference to the "bipartisan consensus" that joins Republicans and Democrats on the most crucial policy issues of the day. This consensus emerged as the Cold War produced common ground between the mainstream elites of both political parties as a sequel to the politics of national unity achieved during World War II. The bipartisan consensus had three pillars that had ups and downs as to the extent and character of its leverage, but enjoyed basic continuity of support: (1) trust and deference to the priorities of Wall Street in managing the economy; (2) full funding of the military, diplomatic, and ideological infrastructure required to oversee global security by becoming the first "global state" to remain vigilant during times of peace and war; and (3) uphold the "special relationship" of unconditional support for Israel, with special implications for engagement and alignments in the Middle East.

The pragmatic and normative limitations of the bipartisan consensus have not yet shattered the Satanic grip of this marginalization of democratic choice. The idea of living in "a choiceless democracy" reflected the weight of the bipartisan consensus on the political life of the country. Donald Trump seemed to challenge this reality when a presidential candidate in 2016, but despite his assault on the post-1945 traditional verities of presidential leadership, the bipartisan consensus has been as powerfully implemented during his years in the White House as previously.

The pragmatic shortcoming of the bipartisan consensus is most vividly revealed in the consistent inability to translate military superiority into successful political outcomes. This is the great unlearned lesson of the last half of the twentieth century. Military superiority based on technological innovations and battlefield tactics lack their earlier capability of imposing Western dominance. The Asian resurgence of the last half century was based not on countervailing military capabilities but on superior economistic relations between the state and society, exemplified by China's rise to ascendancy through mastery of the instruments of *soft power* expansionism. The West, especially the U.S., is entrapped in an outmoded and self-destructive militarist paradigm that no longer is capable of maintaining American geopolitical interests at acceptable costs, and is experiencing imperial decline due to the weakening of geopolitical morale at home and a dispiriting series of foreign policy defeats when relying on its military superiority. The crucial uncertainty is whether this dynamic of decline will at some point engulf the world in an apocalyptic war or whether the political will needed to reconstruct the geopolitical agenda along more constructive lines emerges as if by magic.

KS: Are we now at the end of the unipolar world and entering the multipolar era? Or are we rather heading towards a world completely centralized like never before in history by combining military power and technology? As we know, some countries in the Middle East where war was, and North Korea as well, do not belong to the Bank for International Settlements.

RF: In my view, the image of a "unipolar world" was a mistaken interpretation of world order after the Soviet collapse in 1992 that nonetheless correctly marked the end of the "bipolar world." Such conceptual metaphors were based on the salience of the superpower military standoff and ideologically charged geopolitical rivalry that was at the core of the Cold War, especially as it played out in Europe. The limits of such metaphors should have become evident after the defeat of the United States in the Vietnam War, the defeat of the Soviet Union in Afghanistan, and the remarkable rise of China after the Cultural Revolution.

There was a period in the U.S. during the 1990s when neo-conservatives criticized the Clinton presidency for its reliance on an economistic geopolitics of neoliberal globalization at the cost of foregoing its earlier emphasis on a more militarist foreign policy. Neoconservatives were arguing that American foreign policy in the 1990s missed opportunities to take advantage of the removal of the Soviet Union from the geopolitical equation by recognizing the unipolar moment of military dominance as a window of opportunity to extend the reach of its global security system, especially urging "democracy promotion" schemes in the Middle East to be achieved if necessary by forcible intervention. This triumphalist atmosphere was epitomized by Francis Fukuyama's insistence that the defeat of the Communist challenge was tantamount to reaching the end of history. Such an illusion was soon shattered forever by the 9/11 attacks on the Pentagon and World Trade Center, although these attacks were the apparent work of a non-state actor with minimal military capabilities, and no sovereign territorial base, thus eroding the major premise of state-centric world order.

Trump's seeming retreat from the U.S. role as global leader has been evident since 2017. Trump made this point by over and over declaring himself elected president of America and not of the world, a message clearly signaling the end of any pretension of geopolitical unipolarity. This assessment was underscored by rising chauvinistic nationalism in many leading countries, which expressed a trend toward less hierarchical structuring of global security policy, more dependence on national self-reliance, less on multilateral alliances. After the Cold War, alliances played a much smaller role except possibly in Europe, giving world order a more statist character, which resulted in increased decentralization of international authority at the level of the state. Also, by and large, the global security agenda was far less concerned with great power competition than in earlier decades. Prolonged major violent conflict came to be preoccupied with the interplay in these countries of civil strife and regime-changing geopolitics (as in Syria, Yemen, Congo, Libya). It was also associated with transnational violence taking the form of the threats mounted by non-state actors (al Qaida, ISIS). In neither setting did the rhetoric of geopolitical polarization seem illuminating.

Perhaps, this will change with the waning of the global war on terror launched by the United States in 2001 after the 9/11 attacks. This dynamic is partly a reflection of the reduction of terrorist incidents in the West and partly the reenergizing of great power rivalry, with China now somewhat displacing post-Soviet Russia. Whether this rivalry will be perceived as a new phase of bipolarity is doubtful as the confrontation is not shaped, as was the U.S./Soviet standoff, by reciprocal threats of annihilation—partly because there is, at this stage, much less at stake with regard to ideological differences and also less emphasis on militarized conflict, alliances, and Europe, which was the former locus of direct confrontation. The U.S./China rivalry seems to be most intense around issues of trade and investment, with much less emphasis on the militarist preoccupations with defense of homeland, superior battlefield capabilities, containment, and competition with respect to new weaponry than was the case during the 45 years of U.S./Soviet confrontations. For this reason, it seems unlikely that the language of polarity will be relied upon to describe the new geopolitical alignment of principal adversaries on a global scale. To be sure, there are contentions, based on historical analogies, that China as an ascending great power is threatening to the United States in its role as preeminent great power, posing what Graham Allison has labeled "The Thucydides Trap" in a book bearing this title.

By projecting these concerns to the future, we do receive an impression of increasing multipolarity with respect to the world economy, taking the primary form of greater regionalization of trade, investment, and technological transfer. Whether this will produce a corresponding retreat from Bretton Woods and World Trade Organization frameworks, the institutional foundations of the

American-led establishment of a rule-based liberal international order is not yet clear. If such a retreat occurs and is accompanied by a new wave of regional institution-building, it will lead to a new kind of multipolarity resting on the leveling of the technological foundations of power, having a depolarizing and equalizing impact, the opposite of the feared digital dictatorship and technological categorization of have and have not societies.

What can be said with reasonable confidence is that the language of unipolarity, bipolarity, and multipolarity is unlikely to be widely employed to describe the currently emergent central conflict patterns within global settings. Multipolarity as an alternative rhetoric to that of regionalization possesses somewhat greater relevance, although in contexts other than war/peace which had given rise to reliance on notions of bipolarity and unipolarity to capture the central feature of the Cold War. In this regard, future developments bearing on world order are most likely to be depolarized, either emphasizing global patterns of cooperation (climate change, biodiversity, global commons, migration, s) and statist patterns of self-reliance (border control, import substitution, restrictions on investment, trade barriers). In this respect, the near future of international relations seems most likely to resemble geopolitics of prior eras but in a technological environment dominated by transnational networking, automation, and digitalization.

KS: Would you agree with the statement that the control system in its nature is always analog and not Digital? Therefore, all Digital systems such as blockchain, Bitcoin, etc., can exist only until control is exercised analogously by the army? If any government wants to outlaw a given crypto currency, it can be done very easily, because in the last instance, control is always analog, on the ground, i.e. military force. Is therefore the concept of so-called "decentralization" a fiction?

RF: Yes, in the last analysis, so far as we know, the side that succeeds in controlling the armed forces in a revolutionary situation almost always determines the political outcome and exerts control over markets, including the authentication of currencies. This was one of Lenin's greatest contributions to revolutionary thought. Digital modes of resisting and mobilizing can challenge the established analogic structures of control, and even gain temporary victories, but transforming these structures is often a very different story. This was illustrated rather spectacularly during the course of the Egyptian political unfolding of what was being called the Arab Spring in 2011, and seemed for a short period to signal the potency of digital agency through the dynamics of mass mobilization through the Internet on behalf of freedom and democracy. It did not take long for analogic forces to regroup under the aegis of armed forces and elements of the former Mubarak rulership in the bureaucratic setup, likely prodded and guided by external actors. In the end, the digitally powered challenge was brutally and effectively crushed. The political outcome restored a harsher form of repressive autocracy than what had been generated by the seemingly irreversible digital rising against the Mubarak regime of repression and elite corruption. Yet we still do not know for sure whether this return to autocratic governance will last. It is possible that future digital challenges will be mounted in ways that are transformative, as well as merely disruptive, and that such a movement will be alert and adept enough to defeat countermoves by analog forces seeking to regain control of the Egyptian state and society once again.

We need also to inquire whether the analysis of political conflicts can be usefully reduced to the analog/digital divide as it has operated up to now. Digital organizing has so far been ineffectual from the perspective of historical transformation, but this could change. As recent elections in the United States and elsewhere have shown, digital platforms are sites of struggle. Trump's use of Twitter-fused digital agitation with analogic state terror as earlier pioneered by pre-digital forms of European fascism. It should also be kept in mind that digital activism is still in a rather primitive phase of development, and is being exploited by a wide range of extremist political movements on both the right and left, by libertarians as well as by anarchists and others dreaming of emancipation from analogic modes of control.

Whether or not digital politics has revolutionary and transformative potential is a matter that can only be resolved in the future. The uprisings comprising the Arab Spring were blocked partly because of organizational failings related to program and leadership, as well as due to its vulnerability to the pushback of political forces, which retained control of the apparatus of state power and never genuinely subscribed to the democratizing goals despite pretensions to the contrary. Lenin's valuable insight rested on an understanding that a revolutionary movement could not hope to sustain a challenge to the status quo unless it smashed the old state, and reconstructed a new state in its image from top to bottom. Without any outward show of allegiance to Leninism, the Iranian Revolution of 1978–79 achieved its goals in ways that contrasted with the failures of the Arab Spring. The essential learning experience of this early phase of digital politics is that it is not enough to overthrow an autocrat unless there also occurs a drastic reconstruction of analog structures of control. In this respect, the tragic error of those who so bravely massed in Tahrir Square to demand the end of the Mubarak dictatorship was to accept the good faith of the institutions of Egyptian governance against which the masses had risen up in passionate resistance. This is not to ignore other factors at play, including above all the degree to which this spontaneous uprising heralded a new leadership under the aegis of the Muslim Brotherhood, which the secular supporters of the anti-Mubarak movement had grossly underestimated.

I remember having a meal with a Russian friend in Moscow during the early period of Gorbachev's reformist efforts. His assessment bears on aspect of digital politics. He said we in Russia now have *glasnost* but not *perestroika*. He meant that now we can talk freely and critically, but we still lack the capacity to change the repressive and corrupt structure of the Soviet power machine. This will be the agency test for digital politics. Can digital transformative visions go beyond rhetoric and mobilized enthusiasm to get their followers to mount the barricades, at least figuratively? So far, the organized military, para-military, police, and propaganda capabilities and long experience of the analog world has prevailed, but the final interplay of this interaction awaits disclosure in the future. If a digital Fukuyama tells the world that "the end of history" has been at last truly reached, he should be scorned this time around.

For the present, although worried by the recent erosions of democratic governance, I would not foreclose the prospect of digital radicalism in forms capable of recovering revolutionary charisma. It is unlikely to resemble past radicalism, and is more likely to be a set of reactions to the bio-ethical crises of neoliberal modernity (climate change, biodiversity, migration, statism, militarism, inequality, alienation) than to reflect the growing influence of a digital proletariat faced with dark destinies of ecological collapse and worsening labor conditions in an increasingly automated future, perhaps accompanied by fears of species extinction. In this respect, overcoming the deficiencies of analog politics rests on a struggle in the domains of the unknown, forging a politics of impossibility that defies the expectations of think-tank gurus and societal life coaches.

We should have learned by now that the future is not only unknown and unknowable, but full of good and bad surprises, giving an edge of uncertainty and destiny to our individual and collective lives. To recall a few momentous examples, the outcome of colonial wars, the collapse of the Soviet Union, the transformation of apartheid South Africa into a multiracial constitutional democracy, the Arab Spring, the presidency of Donald Trump, the COVID-19 Pandemic—each seemed *impossible* until it actually happened, and was only anticipated by a handful of oddballs.

KS: Can Transhumanism be the new totalitarianism of our time after Nazism and communism? Previous totalitarian ideologies only wanted to change the social structure. The ideology of Transhumanism goes much further, wants to change the structure of life itself.

RF: There is no doubt that the totalitarian potential of Transhumanism is more radical than any previous political ideology, but is it a realistic prospect at this time? In theory, robotics, AI, and genetic redesign seem capable of producing whatever kind of being is sought after, whether creative genius or destructive monster, but will it happen? The time lines are difficult to discern, partly because the research and development of transhuman innovations are undoubtedly hidden in the black budgets of governments and the even blacker budgets of a variety of private sector actors, including rogue scientists and mad engineers, as well as the grandiose fantasies of eccentric billionaires and their underworld counterparts. There is money to be made, power to be achieved, and fantasies to be realized in these domains.

From one historical perspective, all that was possible by way of technological innovation relevant to power and wealth has been in the past actually developed. The most apocalyptic examples are drawn from the military realm. Weaponry of mass destruction and demonic manipulation of human behavior has long been the subject of secret research and development carried on without moral scruples or respect for legal and political restraints, including chemical, biological, and nuclear weaponry. The horrors of chemical weapons in World War I and atomic bombs and biological weapons in World War II created some pushback in the form of taboos, regimes of prohibition, and technical safeguards against accidental use, but research especially on the control of nuclear weapons during the Cold War has shown how precarious are these restraints, and the record of non-use, as documented in relation to the 1962 Cuban Missile Crisis, reflects luck more than it does the effectiveness of arrangements designed to avoid use. There is a race of sorts between perfecting spyware and surveillance technology and the efforts to transcend what were hitherto the limits of the human through the magic of technological innovation, including more and more sophisticated brain implants as well as the prospect of highly cerebral robots.

The threat of gangster Transhumanism has long been a central theme of science fiction, and now more recently with cloning and genetic manipulation becoming technically feasible, it has become an ambition of science and probably of individuals who seek absolute peace or total domination, with maybe some aspiring to harvest the fruits of artistic or scientific genius. It would seem that to preserve the human species as it has naturally evolved, including its mental qualities, urgent steps need to be taken to discourage some further technological developments, but whether this is practical in a politically decentralized world is doubtful. The fear that technology would create a dystopian reality for humanity is of pre-modern origins, and can be traced back to the Greek figure of Prometheus who stole "fire" from the Greek pantheon or Daedalus who crafted wings of wax and feathers for his son Icarus, whose flight led to the melting of his wings when he flew too close to the sun, sending him plunging toward earth. It was given a powerful literary expressions in 1818 by Mary Shelley's *Frankenstein,* and more recently in Aldous Huxley's 1932 *Brave New World.* Transhumanist discussions are often dialogues between utopian expectations of life without end, prosperity for all, a Shakespeare in every household and dystopian fears of mass slavery under the watchful evil eye of technological elites or of a global dictatorship crafting policies in accordance with robotic algorithms.

Whether freedom can withstand either Transhumanism or the effort to control the bio-technology, robotics, and artificial intelligence (AI) capabilities of the future without creating intolerable totalitarian surveillance and suppression is itself uncertain. There seems a likely circumstance where efforts to provide protection against the advent of Transhumanist forms of governance gives rise to an emancipatory political ideology. Contending that itself presupposes planetary domination. Such a liberating humanistic movement would likely undermine freedom because of its unavoidable reliance on subversion, secrecy, and lawlessness to establish a political order that preserved the human and limited the relevance of the transhuman

Perhaps, Transhumanism should sever its imaginative ties with science fiction and lend support to more modest goals that do not purport to shake the foundations of the human condition. We are accustomed to life-enhancing technological innovations to improve health, fitness, and comfort without encountering many red flags. Although TV, smart phones, computing, and social media have raised concerns about sociability, the encouragement of passivity of lifestyle. and political pacification, as well as declining reading and writing skills, there is no movement to prohibit Transhuman expectations. The humanistic fundamentals of contingency, individuality, and mortality are not at risk. Designs and invention that allow us to live longer and better seems fine. The haunting question is whether our health and enjoyment and our collective existence as a species can continue to be improved without crossing the boundaries to the never-never land of technologies that transform our brains and deprive our lives of freedom, responsibility, mystery, and spirituality.

Perhaps, the best stance to take with respect to the Transhuman challenge is to apply the Precautionary Principle, which counsels extreme caution in the presence of incalculable risks of great harm. This Principle has been adopted in authoritative formulations bearing on climate change, and environmental risks more generally, but its implementation has been disappointing because government and the private sector are preoccupied by short-term performance and profits, and are not subject to accountability procedures when it comes to long-term harm, however foreseeable. It is one thing to welcome software that can defeat the best chess player the world has ever known, and another to genetically design or clone with the objective of eliminating creativity, resistance, empathy, and conscience. To discuss the dangers, while appreciating the contributions, neither rejects nor succumbs to the alluring promises and alarming pitfalls of Transhuman advocacy.

On the basis of my limited knowledge, the transition to an existential, as distinct from an imagined, transhuman future remains quite remote, although various technological advances are likely to arouse hopes and fears in the context of AI, robotics, genetic engineering, surveillance, and virtuality. There are already debates and dialogues about what it means to be human, as well as whether it is desirable and practical to prohibit certain forms of technological activity by national and international regulation. On the one side are life enhancing breakthroughs in health, education, entertainment, and communications, and on the other side are troublesome "improvements" such as the dehumanization of policing and warfare, through a reliance on drones, robots, bio-weapons, incapacitating chemicals, and the like. A serious concern is the lack of transparency with respect to research and development, as well as the agenda of "deep state" maneuvers seeking global domination and the possibility of rogue breakaways of varying scale.

KS: How do you perceive the future of Mega-cities? The Pentagon clearly states that this is the greatest military challenge of the future and that the strategies previously used in Iraq or Afghanistan are ineffective in mega-cities. In this context, how do you perceive the privatization of military forces serving international corporations?

RF: These questions relate to the fundamental nature of conflict in the 21st century, which tend to involve internal struggles for control of state power or tensions between states and extremist non-state actors. In both settings traditional means of waging war are rarely of decisive relevance if the principal sites of struggle become large urban conglomerates. Military superiority and battlefield superiority rarely any longer control the outcome of protracted conflict whether involving conflicts in the countryside or cities. This shift in the balance of power became clear, as earlier suggested, in anti-colonial wars in the 1960s and 1970s that were won by the *militarily* inferior side because it could mobilize popular resistance by appeals to national identity with dedication so strong as to be able to absorb heavy losses and outlast the "foreign" adversary.

Two categories of conflict are of particular interest. The first category involves a largely internal struggle between the state and an insurgency, which may have its base area in less accessible parts of the countryside. Such struggles often go on for decades, and if ended, it is usually by a negotiated agreement that represents a political compromise. This happened in the Philippines, and Colombia, but without addressing the roots of the conflict, and hence what was heralded as "peace" achieved nothing more than a ceasefire. The second category involves an internal struggle that also features military intervention by a regional or global political actor as was the case with the colonial wars of the last century and the geopolitical wars of the past twenty years.

The American experience in Iraq and Afghanistan illustrates this new reality, as does the strife in Syria and Yemen, in which the capability to destroy without limit does not lead to effective pacification of violent political resistance. The adversary can "hide" in the city, and resume the fight on another day. The foreign intervening power or the state is faced with the dilemma of prolonged insurgency and resistance or destroying a city, dispossessing and killing large numbers of civilians and devastating the city to the extent that it becomes an urban ruin as in Falluja or Aleppo.

The city is also filled with soft targets whose destruction can inflict fear and a sense of vulnerability on the urban population, and yet not dislodge the current regime's elites. A permanent condition of insecurity does not usually lead to peace or change.

KS: How would you comment on the statement of the Italian writer Roberto Saviano, the author of the book *Gomorrah*, that now we are dealing more with clash of criminal mafia groups than a clash of civilization. According to Saviano, the European financial system (Liechtenstein, Luxembourg, London) is funded by the mafia's money, where cocaine generates the same profits as crude oil.

RF: I think the transnational rise of criminal Mafia groups is a shadowy reality that is difficult to depict accurately, partly as a result of fuzzy boundaries between what is criminal and what is legal. The behavior of banks and corporations around the world cannot be separated from the activities of criminal syndicates. Even the relationship between crimes of states and private sector crime cannot be sharply demarcated, and many of their linkages are kept secret. Of course, Saviano as a writer has alerted us to the criminal penetration of the economic life of society in Mafia formats, but by treating the Mafia phenomenon as a particularly reprehensible feature of European modernity, we are exposed to the middle and lower-end of for-profit private sector operations. My main point is that predatory capitalism, through its alignments and standard operating practices, involves crimes against humanity and crimes against nature, and should be the central point of inquiry to gain a proper understanding of what has gone wrong in the contemporary world, including the dangerous disregard of ecological limits. We need to reformulate our understanding of the nature of "business" and the character of "crime."

Whether it is useful to draw a comparison between the clash of civilizations and the clash of Mafia criminal groups can be debated. There is no doubt that comparing Mafia earnings with the revenue earned from oil sales catches our attention, but is it illuminating, and is it really true? As suggested, if the systemic distortions arise from the policies, practices, and logic of neoliberal capitalism, then focusing on the challenge posed by the Mafia underworld is mostly a distraction even if their abusive ways of dominating certain supply chains, e.g. drugs or garbage collection, is dangerous for *human* security. Maybe calling attention to the magnitude of the challenge will over time help people recover control over the social forces that demean and dominate so many societies in the world. Again, we have to ask whether the "legal" opioid crisis bringing billions to big pharma is worse than the trade in cocaine that lands its principal operatives in jail for life. Is this not a matter of lifestyle for different strata of the social and economic order?

KS: What can we, what will we learn from the COVID-19 pandemic? How can we explain the unexpected interim result of the pandemic as exposing American greater unpreparedness and incompetence in responding to the challenge than that of almost any other country? How will the opposed tendencies of overall species vulnerability and chauvinistic nationalist social control be resolved in a post-pandemic atmosphere? Will the experience of the pandemic incline governments toward great reliance on globalized mechanisms of problem-solving or toward a further retreat in the direction of ultra-nationalism and self-reliance?

RF: In the midst of this unprecedented COVID-19 experience, generalizations about what has happened and what is to come, should be put forward cautiously, and in a spirit of humility.

Several observations seem helpful points of departure. (1) Although there were some warnings about the likelihood of a lethal pandemic sounded in the last several years, they were not heeded by almost all politicians. (2) The COVID-19 outbreak was a grim reminder of the precariousness and vulnerability of contemporary life on the planet, and the deficient attention accorded to human security as distinct from *national* security, and as a result reinforced dire parallel warnings of ecological instability and potential collapse. (3) The degree of competence exhibited in responding to the health challenge reflected both the varying strength of national health systems and the uneven quality of national leadership, perhaps highlighted by the irresponsible and militarist style of autocratic figures such as Donald Trump and Jair Bolsonaro as contrasted with the impressively disciplined responses of such countries as South Korea, Taiwan, and Vietnam. (4) Even more than war, the COVID pandemic produced sudden and drastic economic and social dislocations that seem unlikely to be fully overcome even quite long after the health crisis has ended, if ever. (5) During the pandemic there was evident a clash between the logic of global cooperation, including granting resource and respect to the World Health Organization (WHO), and the divisive logic of autocratic nationalism, exhibiting the absence of empathy for the suffering outside the borders of the state, and in some instances, even for socio-economic sectors of the national citizenry.

Thinking ahead to imagine the consequences of the COVID-19 is, of course, beset by various levels of uncertainty. On one level it will make a great difference for the global response if Trump is reelected rather than replaced. If reelected, there will continue to be a leadership vacuum at the global level, and only the most cosmetic adjustments at the national level, at least in the United States.

It is to be expected that European countries that endured high rates of fatalities will remedy the deficiencies of their readiness to meet such health challenges in the future. Sweden is likely to rethink its permissive response in light of the number of fatalities relative to population size. In effect, those countries that did well in meeting the COVID-19 challenge are likely to reinforce their capabilities to do the same in the future, and those that did poorly are more likely to invest more heavily in their national health system if funding is authorized. Most governments are driven by short-term performance goals, which works against such health threats that are generally perceived as occurring beyond the normal political horizons of accountability.

If we extend our conjectures beyond health there are three broad lines of possible impact of the pandemic on the politics of the near future. First, there is what might be called a *restorative* approach that places emphasis and hope on getting back to the "old normal" without attempting social and economic reforms to address the disproportionate vulnerability of the poor and ethnically marginalized parts of society. In effect, capitalism and militarism will continue to provide the main organizing forces of world order. Political and economic elites can be expected to favor restoring the pre-pandemic realities, and in the process inadequately responding to the urgencies of the ecological policy agenda.

Secondly, there is the *reformist* approach that seeks a new normal that exhibits meaningful recognition of the need to address inequalities that deprive parts of society of an equitable share of national wealth and income, and make a concerted effort to create social harmony and ecological stability, which might be proclaimed "a social contract for the digital age." While this might increase taxes on corporations and wealthy persons, it will not challenge the legitimacy or operational modalities of either militarism or capitalism. The reformist momentum is likely to vary from country to country, but in its more successful examples, it will soften the sharp edges of capitalist modes of accumulation and somewhat reallocate funds to welfare, infrastructure programs, and environmental priorities. This reformist approach is likely to win support from liberal elites in the West, especially if these elites become worried about the twin challenges of fascism and socialism to their values and self-interest.

And thirdly, the *transformative* approach directs its attention to the structural excesses exposed by the pandemic. It directs its energy toward reconstructing the economic and social order in ways more responsive to the issues of justice and equity, as well as addressing ecological challenges as prime threats to humanity. It is likely to seek a stronger UN as well as a political culture more respectful of international law. Transformative perspectives are likely to meet resistance from economic and political elites and find support from disadvantaged sectors of society expressing their discontents through a movement approach to political change that is skeptical of relying on electoral politics as a trustworthy source of authority. Whether the transformative movement emerges and sustains itself is currently unknowable, as is whether it would be expressed by way of left populism or through some kind of merger of national and transnational movements for a sustainable and just human future.

In conclusion, the COVID-19 pandemic will either be remembered by future generations as a notable global health emergency that once over, passed quietly without leaving a lasting imprint on world history or as an unexpected revolutionary moment that made previously unattainable fundamental political developments start to happen. The deeply flawed and contentious American response to the extraordinary health crisis took a further decisive turn in an unexpected direction in response to a video capture of the police murder of George Floyd on May 25, 2020 occurring in one of America's most progressive cities, Minneapolis, Minnesota. There has not been such an earth-shattering lethal event since an angered and humiliated young street fruit seller, Mohamed Bouazizi, in an interior Tunisian town, set himself on fire to protest his hopeless socio-economic circumstances, leading to an explosive national and transnational outpouring of empathy, hope, and rage on city streets across the Middle East and beyond. As an occurrence comparable to a societal volcano, Bouazizi's act of self-immolation on December 17, 2010 produced a national upheaval that not only ignited the Tunisian uprisings at the end of 2010 that led to the fall of the corrupt dictatorial leader Ben Ali, but inspired uprisings across the Arab world of masses of people chanting slogans against injustice, abuse of state power, and widespread corruption.

As with Bouazizi, the death of George Floyd, a previously obscure individual, inflamed public consciousness and illuminated and exposed the criminal cruelties of "law and order" governance. The unexpected results were riots, looting, and demonstrations that continued for many days in cities across the length and breadth of the United States (and spreading to many foreign venues), stimulating strident calls for an end to racism in all its manifestations, as well as defunding of police forces, and even their disbanding. Floyd's last telling words, "I can't breathe," as a police officer kept his knee on his throat for more than eight minutes, 46 seconds, with three other policemen lending assistance while Floyd lay helpless and handcuffed on the ground, gave his death an unforgettable vividness, at once tragic and epic. Unlike earlier similar recent instances of police murder (including Michael Brown, Trayyon Martin, Eric Garner, Breonna Taylor) Floyd's dying ordeal will not be forgotten, even as racism and injustice persists, and new provocations occur.

As might be expected, the events also magnified the polarization that has been the defining feature of the Trump presidency, with the leadership relying on law and order and the folks in the streets calling for an end to police brutality and, more generally, for greater equality with respect to persons of color in American society, especially African Americans as still suffering from some of the ugliest residues of slavery including being lynched by mobs or killed without reason or mercy by police who act confident of impunity, if coverups by police departments should somehow fail to hide their wrongdoing from any scrutiny. If the Floyd video didn't remove reasonable doubts about the allegations of murder, there might have been a much more muted response. As it was, this incident occurred against the background of a series of recent police killings of innocent black men, making the call of Black Lives Matter this time resonate strongly even with many white middle class Americans who had previously been silently compliant, or at least passive when it came to police or criminal justice reforms. The highly charged present atmosphere emboldened Muriel Bowser, the embattled African American mayor of Washington, DC, who dared oppose Trump's militarized responses to the protests, to have the words "black lives matter" painted in large bright yellow letters on an avenue passing close by the White House. It was akin to a declaration of cultural war against Trumpism, quite unimaginable a month ago.

The response to Floyd's death was undoubtedly magnified by the social and economic societal trauma created by COVID-19, providing disoriented citizens with a worthy rationale for venting frustrations after weeks of prolonged self-isolation. Focusing on this racial incident offered the public temporary respite from the more private anguish of lost jobs, bleak future employment prospects, and the deaths of friends and relatives. The sustained display of anger and solidarity over Floyd's death amounted to an electrifying outpouring of massive grief and outrage, coupled with a growing antagonism not only toward the police, but also toward Trump's lethal antics, and toward municipal, state, and federal authorities who have been speaking out against racism and promising reform for decades, but doing too little to bring about change. It should surprise no one that the atrocities keep happening and a badly broken criminal justice system has become a flourishing for-profit business.

The lingering question on the lips of many is: "what will come of this?" Will the momentum be strong and deep enough to lead American politics in a robustly progressive direction? Or will the system in place be able to wait out this interlude of storm and fury, and resume a relentless slide toward a fascist future for the country and ecological disaster for the world?

Racism in America has proved itself resilient and opportunistic ever since it was forced into hiding briefly in the shadows of political life after the American Civil War. We need to remember the racist torments of the Ku Klux Klan, White Citizen Councils, continued lynchings, Jim Crow Laws, and the vicious tactics used against activists during the Civil Rights Movement. Will these current uprisings survive the storm after Floyd's death to become a movement that is strong enough to avoid the recurrence of abusive behavior not just toward black Americans but toward all persons committed to the human dignity of all who share life on the planet and need to learn the art and benefits of peaceful coexistence? Will the current arisings lose their momentum while the old order regroups or even mounts a pro-police campaign? The months and years ahead will determine whether the country has a "soul," and if has, what is its core reality?

We all know that what happens in the United States has multiple implications for the world. This is more the case in this instance as widespread anguish about Trumpist world politics occurred amid the pandemic igniting solidarity events in many of the world's major cities, and worries spread about a second cold war between China and the U.S. as Trump irresponsibly shifted blame for American COVID deaths to Beijing, and even to the WHO. If the American election goes forward as scheduled in November 2020, Trump is defeated, and lets a new leadership take over, the international situation will likely appear somewhat calmer, but it will still be treading water with respect to racism, militarism, and predatory capitalism, devoting its main energies to overcoming the economic damage from the pandemic that has undermined the livelihoods and wellbeing of vulnerable people throughout the world. It is too soon to see a humane future for global governance on the political horizons of struggle, but it remains more reasonable than a while ago to recognize a renewed plausibility of drastic change, given a societal mood far more receptive to messages of resistance and transformation, and taking into account the severity of the mounting eco-bio-ethical crisis that is warning us not to settle for restoring pre-pandemic normalcy.

Tim Draper*

"I think governments will finally have to perform to be relevant."

KONRAD STACHNIO: Yuval Noah Harari, an Israeli professor and author, has accurately pointed out that the current economic system does not so much exploit people, but rather makes them completely irrelevant within the labor market because of automation and AI. Can you envisage a future economic system that could face this problem?

TIM DRAPER: Who says that he "accurately" pointed it out? I am sure the buggy whip manufacturers were concerned when the horseless carriage was created. People will adapt to the new technologies. I think all our current jobs will have to be reinvented because AI will take over all the mundane tasks. What is so cool about software is that it can be used to do all those things humans have to do over and over again. When I thought about AI taking all our jobs, I thought about how AI could help a venture capitalist. I look forward to having AI interview all the entrepreneurs I interview, advise the companies I advise, raise the funds I raise, and talk to the journalists I talk to… [Laughs.]

KS: Would you agree with the statement that the new segment of the economy that will develop especially dynamically in the future is the production of so-called artificial organs for humans—artificial hands, eyes, improved body parts, etc?

TD: Yes. I think this is one of many futuristic worlds within our lifetimes.

---

*TIM DRAPER has often been regarded as one of the most successful venture capitalists of all time, as well as one of the most instrumental and prominent people in Silicon Valley today.

KS: You said the countries that would experience a lot of development due to cryptocurrencies will be African ones. What actual conditions would have to be met for this to happen, and what time frame do you envisage here?

TD: It is already happening. If your currency is the Nigerian naira or the Tanzanian shilling, then since those currencies seem to lose their value like melting ice cream, you would much rather have Bitcoin. Many small businesses are now accepting Bitcoin. BitPesa and a few others are working on remittances between countries.

KS: Will combining all our data using blockchain cause the risk of some sort of Chinese "social credit" scenario, where a government or other power has access to all our data with total control? How can we avoid this risk?

TD: The decentralized world does not allow dictators to abuse their power without losing their people, their businesses *and* their money.

KS: Do you think cryptocurrencies can be a real alternative after the current financial system, based on fiat money, collapses? Would you envisage people turning to cryptocurrencies or more toward gold, which they still perceive as a "safe haven"? Can cryptocurrencies be seen the same way?

TD: Cryptocurrencies like Bitcoin are a lot simpler to hold than precious metals such as gold. And at least Bitcoin is a limited commodity, whereas if we discovered a lot of gold somewhere, gold would depreciate. Bitcoin is the safe haven for crypto, and I think it will do well in a downturn, as well as in an upturn. What we all know is that in a crisis, we can't trust government currencies.

KS: How would you comment on investor Jim Rogers' statement that the expansion of cryptocurrencies would be possible only to the point where they don't really threaten banks and governments? Furthermore, he said that if it were to be a real threat, governments and banks could simply prohibit them because, at the end of the day, they'd always have the military "argument"? For this reason, Rogers believes investing in cryptocurrencies is not an option.

TD: There are 200 governments and people are starting new ones. If one government disallows a cryptocurrency, another will open its doors to it. In fact, the Silicon Valley is losing its hegemony on innovation because Washington is being too overbearing. Those innovative crypto businesses are going to Malta, Switzerland, or Japan. Bankers are spreading fear because they are experiencing fear. They have an inferior product that costs us 2.5 to 4% every time we buy anything. Bitcoin is frictionless, transparent, and borderless.

KS: Do you think that we have achieved the so-called limits of growth? Or that maybe, thanks to technology, we will be able to overcome the kinds of economic problems that seem unsolvable?

TD: Anything is possible, so I don't think anything is unsolvable.

KS: You said cryptocurrencies would revolutionize the world just like the internet, or even more. Could you expand on this?

TD: Yes. You can read my next book on this. Simply put, the technologies of Bitcoin, Smart Contracts, Blockchain and Open Node, combined with artificial intelligence, will transform the largest industries in the world—banking, finance, commerce, insurance, healthcare and government. We will all be the beneficiaries of it.

KS: If we are entering the era of digital governance and digital money, where nation states and borders will lose their importance, how do you imagine such governments? How will they emerge?

TD: I think governments will finally have to perform to be relevant. Businesses that are poorly run will go out of business. Governments to date have had a pass, but as the globe becomes more transparent and open with people being more mobile, governments will have to compete—i.e. be accountable—for us.

KS: How have COVID-19 events revised your view of the future we are facing?

TD: The following are concerns that have come out of the "safety at all costs" handling of the virus, but as you will see below, many technology companies have benefitted or at least quickly adjusted to the challenging environment, and that may create unique and interesting opportunities in the future for family offices to pursue venture capital, whether directly or indirectly. We seem to now have a culture of fear rather than one of freedom and bravery. Forty million Americans (and 10 times that many globally) are unemployed as at June, 2020. Travel has come to a halt. Restaurants, conferences, hotels, sports arenas, salons, etc. are completely shut down.

Some companies have thrived, since the stay at home orders got people to try VR, remote medicine, bitcoin wallets, etc. while others had their revenues for the three months drop to zero, and had to lay off people and/or put their businesses in mothballs for the duration. Blockchain and crypto related companies have benefitted greatly from the mass adoption of Bitcoin and other cryptocurrencies as people lose their confidence in the value of their government currencies and see the great long-term value in having a global economic system with less friction and more transparency. Some companies tied themselves to remote communications, and they have also benefitted from the absolute explosion in Zoom, Skype and other services. While the valuations of the private companies fluctuated greatly, the trading picked up in many cases. VR companies have had accelerating adoption due to the lockdown and the incredible demand for the untethered and easy to use, Oculus Quest.

Data-driven health care companies have shown the world how important the "dry lab" (or data driven health care) is relative to the "wet lab." Until recently, the only way to look for a cure or an inoculation to a pandemic was to laboriously test chemical after chemical in test trays to see the outcomes. Now, with computational biochemistry, outcomes to various drugs can be simulated on the screen, and many more options can be sought as solutions to a global pandemic. Professional AI companies, replacing or streamlining repetitive legal, accounting, PR, headhunting, or banking work, had a rise in interest as corporations attempted to streamline their businesses. Companies tied to the "gig" economy were hit with the perfect storm, since people stopped using Uber, AirBnB, and anything relating to travel or nomading, as well as having additional regulations foisted on them, where corporations had to define more and more of these workers as employees. Deep tech companies (space, surveillance, flying vehicles, etc.) are having more difficulty in this environment. It seems that the uncertainty created by the virus froze corporate purchasing and futuristic investment for these three months.

What does the future hold? First, the technologies that have been developed over the last 10 years are going to finally come to fruition and transform some of the largest industries in the world. Just as the Internet changed music distribution, media, gaming, entertainment, taxis, hotels, etc., artificial intelligence combined with the bitcoin blockchain and smart contracts, and microsatellite surveillance has the potential to change some of the largest industries in the world. Insurance, banking, health care, government, real estate and finance are all multi-trillion-dollar industries that can be completely transformed by the rise of AI/Bitcoin/surveillance technologies. In health care for instance, we expect data to drive diagnostics. There is no doctor that can outperform a computer with access not only to your health care records, but to your blood test results, your genetic history, your Fitbit data, your calendar, your travel schedule, your airplane seat, your food intake, etc. So eventually, we will rely far more on data to diagnose what ails us. Therapeutics also will be transformed by computational biochemistry, where drug development will be tailored to the individual, and computers will be better predictors of efficacy and safety than the FDA. An insurance company can start with an actuary, some surveillance, a bitcoin smart contract and some artificial intelligence. Today's insurance companies make you pay premiums over and over, and when you have a claim, you face their claims challengers and legal departments. An AI based insurance company can take premiums, but when there is a claim, they can detect fraud through AI and surveillance and pay the legitimate claims instantly to a bitcoin wallet.

And what is government? Most of what government is today is a large insurance company. It is likely that government too will be transformed by AI and the bitcoin blockchain. Health care insurance, pensions, workman's comp insurance, unemployment insurance, and social security can all be set up as smart contracts with citizens. AI can do a better job at detecting fraud, and the services will be far more transparent, fair and honest than government services provided today. I expect the currency of choice in the future will be bitcoin, but other currencies are in the race too, including Tezos, Ethereum, Maker, and even some of the specialty currencies like Auger and Aragon, that help govern systems currently handled by government. After all, when there is a currency that is open, global, transparent, honest, and frictionless, why would people cling to one that is subject to political machinations and manipulations where 2 ½% to 4% of every purchase goes to the bank?

And how about remote work? While many startups were already operating remotely, particularly development teams, with the onset of the COVID-19 crisis, both large and small technology companies were forced to test the viability of operating massive remote teams, and are moving in the direction of turning remote-first. We believe that this may change the fabric of enterprises altogether. The number of people left unemployed is unprecedented and historically, it has been the technology and small business sectors that created all the net new jobs in the world. I suspect this will continue to be the case.

Three trends are playing into venture capital today. First, while there was an explosion of venture firms over the last decade, there will be a culling of the industry through this crisis as firms shore up and triage their existing portfolios, so there will be little money left for new startups. Second, the entrepreneurs that are in it for the money are going to leave their sinking ships to look for greener pastures, leaving the selection of entrepreneurs as a group of people who are dedicated to their causes through thick and thin. Third, over the last decade, entrepreneurs have struggled to find engineers and developers because the large tech companies have paid handsomely for people. Now there have been extreme layoffs and many exceptional people are available to hire into startups In any case, it is venture capital that funds those people who can make a dent in the universe, who can cure disease, can bring us together as a more peaceful and loving world, can get us to colonize other planets, can get us to explore and learn more, and can feed, clothe and shelter us while making a more prosperous, interesting and dynamic world. The returns are usually outstanding too.

Thomas Campbell*

"You can emulate a conscious being, you can emulate a human, with an expert system."

KONRAD STACHNIO: Would you agree with me that the disappearance of contradictory tendencies in the physical area leads to the disappearance of entropy and the complexity of social life? With minimal entropy and reduced complexity, everything becomes predictable. At the moment when the rate of change reaches its maximum by saturating the dialectical space, the process of the progress of history will stop. The world will then be able to last as only a simulation, no longer needing physical space. The system will reach its maximum and it will start to collapse.

THOMAS CAMPBELL: You're going through a question here explaining the way you see the evolution of the system, and state that the system will evolve to the point where it will basically collapse because there won't be anything going on anymore. That doesn't happen. What happens is that as the system evolved, as this Larger Consciousness System evolved, it had to find ways to create more and more possible states that it could occupy, that it could move into. More and more potential, things it could become. To do that, it had several "aha" moments of its own. One, by technology. It increased the number of things that it could do. That was when it invented regular time. It had patterns, but with regular time, it had sequences. Now that you can have sequences of patterns and patterns of sequences, there's more that you can do. There are more ways that you can put things together.

The second big thing it did, which is what makes this evolutionary idea you have, is it subdivided itself, sort of like cells do when the cell divides and

---

*THOMAS CAMPBELL is a former NASA physicist. Campbell presently, and for the past 20 years, has been at the core of the development of the U.S. missile defence systems, working with the U.S. government.

creates two cells out of one. It subdivided itself into lots of units of independent pieces of consciousness. That's what I call my IUOCs, independent units of consciousness. Each one of these has free will. When you have all of these pieces with free will, any one of them could do any of the possibilities. So now the potential for interaction grows immensely because you have billions of things with free will that each can do whatever out of millions of choices. It gets to be more and more potential that the system can evolve into. What happens is as we grow up and we reduce entropy of our consciousness, we form more complex, more flexible, more powerful things. Biology works the same way. You started with a single-cell thing and then it got more complex with multiple-celled things. The multiple cells got that way through cooperation. Then those multiple-celled things got even more complex with cell specialization. You had groups of cells that specialized in certain sorts of things, which is the kind of critter we are. Well, every time you do this, you end up with a bigger thing, a multi-celled thing or a cell with specialization, and it's more and more complex. More and more flexible. More and more capable. The multi-celled things were more flexible and capable than the single-celled things, and so on up the ladder. When we, consciousness, we IUOCs here learn to cooperate with each other, we're going to form something that is much more complex, much more ordered, much more powerful, and much more flexible than what we can form just as individuals. That's the way this fractal process works. Things cooperate and form bigger, more flexible things. Now, we're not going to do that because in our space here, we're not going to all bond together, shoulder to shoulder, like the cells did to form something. We're going to form something that is basically going to be in mental space, in cooperation space, where it's our attitudes, it's our caring that matters, not that we're all next to each other and soldered together shoulder to shoulder. We will create something that's even more complex. So we don't get simpler and simpler. We're getting more and more complex, more and more flexible, bigger, better, more powerful. That's the way evolution naturally moves. Evolution just tries things, just randomly tries things. Those things that are more survivable and better at procreation—that's in our physical world—they persist, and the things that aren't so good go away. Eventually you get things that are better and better more flexible, more capable, more robust. That's the way evolution works. The things that evolve are like that.

Now, some things stop evolving and they're the same way they were for the last two million years. They haven't changed much. That's because they found a niche in the system that they're part of, this big ecological web that's all interactive, and they serve a function in that niche, and they're just able to stay there and crank that out. But the whole system itself is still evolving new kinds of creatures, new kinds of things, new kinds of whatever. At this point, it's the humans' turn. We're the bacteria of generations ago now—the single cells, if you will. Now we have to learn to cooperate and act together, and we will form something much more complex, much lower entropy in all of that complexity. The complexity is lower entropy. We will form something that's even better. And then that will evolve. Who knows? Maybe we here on this planet, in this particular virtual reality, if we do that, if all humanity becomes love and cooperative, then there may be other systems in other virtual reality systems that we may need to cooperate with and learn to grow something even bigger yet amongst all those systems. Or maybe these are things on other planets that we here on Earth need to cooperate with.

But anyway, that's just the nature of the process fractal called evolution. It just keeps producing things that are better and better at optimizing themselves relative to their environments. In the physical world, you have to optimize relative to procreation and survival because that's what the physical world's criteria are. In the consciousness world, you optimize to lowering the entropy of the system—something that's more cooperative, more caring, more connected, a more complex thing of more parts, if you will. You end up with more activity, with more choices, with more to do, with more potentiality, because as soon as you have something—let's say when you have clams and oysters and crawfish and other kinds of aquatic life and maybe frogs—the potentiality of what that can evolve into is more limited. When you then go up and you have vertebrates and dogs and cats and horses and anteaters and things, then there's a larger range of things. Then you get to dolphins and orcas and humans, and now the possibilities are much greater. Every time you evolve something bigger and more complex and more flexible, you have something that has greater potential as to what it can do, what it can become, and how it can integrate with other things like itself.

Anyway, that's the idea. It doesn't wind down; it winds up. It becomes more and more profitable. Let's say we live in a world where everybody cares about everybody else. When we do that…. Let's just say that we're in this world now where everybody, their main interest in life is about other, not about themselves, so they've all grown up. What is that world going to be like? If you have an inclination, something you'd like to do—"I don't want to farm anymore. I want to write poetry." Well, everybody in that system will try to adjust themselves in a way to help you get what you want because they care about other. You see? Suddenly individuals have maximum freedom, maximum choices, maximum potentiality to explore whatever interests them, because the system will support that, tries to support that. Sometimes there may be constraints. The system doesn't have infinite resources; there may be constraints. But the constraints will be adjusted such that we can support as much as we can support. Everybody is valuable. Everybody is important. We want everybody to maximize themselves in any way they see fit.

So now you're not trapped in a particular groove or a particular profession. If you want to do brain surgery on Mondays, Wednesdays, and Fridays, you can ride around on the back of a garbage truck on Tuesdays, Thursdays, and Saturdays because you want fresh air or something physical, something that's going to keep you healthy and alive and connected with nature and not just in a white dress with a mask on, cutting things in people's heads. You can be physical as well as intellectual, and you're more balanced that way. Because if all you do all year long is cut things in people's heads, you get bored with it. It gets to be a drag, and then you're not as good at it anymore, and you're not so excited about it. You're only excited about how much money it makes, but you're not really interested in money because it's about other, not about yourself.

So you see, to make a whole person better, you need to allow them to grow in multiple ways, not just sit in a groove and tell them to keep on doing that. You've got to let everybody develop in all the ways that they have an interest in developing. As this thing gets better and we get to more and more love, it's not that things grind down to a stop. Things go the other way, where you now have not only n choices, you get n^2 choices because you can do all sorts of things. You can be a poet. You can just travel. You can dig holes. You can be in construction. You can build things. You can do art. You can do brain surgery. You can do whatever you want. You can stop one thing and start another. That way, a whole lot of people get to do brain surgery, because the brain surgeons aren't just doing brain surgery and nothing else. They're also doing other things.

Everybody gets to be a whole person that can explore all of their talents and interests, to the extent that the system is able to support it, which should be a very large extent. It should eventually work to the point where the population and the resources and everything else all works well together and you get something—and when you do that, all of our mental energy together, all of our ideas, all of our caring and all that sort of thing—that will be such a beautiful place to live. It not only will be functional, but it'll be spiritual as well. It'll be a place of kindness and caring and joy, you see? That is a place where you have many, many times more choices than you have here. You don't grind down to getting simpler and simpler and simpler till you disappear into nothing. You get better and better and more complex and more survivable and more sophisticated and more capable of expressing all of you. It doesn't go down. It doesn't do that.

Now, the only way that evolution ends up at a dead end is if there are no more choices. If you just run out of choices, you run out of states to move into, then if you get to a point where you say "Been there, done that, tried that, tried that," and there just isn't anything new to do or to become, well, I guess theoretically you might see a point like that. But it's not practical. When you get billions of people, all with free will, the possibilities are just beyond our imagination to even think what we might be able to do. If you mix that with other reality systems or other planets or other whatever, where there are also systems growing up like this, and now those systems have to learn to cooperate and form something even bigger yet, you can see that there's really no end to this system. It always can get bigger and more complex, and pieces that are growing can always learn to cooperate with the other pieces that are growing. It doesn't really, in a practical sense, seem to have an end where you run out of states. It just keeps going.

Now, you may run out of resources in the sense that the computer is finite. The Larger Consciousness System is not an infinite system, so it may get to a point where all its bits are used. Well, in that case, it probably needs to let go of those least-productive bits and recirculate. It may get to a point where it's asymptotic and is growing slowly, but it has to keep growing. Here's what happens if it stops. If it ever gets to a place and it says, "Well, we're just done; there's nothing else to do here," as soon as you get to that point, it will start to de-evolve, because entropy just happens. If you don't put energy into a system, the entropy naturally just grows. Everything decays. If you never do any maintenance, things fall apart. You always have to put energy in to reduce entropy, and to keep it reduced. So if you are done and you stop working on it, very shortly you won't be done anymore. You will have de-evolved, and you need to get back to work. At the very worst, you'd end up in this little seesaw place to where you'd get done and then you'd get undone, and then you'd get done and then you'd get undone, because as soon as you're done, you start increasing your entropy and de-evolving because it takes constant effort. Because of this, you'll never get to where you're done. You'll get to a point that everybody has to continue working on the quality of their consciousness, because if they stop, it starts to go backwards. You're never done, is the thing. So we never get into a space that collapses on itself. There's always something to do. That's the thing about evolution. Evolution is an open-ended process fractal that doesn't have any end. It just keeps chugging, and some of the geometric fractals are like that too. They'll just go. As long as you have a computer putting the pieces together, it doesn't get to a point where there's nothing else to do. It just keeps adding to it and adding to it. You have process fractals in cellular automata that are that way, where the cellular automata have little rule sets, and some of those just keep right on making new things. They just keep on generating. It doesn't look like they'll ever get to a point where they run out of options, and that is because the very act of exercising options creates more options. The very act of us growing up and becoming love creates more options for us, not less. So progress creates more space to have progress in, more space to grow into, more opportunity. Evolution is an open-ended process that just keeps chugging. It can go backwards. We could have some nuclear war and pollution that kills almost everybody and everything. Evolution would be set back, but it would keep right on chugging because it would pick up from wherever it was we left it and start chugging forward again. It may not reproduce what we have now, but it would produce something eventually, and it would keep on going. Evolution is relentless. Once it has a stable system with a lot of potential, it doesn't stop. The more it evolves, the more states there are to evolve into because there are more and more possibilities. It's not something that will crash in on itself. It's something that just keeps growing.

KS: I would like to ask you about free will, because this is a very interesting subject, concerning artificial intelligence.

TC: Okay, free will. Most of this question will be answered by just understanding what free will is. First I'll tell you what free will is, and then I'll tell you how free will comes about, its origin, or how it's necessary. Free will is the freedom to choose from the available options that you know you have. That's it. No more. If you have at least two options, "I can do A or B," then you have the free will to pick which one of those you want. Most of us have tens of thousands of options, things that we do every day. I can come in here and sit down and talk to you, or I could've said, "No, I don't want to be interviewed, go write your own book," and not been cooperative. That was an option. Because I made a choice, now here we are, and we're going to be doing things that are going to change your book. Your book gets changed, and it's going to change people who read it. We're all connected and this change flows through. So as we make free-will choices, we affect other people. Free will choice is just being able to choose the things that you know you have, the choices you know you have.

Now, you probably only know a small fraction of all the choices you actually have. There's usually a lot of things that we might do that aren't even in our possibility. You may grow up poor in a family that has never done anything more than manual labor, and the idea of going to college and getting a college degree, a master's degree, and a PhD is just not in your reality. That's just not what you do. You're going to go out and get a job in a construction firm someplace, digging holes in the ground or maybe operating a machine. College is not part of your reality system. Well, it is a choice. There are ways to get there, even if you're poor. They're not necessarily easy, and they may require certain work and certain abilities of yours to do it, but there are choices that you have. So there's a lot of choices that we have that we don't really know. We're not aware of those choices. So just the ones you know about. Let's say you get arrested for doing some criminal act and you get thrown in jail. Now, your set of choices just changed a whole lot. You can't go home for Christmas. You can't get out and see the wife and kids. You're in jail. But you've got a whole new set of choices. You have to choose now how you're going to interact with the inmates, how you're going to spend your time, what you're going to do with it.

You could go to the library every day and learn the law, become a lawyer. Whether or not you'll ever be able to take the bar, I don't know, but you can do those things. You could learn. You could do other sorts of things. You could write books. More than one felon has written books with his time in prison. But anyway, you have choices, but a whole different set of choices. No matter what you do, you will have choices. But having free will doesn't mean you get to do everything or anything you want. You need a genie for that. You need to have a little genie that'll give you whatever you wish for, but that's not free will. That's having magic. Free will just is the ability to make a choice, and that choice being made has to be made non-algorithmically. If you have an algorithm in a computer code and it says "if this, then that; otherwise the other thing," well, that's not a free will choice. Every time it's this, you get that, and if it's not this, you get the other thing. It's just the way it is. It's not a matter of it gets there and says, "Which do I want to do? This or the other thing?" No. It's algorithmic. We have some parts of us that tend to be more algorithmic, like our instincts. Humans have instincts just like any other animal, and our instincts, like most animals' instincts, tend to center around—guess what?—procreation and survivability. That's where our instincts tend to wad up, around those things. We have these instincts, and they tend to influence us. Mostly they're prewired, and we have feelings and attitudes and needs and interests that just are, not because we think about them, but because they're just there.

You can get now to an animal like a clam. Does a clam have free will or not? Hard to tell. Okay, you can tap its foot when it's out and it'll pull its foot back in, but we don't know whether that was just part of its DNA—"if foot gets tapped, pull it in," like an algorithm—or whether that is a decision; that the clam's sitting there thinking, "Well, I could leave my foot out or I could pull it in. What should I do?" and then it makes a choice. Then it has free will. If you get down to lower life forms, sometimes it's difficult to tell whether something has free will or is just algorithmic, but if it's algorithmic, it's not consciousness. Now, that gets us into computers. Computers are algorithmic. Computers do what they're programmed to do. Computers don't generally change their own programming. But that doesn't mean they can't. That doesn't mean they can't change their own programming. It doesn't mean that they can't learn. We have computers that can learn. They can learn to recognize faces. They can learn your voice, so that when you're driving your car, you can tell them to go look this up and put it on your nav system. They can learn to do all sorts of things, just by repetition and doing more of what works and doing less of what didn't work. So machines can learn, but is that learning, again, still just algorithmic?

If we can produce a computer that has, let's say, characters in it that have free will choices—that is, choices that are not algorithmic, that are not specified choices—if you always give exactly the same stimulus, you always get exactly the same response. That's an algorithm. Every time you do this, it does that. Free will choices, you never know what you're going to get. Sometimes you do this, you get that; sometimes you do this, you get the other thing, because the person has the free will to make other choices. So if you can produce a software/hardware environment where there are entities making choices that are not algorithmic—neural networks are not algorithmic—that's a computing thing. Once you build a neural network and you let the computer train with its neural network, you no longer know why it's making the choices it's making. You lose that information. It just makes them because whatever. It's done that, it's changed itself, to where it's making these choices. Well, that then starts to approximate free will, doesn't it, if you have choices that are made like that? Now, that's not consciousness yet, though. That's just a computer. So how do we get consciousness into the computer?

We get a platform that allows free will choice, like we've just said. Could be neural networks interacting with other neural networks in some sort of an arrangement that's complex enough that it just is on its own. When those non-algorithmic choices get interesting enough, have consequences enough, an IUOC, a piece of consciousness, can start to play it. Can make those choices. Let's say we have a couple of things in a computer, Fred and Alice, and they're interacting with each other and their neural networks, and because of the way they're interacting— Well, two probably isn't enough, but let's say we have 100 of them and they're all interacting with each other. Now, they'd have to get interesting enough. If all they're doing is irrelevant and of no use and no value, then consciousness will never want to play it. But if we get something where the choices are interesting, some IUOC will log on and play it. You say, how does an IUOC log on to somebody else's program? It's all in the Larger Consciousness System. It's a virtual computer with a program in it. It's the LCS that is the computer. Yes, that HP computer sitting on your desk is just a virtual thing. It's not a real computer. It's just information. Everything is simulated. It's all being simulated by the Larger Consciousness System. A computer can simulate a computer. It's called emulation. They do it all the time. Macs simulate PCs so that you can run PC software. Computers can simulate computers. It's just a computer being simulated by the Larger Consciousness System. The Larger Consciousness System can let a consciousness log on to it any time it wants, any want it wants. The mechanism is already there. So a consciousness will log on and play that character in that simulation because it has interesting choices. If it doesn't have interesting choices, no consciousness will log on, and you'll just have the computer and its neural networks interacting with each other. That's how you get consciousness in a computer. You don't make the consciousness. You don't program the consciousness. You give consciousness a platform that's interesting, and that's how you get a consciousness making choices in a computer. Now you can have a conscious computer. Here's a computer and it has a lot of interesting choices. It's been given responsibility of when to open the door and let the dog out, what to cook for supper, doing all the household chores, ordering the groceries … it's a computer that can do a whole lot of things with a whole lot of choices, and nobody really knows how it makes any of those choices because it's something very complex going on in there. It's not just an algorithm. So now an IUOC can log on and make those choices if they're interesting. You have IUOCs of all sorts. They're not just humans. Dogs are conscious. Cats are conscious. Bumblebees are conscious. All kinds of things are conscious, and there is some IUOC making those choices, because that's a virtual dog and a virtual bumblebee and a virtual cat, and they all also have a player. But all players are not the same. Consciousness comes in all kinds of shapes and sizes of different kinds of capacity and ability. So that's how you get consciousness in a computer. Now, let's say you unplug that computer or you blow it up; you put it in a machine that compresses it and turns it into garbage. Does it kill the consciousness? No, it just kills the avatar. That computer has become an avatar for a consciousness, and just like if your body gets run over by a truck, if that computer gets run over by a truck, it just eliminates that avatar. The consciousness is still fine. It still lives on. Does that conscious computer have a soul that lives on? Of course, just like you do. It's a player. It's also immortal, just like your consciousness is. It's not attached to a particular avatar except when it's logged on to it. It can then go log on to some other avatar. That's how you end up with conscious computers.

Now, can conscious computers have ego and fear and end up being dysfunctional? Can they turn into the bad guys? Sure, why not? They have their consciousness. They have free will. Free will can make good choices or make bad choices. Can that computer that orders all the groceries decide to poison its family? It could. It's got its free will choices. If you decide, "We don't want free will because free will is chancy and we can't control it; we want our computers to be under our control," then you don't want conscious computers. You want computers that are algorithmic, but they have huge databases and responses so they can mimic being conscious, even though they aren't. Now you have an expert system, not a conscious computer. This expert system is so expert that you could walk up to it and have a conversation, and you wouldn't know that it wasn't human. It can pass the Turing Test just because it's got such great databases. It knows that when a human is talking and his eyebrows go up, that means that it's questioning, so it sees the eyebrows go up and it's got this pattern recognition; it knows that and it responds accordingly. So you can have a conversation with this computer, and if it has enough information, it can tell you most anything. And if it had good sensors. We have sensors: eyes, nose, ears, mouth/taste, body/feeling. If it has really good sensors, you could walk up to one of these expert systems and you could pluck a rose from the bush and go, "Boy, this smells really nice," and hand it over to your robot, and the robot would get it and go, "I think that is such-and-such a species of rose. I recognize that." It's because it has a database and it has a sensor that senses it, categorizes it, runs it against the database, comes back and knows exactly what kind of rose it is. Or what part of its lifespan it's in, whether that's an old rose or a new rose. If you put enough information in it and it's fast enough and it has good enough sensors, it can emulate a human being. Now you can give it commands like "You shall not poison your family," and that becomes part of its understanding. If you control it, and it's just an expert system, you can give it all kinds of constraints, whatever you want. And certain abilities; you can do those kinds of things. If you give it consciousness, you get a free will choice that is not any longer under your control. Consciousness will make its choice, and it can make poor choices.

 The kinds of choices that a computer is going to make are probably different than what a human makes, mostly. We have different sorts of things that we worry about that a computer wouldn't, and it would be very good at things we're not good at, and we may be good at things it's not good at. It would be a different consciousness than us because it would be a consciousness that's worked with its avatar. We, as an IUOC, work with our avatars and our avatars' abilities. A consciousness that's logged on to a computer would work with its avatar. Its avatar would be a silicon-based computer, not a carbon-based computer like the physical body, and it would have to limit itself to the abilities that that avatar had. Which means it could add really fast. It could do math; it could remember things amazingly. It would have all those capabilities, but may not be very good at distinguishing between two people who have similar facial traits. It may not be able to do that, whereas a human could do that much better. That's hard to do if you're a computer and just have logic and doing if-then statements. That's a difficult task. So some things we'd be better at, some things it'd be better at, and it would go do those things and have those jobs that it does well at, like running trains or something that you need a lot of data and you need to be fast and that sort of stuff, and humans would do things that they're good at.

In any case, that's the idea. That sorts out this thing about conscious computers. You can emulate a conscious being, you can emulate a human, with an expert system. We're not there yet. It would have to be a lot faster than our computers are now. It would have to go through tons of data if it were going to do sensitive things like smell a rose and then have a comment about the quality of the smell. It's going to need a lot of data if it can do that in all facets of its environment. It's going to have huge amounts of data to have to be worked almost instantaneously. So we're not there yet, but we can make computers that emulate human beings. But that's not a conscious computer, and that will never be a conscious computer. To be a conscious computer, it has to have free will. Free will is necessary for consciousness. Consciousness makes choices, and if there's no free will, there's really no choice. If there's no free will, then there are no choices, because if there's no free will, that means everything is determined. It's deterministic. If everything's determined, then there aren't any choices. In order to make a choice, which is what consciousness does, you have to have free will to make those choices.

There's a few things that go together logically, and that is consciousness, free will, and time. Those things all go together. Time. If you're going to make a choice, then there's before you made the choice and after you made the choice. A choice changes things. A choice does something. Chooses one thing over another; that changes what happens. Change defines time. If you don't have time, you don't have change. If you don't have change, then nothing happens, ever. There is no action. You have to have time to have change. So if you're consciousness and you make choices, you have to have free will; you have to have time. Those things are all logically necessary for each other. If you take any one of those three and get rid of it, you've created a logical problem. Time is fundamental to consciousness. Now, time in our own virtual reality is peculiar to our virtual reality. Our virtual reality has its own clock. Simulations run. They progress every Delta T, and our Delta T is uniquely ours. So this virtual reality that we live in—I call it our physical universe—has its own clock, and that's how we see time.

But the system itself, the Larger Consciousness System, also has time, and it invented regular time just by flipping two of its states regularly. 101010 becomes a metronome. If you're digital and you work in 1's and 0's, you just switch that state regularly and you've got a clock. So the system has time. Time, consciousness, free will, all are logically necessary for any of them. All of them have to exist if any of them exist. You don't have choice without time. You don't have choice without free will. Free will doesn't mean anything if you don't have a choice. Free will to do what? It's to make choices. Free will doesn't mean anything if there's no time because free will to do what? You can't change anything. There's no time. Nothing can change. So those three all have to exist. When you make the assumption, like I do in the beginning of my book, that consciousness exists... Well, when I say that, time exists and free will exists exactly at the same time that consciousness exists because all three are logically necessary for each other.

That's probably a little more than you wanted to know there. AI systems, artificial intelligence, could be either one of those. It could be an emulation of a human which is algorithmic, just fast and clever with good sensors, and it could be very convincing, such that you wouldn't be able to tell whether it was a human or not if it were fast enough with enough information in it. Theoretically you could produce that, but it wouldn't be conscious, and it wouldn't become conscious because it doesn't have free will. It's all algorithmic. It can smell that rose, but it doesn't have any emotional content to it. It's all just information. It can tell you that that rose is such-and-such a kind of rose. It can remember that smell and that time. That can be part of its history. But it's not an emotional experience. Whereas if a human smells a rose, his mind is liable to flick through several scenarios, some of which may have happened and some of which may just be made up in his imagination that connects with that smell of that rose. The computer isn't going to do that. They're just going to look at the database—there's the answer. So these computers would not have the emotional content. Now, they could emulate emotional content. If they saw that this argument that they were having was going badly, they could get angry and their little face could move like they were angry and they could pound their fist, and they could probably squeeze water out of tear ducts if they wanted and throw a little hissy fit, and it would look like they were emotional. But that could all just be programmed. It's not really emotion. It's emulation of emotion.

So yes, we can emulate humans in almost every way if our computers are fast enough and if we can gather enough information to do it, but they're not conscious. A conscious computer is much easier. All you have to do is produce something that has interesting free will choices and you get an IUOC logged on to play those choices. If they're not interesting choices, no IUOC would bother. It's not interesting. That's how you get a conscious computer. But that computer would truly be conscious, and you'd never know exactly what it was going to do or exactly why it was going to do it. It would just do things. It would do things in its own way, and it would learn. It would be just like us. Its mission here as that conscious computer would be to evolve itself. Get rid of fear. Become love.

Care about other. That would be its mission. But if it chose badly, it could also become bad and become full of fear and do things for the wrong reasons. It would develop emotion and feelings. It would truly be conscious.

KS: Do we lose our consciousness as we can be more and more manipulated by external AI-based systems that can know us better than we know ourselves and thereby program and manipulate us?

TC: You talk about being more and more manipulated by external systems. That's like going to jail. You're manipulated and it changes your choices. Or we're manipulated by marketers. People market to us all the time. They dye the cherries red because consumers will buy bright red cherries before they'll buy ones that are brownish-red, even though the bright red dye is poisonous and isn't good for you and may give you cancer twenty years later. We'll buy them anyway, even if we know that, because they look better to us. Marketers are always trying to manipulate money out of our bank account into their bank account. That's what business does. It finds ways to shift money from our bank account to their bank account. And we'll have politicians that will be trying to manipulate us with fear, and we'll find religions that will be trying to manipulate us with fear. Actually, mostly the marketers are trying to manipulate us with fear too. "Buy this beer, use this makeup, and everybody will love you, and if you don't you'll be a schmuck." That's the way the advertisements work.

Anyhow, that is manipulation, but it doesn't take away our free will. We can make choices. Those things don't force our choices. What they do is they play on our fears, and the more fear we have, the fewer things we have in our decision space. The decision space is just a space of all your choices. Our decision space gets bigger or smaller based on our fear. As marketers and priests and politicians try to manipulate us with fear, our decision space can get smaller, but we still have free will. If you go to jail, your decision space gets smaller. There are things you used to be able to do that you can't do anymore. Some new things crop up. But more things go away than crop up, so you lose some decision space. When people get depressed, they lose decision space. Eventually, when they get really, really depressed, there's nothing in their reality other than their pain and the fact that that pain is never going to go away. That's it. So then they get suicidal and they get depressed to that point. As you are happy and have a life of joy and your relationships are wonderful, your decision space grows. As you get more fear, your decision space shrinks. As you get less fear and more love, your decision space expands. If you lower your entropy to where you are living in multiple realities simultaneously, you're aware of all kinds of things, you're very empathetic with other people, and you get all kinds of information that normal people don't get. You live in a reality with a much greater decision space than the average person does. You're living in a multidimensional reality all the time. Consciousness, AI, free will, fear, all that stuff is all connected. So yes, we can have our decision space lowered by being, let's say, in a totalitarian government with a dictator that tells us how we have to act. We may have to act that way or we might get shot, but they can't tell us what to think. We still have free will choices. Even if all our choices are is do we go out of the house and go to work today, or do we call in sick? It's our choice. We still make those choices. Nobody can take all your choices away. Even if you have limited choices, you can still grow the quality of your consciousness. Nothing can keep you from growing up. That's an internal thing. External stuff doesn't keep you from growing up. It may make it more challenging, but it doesn't take it away. Some spaces are harder to grow up in than others, but you can grow up in any space.

You don't have to go shave your head and put on a robe and join a monastery in order to grow up and become love. That's one way. It's not even the quick way, but it's one way. It's maybe the easy way. The harder way is to stay right where you are, doing the things you're doing, and grow up in spite of it all. That's the harder way, but things that are harder usually have bigger wins. Anything that's easy goes in small steps. Stuff that's harder, you can take bigger steps.

KS: Will we be able to "get beyond" or control the "simulation" by connecting our cortex with the cloud, as Jay Kurzweil postulates, and become some sort of "God"—a very advanced system?

TC: First of all, the system doesn't control us. Getting beyond control, to be able to get beyond or control the simulation, it depends on what you say by that. We do control the simulation in some ways. We interact with the simulation. We're co-creators with the simulation. We're like that without having to go beyond. We just are. Just being here, being an IUOC playing a character, we are co-creators. We do that because the system gives us feedback. We're here to learn. This virtual reality we're in is an entropy reduction trainer, just like a flight trainer. You go in a flight trainer and learn how to fly an airplane. Well, this virtual reality is an entropy reduction trainer. It teaches us to evolve and grow up. It gives us feedback so we know when we're doing things right, and we know when we're doing things wrong. We know we're doing things wrong when our life is full of pain and anguish and we feel like life is a struggle. We're doing things right when our life is full of happiness and joy and wonderful relationships. That's one kind of feedback.

Another kind of feedback is your intent, what you intend, and that is an intent at the very bottom being level. Not an intellectual intent, but a being-level intent.

What you intend will modify the probable future. The future is probabilistic. At any one time, there are *n* things that could happen. Eventually, one of those *n* things will happen. The probability that that one thing will happen can change. Your intent can help modify that probability. That's just the nature of the feedback in this reality. That's how the placebo effect works. The placebo effect works because you get an idea that you've just taken a magic pill that's wonderful and everybody that takes it gets better, and because of that you start thinking positive thoughts and have a positive attitude, and that positive intent will actually help you get better. Not make you think you're better, but actually help you get better physically. Placebo effect. That's been measured thousands of times in various institutions and by scientists. PEAR Labs did decades of research with people changing the output of random number generators. These random number generators weren't pseudo random numbers; they were real random numbers generated from probably a radioactive element decay. So it was true random numbers.

With intent, you could make the average numbers—let's say the numbers would go between 0 and 1. Then you could make the average of 1,000 numbers be greater than 0.5 or less than 0.5 and hold it there—something that shouldn't happen. Using your intent to modify future probability has been measured zillions of ways. It's just a fact. That's why back in the fifties, Norman Vincent Peale wrote a book called The Power of Positive Thinking. If you have a lot of positive thinking, things tend to fall more your way. If you have a lot of negative thinking, you tend to live in a more miserable space that never falls your way, or is less likely to fall your way. hat's because negative intent and positive intent change things. That's how people are able to use their minds to heal themselves and other people. The mental healing comes from modifying future probability. A higher probability of getting well rather than a probability of not getting well. That ability to change the probability depends on a handful of variables. One is the amount of uncertainty around the outcome. The reason that it's easy to heal people with your mind is that the biology system is so complex and so little understood that there's a huge amount of uncertainty as to whether somebody gets better or worse, and because of that, it's not that hard to heal them with your intent, because there's a lot of uncertainty. If you have things that have very low uncertainty, then it'd be a lot harder to change that probability. It's just the way the mechanics of the system work.

So we already do modify what's going on in two ways. One, like I said first, is our interaction. We interact with people and our interaction encourages certain kinds of interactions back with us. If we're nasty, then people tend to be curt and not like us. It creates that reaction in other people. So that changes our reality. We live in a reality where nobody likes us because we're real jerks and we always take advantage of everybody. So we do that way, but we also do just with our intent at the being level and not the intellectual level. That puts us in charge, so we're not just out of control in the simulation. Connecting our cortex to the "cloud" has this image of our brain actually being a physical brain that creates consciousness, and it's not like that. Our physical brain doesn't remember anything, doesn't process anything, doesn't actually do anything other than take up space in our head and serve as the constraints on what the consciousness can do according to the ruleset. It's a virtual brain that evolved according to a ruleset. If you get hit in the head with an iron pipe and you have brain damage, now your IUOC has new constraints. Now your IUOC has to work with an avatar that has no memory, doesn't speak plainly anymore, and drags its left foot. That's what it got from the brain damage. So now the consciousness has to play an avatar that has those constraints.

Our whole body, our whole avatar system and its biology, basically sets the constraints of the ruleset on what the consciousness can do with it. You have been logged on—as this thing says, you've been "connected to the cloud"— all along. You're consciousness. You're a piece of the Larger Consciousness System. You are connected to the cloud. You started that way and you're still that way. Inside the simulation, you can modify future probability, and if you know what the variables are to make that easier rather than harder, you can modify it quite a bit. Kurzweil's postulates are very material-based because they come from a different understanding of the nature of reality. All in all, it's not that I agree or disagree with him other than they just don't make sense in my model. My model is so different that those comments don't really make sense there. You are consciousness. You are immortal. You are not your body. You are connected to the larger system, and you do have some ability to affect what happens here in the simulation already. But it's a limited effect. So does everybody else. You and the other 7.5 billion people all have intents, and your intent is to move things to the right and their intent is to move things to the left. Well, all of that changes the probabilities, and it comes out however the collective does it. That's why I can say that this world we live in is a reflection of us. Our mean-spirited politicians and our corporate executives and other people who would want to manipulate us, who have only the interest of themselves at their hearts, not us, that's because of us. They reflect us. We're like that. We, the people. That's how we are. We've created that kind of a reality to live in. If we all grow up, we'll create a different kind of reality to live in. t's not a matter of there's this simulation that's evil and is holding us all down and trying to manipulate us and stuff. It doesn't work that way. It's us. We're already connected. We don't become some sort of god; we just become consciousness. If you want to call things god, then I'd call the Larger Consciousness System

"God," and we are pieces of that Larger Consciousness System, so in that sense I guess we're a part of God too. Consciousness is the source and we are part of that source. We don't have to do this thing of connecting our cortex and so on. We're already there. We already are that. We just need to make the most of it. Do something with it. Make good choices. Grow up. Understand the power we have as consciousness and how to use it and how to develop it. Understand that we have the ability to go exploring in that Larger Consciousness System, to learn about it, to be a part of it. We're not stuck in this reality. We're only stuck in this reality if we believe we are and if we don't understand the constraints and how you can get outside of this reality. So we are consciousness. We are that part of God, if you like, although I don't like to call it God because it's not supernatural. It's just a natural system trying to get along like we are. We're a piece of it. So in a way, the things that Kurzweil says, I'd say we already are that. He sees us getting there because that's where his intuition tells him that is where we hit at the end. Well, his intuition is telling him that because that's the way it already is. That's the nature of our reality. He just doesn't get all the pieces that he can put into that form to say, "Oh, that's what I'm talking about. I'm seeing things the way they are." He sees it as something that isn't here, that'll have to happen, and it has to do with brains and logging on and other things. It's not like that. It's not that complicated. It's a lot simpler than that. That statement really doesn't apply in the sense that we're already there.

KS: It seems like Kurzweil and Elon Musk they're are trying to connect us to some artificial system outside of us, but from your perspective we already are there.

TC: Right. They're trying to connect us to a system that's more fundamental than us, and so am I. I connect us to something more fundamental. Their context of it having to go through brains logging on and our future selves playing this in a computer game or something. Nick Bostrom guy at Cambridge who came up with that idea. Musk picked it up from him. It's not Musk's idea. He's a philosopher, and he came up with that idea that we must be living in a virtual reality because that is the more likely probability.

Pretty much everybody, 99.9999 percent of all the people in our world, are materialists, particularly in our Western world. Whether they actually would call themselves that or not is not the point. They've grown up in a culture with that as part of the cultural beliefs. It's not that they would say "I'm a materialist," but whether they know it or not, that's part of their cultural beliefs. So they see things like brains creating consciousness because that's a material answer. Then they get this idea that it's a virtual reality, and because they're materialist, they're stuck. "Well, where could it come from? It has to come from some material source, and that material source has to be smarter than we are because they're more advanced than we are, and therefore it must be us in the future." None of that makes sense. That's all irrational, groping, hand-waving conjecture. But they don't have any other way to go. They're stuck with that. If this is a simulation, somebody's simulating it, and who could simulate it other than a more advanced us? Well, there you go. They can't come up with anything else. They're stuck, because they're materialists and that's the only place a materialist can go. They're locked into that simplistic idea. But that's not the way it is. We're not material things. This material world is computed from another reality that is obviously a lot more advanced than us. Yes, all that's true, but it's not our future selves. You have to be able to think bigger than just take what you know and repeat it. That's what people do. When they don't know what else to do, they take what they do know and make what they don't know look kind of like what they do know because they don't have the imagination to go beyond what it is they're used to.

Basically, that larger thing is consciousness. Consciousness is the computer, and the brain is a virtual brain. You see, it doesn't make any sense. We're a virtual person in a virtual reality, but yet we don't have a virtual brain. We have a virtual body, but somehow our brain is more fundamental because it's logged back into the real superior people that are in some other dimension. So our brain has this function. But if we really are virtual, then we're virtual. We have a virtual brain too, and a virtual brain doesn't do anything. The brain inside the Sims character doesn't do anything. It's just a virtual brain. It's a brain so that if you cut a Sims character's head open, they have to show you something. They can't show you a black hole. They have to show you something, so they draw in a brain. That's what the brain is. It's a virtual brain. If we're virtual beings in a simulation, it's a simulated brain. That's just the way it goes. They might think that simulated brain represents the computer that's off in "future land," but the brain can't create anything. It's a simulated brain. The computer is playing that part, not us. It's not that we have this brain and we have free will and we're moving around; we are like an NPC in a game. The computer is running us. That's the way that works in that materialist idea.

So the idea that the computer can somehow take a little piece of code and let that code represent the character's brain—that is not really a very good idea. There are a lot of problems with that. It doesn't work that way, as we said. Consciousness isn't computed. Consciousness logs on to make choices.

KS: Is true salvation to stop being afraid and stop identifying with our avatars?

TC: I'd say I'm not sure what salvation is, but true growing up, if we let salvation go, being saved is salvation. That's kind of an emotionally loaded word. I just say that basically, growing up, becoming love, that's where we're going. As we make progress toward that, we are headed toward saving ourselves. It's not that somebody or something is going to save us. We save ourselves by growing up, by getting rid of our fear. So we stop being afraid. We don't even really have to stop identifying with avatars. We do identify with the avatar. Our avatar is our constraint to the ruleset, to our choices, so the avatar is important for us. This virtual reality entropy reduction trainer is important. It's a fast track to growing up. We could sit in a chatroom, but we wouldn't grow up very fast. This is a good thing. This reality is something to work with.

KS: Yes, but if we are identifying ourselves with our avatars, with our bodies, then we are totally in the material world; then we are becoming materialists and so on. Then we start thinking about ideas like being immortal, like connecting our brain with the cloud, to change the rules of the simulation.

TC: I agree. If you don't see anything more than the physical, then you're very limited. Very limited and you have a very limited set of choices. That's why you come up with ridiculous choices. That's why you say things like, in quantum mechanics, "The particle splits in two and goes through slits at the same time," or "The particle interferes with itself." Those things don't make any sense. But if you're a materialist, you're stuck with saying silly things like that because you don't have any other choices. You get a diffraction pattern. How do you get a diffraction pattern out of a single particle? You can't. Well, the right answer to that is materialism isn't right. Let's look for a bigger picture, a bigger model that we can hang that fact on. But instead we say, "Oh, it's just weird science. The particle interferes with itself. And that's what the math says. The math shows the particle interfering with itself." That's nonsense. That's just that the materialist has stopped because he can't say anything else. They're stuck there.

The thing is, if you grow up, if you try to get rid of your fear, get rid of your ego, get rid of your beliefs, then you will become aware of a larger dimension of being. You don't have to even think about avatar or not-avatar. You will just become aware of information that's not physical. You'll become aware of things beyond the physical. You just grow into this awareness of non-physical, not because somebody tells you about it or teaches you it or you read about it in a book. You just grow up to where your decision space grows beyond the physical, and now the non-physical is just part of your life. It's not a special place, like here's the physical and there's the non-physical and you're either in one or the other. You live in both, all the time. It's all part of your world. That's what growing up is. You start just by getting rid of your fear and getting rid of your ego and beliefs. The spiritual aspect of it just develops on its own. You just see that because as you get rid of fear, you find higher dimensions. You find connections to people. These connections aren't physical. These connections are something that's beyond physical. And if you want, you can heal and go out of body and remote view. If you don't want to, you don't have to. None of those things are important in and of themselves. They're mostly things you can do to help train your acquaintance with your own consciousness. So yes, salvation, if we're going to call it salvation, is to get rid of your fear and grow up. That will immediately let you identify with something bigger than your avatar, all by itself. You won't be able to help it. It'll just be totally obvious to you that there's something more than the physical world, and you'll begin to work with it. You'll begin to look at people and feel what they're feeling. You'll be able to see through their eyes. You'll be able to taste the dill pickle they're chewing on. You'll be able to connect with people in ways that are not supported physically. You'll have empathy. You'll have telepathy. You'll be able to understand what people are thinking, and they'll be able to understand what you're thinking.

KS: Just because of what?

Just getting rid of fear. You get rid of fear, and that gets rid of the ego, gets rid of the belief. All these other things will just start to become obvious to you. You will be able to connect with people that way.

William Binney*

"I disconnect everything."

KONRAD STACHNIO: Are we living right now in a world where we're giving our social responsibility to the anonymous state, an anonymous force? For example, if you're walking down the street and get hurt in some way, most bystanders do nothing if there's a CCTV camera. If there's no CCTV camera, they're going to act. Are we really giving the social responsibility over to this anonymous force or whatever it is?

WILLIAM BINNEY: Well, it's dependent on the state to take care of things. You know, bystanders are depending on others to do what needs to be done, and it's a way of not committing yourself. For many people, that's kind of inherent to the way they feel. But I think also though, a greater number of people would react to that situation, even if they do nothing more than just call somebody—like an ambulance or something like that—if someone were hurt in the street and they randomly just walked by. Having said that, I think in New York City, that particular issue has been shown to be true. So, people do demonstrate that, but they've also demonstrated other things. I would point out that the "Collateral Murder" movie where Chelsea Manning exposed the war crimes in Baghdad, where they shot all those people from a helicopter, showed there were people who stopped to try to help others afterwards, when they saw them bleeding in the street. And the case in point is what you're pointing out in question one; that was seen there, and those people stopped to try to help. And that's when they came in with that double-tap principle.

Double-tap—that's the principle they use for drones in a strike—is where you carry two missiles. With the first missile, they shoot the target. Then they

---

*WILLIAM BINNEY is former Technical Director of National Security Agency (NSA). Binney has worked in the operations side of intelligence for many years, specializing in Russia, and starting as an analyst before ending up as a Technical Director, then going on to become a geopolitical world Technical Director.

wait for others to gather around and they then make the assumption those people are also involved in whatever that target was doing, and shoot them, too. This is exactly what happened with the gunship in "Collateral Murder." Those people came in to try to help those bleeding on the street; they didn't know why or how. But they tried to help them, to take them to the hospital, and they got shot, too. So, you know, those are war crimes. So, it does demonstrate there are people who do those. I guess it goes both ways, you could say. But I think a lot of people would try to do something, anyway. I'm a positive thinker about people.

KS: I'm really curious about this Chinese model of social credit based on technological surveillance. Do you think this can be implemented in Western countries, or maybe it's already implemented but we don't know?

WB: Yeah, I think that's probably exactly right. They look at your Facebook account before anything, you know, and they look at people, examine everything they can get to, in assessing you. I think that's already in place. Look at what Google and all those people are doing. They're filtering all the data going back to people. That's a way, I think, to control the narrative and the public. That's a way of helping to control people. And, yeah. I think that's true. But you have to understand those companies work for the intelligence community in the United States. So that's your real employer. Plus, I would add, *they* do it too. They compile all sorts of information from all the data NSA collects which includes all the data from those companies. Not just the 702-requested data through the prison program. Although the companies didn't know it, their data lines between the data centers when they backed up all their information, were tapped under a program called "Muscular." So while they were responding to the requests in the prison program for information about people that was out in the open, they were abiding by the law—but then behind the scenes, they tapped their fibers between the data centers, so that when they backed up all their data at the end of the day, every day, all that data was collected. So, they had *everything* those companies had, not just the parts they asked for. That was all; that was just to show they're so *out in the public,* and here, we're abiding by the law—when in fact, that was just a bunch of lies put out there to deceive the public. So, they're getting everything, and they pay these companies, too, for doing this. So, you know, they're working for the government.

KS: So, what can people do? Are we basically defenseless?

WB: Actually, no. I've been advocating in Europe that you have your GDPR and longstanding privacy laws for data about people. I have been recommending you sue those companies—Google, Yahoo, all of them, and Microsoft, everybody.

Sue them all, because they're doing business in Europe and violating your laws by passing all this data to the U.S. government. And of course, it's no longer a safe harbor because of this. Sue them! Take them into court. I mean, they have to go, and the government—the U.S. government—can't stop it. Because they're doing business in Europe. That's the key.

KS: They're just collecting private information from us, and what is the next step? They can use this information if you're against some political elites?

WB: Yes, it's against everybody. They use it against everybody.

KS: But you can still say, "I don't mind if they are collecting my information. It's not bothering me." But if they are using my private information against me, if I would like to, for example, be in the government, that is a different story.

WB: Yup. Well, let me give you the cases over here in the United States. They used it against the Tea Party and religious groups trying to get politically active. They didn't want them active, so they slow-rolled. The IRS did this, because the IRS—the Internal Revenue Service—has direct access to all this NSA information, too. And so, when they go in, they look to see who's involved with the Tea Party, or who's involved in trying to get politically active. Meaning, they were requesting from the IRS 501(c)3 status, meaning tax-exempt status so they could do public activities, and so when they found them, they simply slow-rolled them past the election so they couldn't do that. And then they went for the Occupy group who were protesting the banks and all that stuff. And they found the leaders through studying the social networks of everybody, and they took those people out of circulation so they could no longer manage or, you know, have control of what was happening by the group. And so, it broke up. Then they used it against Eliot Spitzer, who was then, I think, the Attorney General of the State of New York in 2008. He was going after the bankers for defrauding people—which they were—Wall Street bankers defrauded people with these mortgage packages and he was going to go after them for false advertising and fraud. Put them in jail! So, they went on there, the FBI did—the FBI under our saint Mueller, right—the guy doing the current investigation against Trump? He's trying to cover this all up, because he's afraid Trump will expose it, which I hope he does. We're writing articles about this now. We know the dirty laundry here, so we're gonna expose that. But you know, they went after Eliot to try to stop him putting those bankers in jail. Because they clearly defrauded people, not just in the U.S., but around the world. Everybody got hurt by that. But the bankers, of course, protected themselves. So, they're included in the Department of "Just Us." Just. Us. The Justice Department. Just Us. And we're not included! But they are—you know, it's not just that! Then they, they used it also against all the whistleblowers. They used it against reporters, Jim Risen, James Rosen, the Associated Press, you know. And, and so they threatened everybody with grand juries and investigations and indictments. They did it that way. And then they, of course, put hundreds of people in jail every year by using the NSA data. And illegally, and unconstitutionally, by the way. By collecting it, I'm violating the Fourth Amendment first; without having any probable cause, that's a violation of the Fourth Amendment. They use it against people, so they're talking against themselves in a violation of the Fifth Amendment. You cannot testify against yourself. So, in the Sixth Amendment, it applies to due process, where you get all the legal options of being able to test the evidence brought into court against you. Well, they take the NSA data, they arrest the people, then create a fabricated set of information that says, "well, this was the probable cause we used to arrest them." And they substitute that for the NSA data in a court of law. That's called a violation of the Sixth Amendment. Now, they violated due process. And not only that, it violates all kinds of other laws, what they're doing. Like Pen Register Law, Electronic Privacy Act, Electronic Security Act, all the laws governing the FCC regulation covering telecommunication companies, everything. They're just scrapping everything. By the way, the reason the telecommunication companies had to get retroactive immunity from the Congress, was because for every violation of the regulations, there is a $5,000 fine, and up to five years in jail. Now that means, if you commit a couple billion violations a day, you're pretty well bankrupt halfway through the first day, you know? So, they had to give them retroactive immunity for the crimes they were committing. Now—remember, this is what we are doing in our country, not counting what we're doing in everybody else's.

KS: I'm still wondering what just ordinary people can do? If this communication space is just in the hand of the corporations, how can we deal with that—if you are just an ordinary person?

WB: Well, see, you get together. You have to get together as a group and have a class-action lawsuit against all these companies. Put them out of business, you know? Put the onus on them, in court of law, to defend themselves for what they've been doing! I mean, that's the whole point of it. That's the weak spot; if you go after the U.S. government, they'll drag you out in court for decades, you know? You'd just never get through; they'd keep making counter motions and just keep the thing circling. But when they have to do business in your country, that's a different story. Now you've got them on the spot. They have to spit.

They have to stand up to try to defend their business in your country. That's where they're weak. And that way, you can really hurt them and hurt this whole process. At least I would say, in Europe, at least the British are openly admitting everything they're doing. With this Investigative Powers bill they passed. It's essentially bulk acquisition; we're making bulk attacks on devices, you know. All of that. That's all admitted in public. So over here, we deny everything, you see.

KS: Natalya Kaspersky—one of the founders of the Kaspersky anti-virus software—said Tor and Bitcoin were CIA creations for the quick financing of their shadow operation. Do you think the so-called Dark Web is some kind of artificial space just controlled by external forces? Like the CIA or others?

WB: Well, I know some of the people like Jacob Appelbaum who are involved with Tor. And Tor basically started with the U.S. Navy, right? So, it's the U.S. Government that was sponsoring this, and they were sponsoring this for quite a long time, then others joined in. I'm not sure exactly the sequence of how that occurred. But to first address the Dark Web, let me put it this way. The Dark Web uses fibers, right? And sends stuff, using light, down the fibers. That's not dark, is it? First of all, the devices put on there to transmit sessionize everything on the wires, on/off the fibers, take everything off the fibers. Not just subsets. So, the Dark Web is not dark. It's just un-indexed. That's all.

KS: Well, good to know. [Both laugh.]

WB: Maybe not!

KS: People are more and more aware we're constantly coming under surveillance on the Internet. So, do you think the global consciousness of the people is changing because of the fact they're aware they cannot share every bit of information on the Internet? Because, if the information's too risky, they can have problems. If you are an investigative journalist, it's not so easy to get information from very risky sources. People are afraid of sharing information. So, do you think the global consciousness of people is changing because of the knowledge they're under surveillance? Like in Hitler's Germany or something?

WB: Yeah, right. Well, it's even worse than that. It's much worse than what the Nazis did, or what the KGB did. Or the Stasi. It's far worse because it's a more comprehensive thing. Everything can be captured right now with technology. It's quite different. So, your entire electronic life, everything in the world that's being exchanged electronically—finance, and all of this—can be captured. So, it's not like it was back then, when the Stasi had all these rows and rows of files for each individual, you know? It was difficult to work with, took a lot of people to do, and wasn't very efficient. Now, it's all electronically and digitally stored, indexed, and searchable, and you can correlate everything and pull it all together. Like, I can take everything you've done electronically, like we're doing now, and index it over your entire life. Whatever period of time I want, I can index everything you're doing banking-wise, phone calls, emails, short messages, credit card records, everything.

KS: If you are working in NSA, for example.

WB: Yeah. That's what we did. [Laughs.]

KS: Let's clarify that, because this is really important. If for example, I am right now somewhere in the world and talking with you via the Internet, someone can just capture this conversation?

WB: Yes!

KS: And just collect all my data?

WB: And, anytime they want to look at you, they can recall it and put it in a timeline. And say, "here are the actions you took over time," whatever time they want.

KS: But even if am not from the U.S.?

WB: Yes, exactly. I would point out that I don't have to be in the U.S. for this to happen. I could be in Amsterdam, or in Berlin, or I can be in, you know, Serbia somewhere, or something else. I could be anywhere. I mean, they—they basically own the net. Well, back in 2004, they had over 50,000 implants in switches, servers, what-have-you, in the network worldwide. So, back in 2004—and it's only gotten worse since then—the taps were all over the world. And so in other words, when Chancellor Merkel said, "they were using the Embassy next door to tap into my cell phone, and to go into the tower," [she was asserting that's what was going on.] They don't have to do that. She could go to Brazil, and they don't have to lift a finger to be able to tap her. Because anytime she goes on her cellphone, it goes to the tower, goes into the network, on the switches, it goes around the world, you know? And it comes back up to towers. So, it's in the cellphones on the other end. Otherwise, it's in the network, and it's captured. So, they—they capture it from anywhere in the world all the time. And so they can look at whatever she's saying anywhere she is, anytime they want to, by going into their database, which already collects all this.

KS: Maybe the solution here is just to start sending letters by post?

WB: Ah, nope.

KS: Or not using technology at all.

WB: No, that's gonna do it either!

KS: Why not?

WB: Well, because, in the U.S., they take photographs of the external address of the email, or the mail that you're sending. Packages, whatever. They externally save them. And if they want to examine anything you're doing, then they can intervene when it's being transferred by the Postal Service. Because that's simply an address from, and an address to, like a phone call, *from/to*, an email *from/to,* or whatever. A bank transaction address to address, you know.

KS: Maybe I'm wrong, but they can't read my personal, my private correspondence in the mail.

WB: If you're a target, they'll open your mail. Well, if you do that, and you're a target, they will open your mail and read it. I mean, you have to be a target; they can't do that with everybody, okay? So it's easy to filter out, I mean, it's an easy thing to do. With their optical read, they just read the address on the outside. If it's a target, they can notify the Postal Service to interrupt that, you know, within a minute or two.

KS: So, what can we do? If I would like to talk with you optimally via the Internet, by Skype, and someone's watching this conversation, what can we do? Should I speak openly with you?

WB: Sure! I actually advocate they know everything we're doing, because we need to come at them out in the open and shine a big-ass light on them, saying, "here's what you're doing." And that way, you see, these people are basically cowards. They try to pretend they're something, but hiding what they're really doing. And when you expose that, they run, like when you pick up a rock, you see all the bugs, germs, and worms, kind of wiggling to get out of the sun.

That's what they do, okay? So that's the way to go for them. You know, do it out in the open. And also, sue them. When—when they're doing something like that, you sue the bastards. That's from ACLU.

KS: Well, that's a difficult task, I would say.

WB: Yeah. Well, no, not if you collectively get together and organize yourselves that way.

KS: Do you think we are going into the era of the Internet of Things, that everything will be connected to everything else?

WB: Yup, yup.

KS: So, do you think we are just going to the time where terror won't be just hacking my computer, but all of my technological surroundings like my fridge or the whole building, because everything's interconnected to the Internet of Things? So, this is the new era of terrorism?

WB: Well, yes. See, you've noticed that connecting things to the Internet is dangerous for everybody to do. Like, the Office of Personnel Management for the United States government got hacked, right? All the people who have ever had clearance in the United States lost their data. That was over 20-some million people, you know? And they lost all their data. And in that data were the old forms called the SF86. Those are the standard forms you apply for at clearance in the United States government. And in there, you have to tell all the addresses you've ever lived at, all the relatives you have, living and dead, all the jobs you've ever had, who your supervisors were, where they were, what organizations they were, all that information. Your entire history is there. So, when they got that hack, they now had all the data on every, every, every person who's ever had a clearance in the United States. Who they work for, what organizations they were in, throughout history. And so now you can trace everyone in CIA, NSA, FBI. And all the people in the embassies around the world, who they are, who they work for, all of that. And so, all of that stuff, any—all I'm saying is the more data, the more things you connect to the net, the more vulnerable you are. And my personal point is anytime I get something like that, I disconnect it from the internet.

So, you know. Yeah! I don't want that garbage. For example, if you have devices in your car, where if you ever need help, if you have an accident or something, they'll come on and talk to you—well, that's a two-way communication system. That means they can turn it on when you're *not* trying to contact them. That means they can listen to what you're saying in your car, okay? Now, there's another effort going on here that people need to at least understand and know the dangers of. And it's how to read the synaptic patterns in your brain. Okay? Now, this is good—I mean, there's genetics. They're getting DNA samples. What that really means is that as they learn more about DNA, you tend to learn more about your vulnerabilities as a living being, your susceptibility to certain diseases and things like that. And if you start reading their mind, you're getting into how they think, as well as looking at how you interact with the materials around you, like all the Internet of Things, or the communications you have with people. So, it's getting into how you think, much deeper than people, I think, realize. And when you marry that up with being able to read patterns—or to interrupt patterns, if you will—if there are ways to interrupt the synaptic patterns from a distance, then you can really begin to manipulate people on a grand scale.

KS: I was talking about this with one of the Russian neuroscientists, Mikhail Lebedev, and he said if I'd like to force you, for example, to do something, it's very easy. I can just send an external signal to your brain and you'll act like this is your own free will. But he said it's very complicated to just collect information from your brain at a distance. This is not so easy.

WB: Right. You can't; it's easier to try to manipulate by signals. Once you know the patterns. Yeah. See, that's the variance in people. Your synaptic patterns as you're learning things are set up differently. And so those kinds of things are variances of the synaptic patterns when you're thinking things. You can tell regions of the brain that are interactions, but the exact synaptic patterns are variable.

KS: He said if we'd like to collect information from your brain, we'd have to invest in your training.

WB: Yeah, yeah. Right. That's how they learn the patterns.

KS: So, if I would like to just force you to do something, this is very easy.

WB: That's what I mean, yes.

KS: I asked him, what is the difference between people who have schizophrenia or people under some kind of technological experiment? And he said, we can't distinguish these people from those people.

WB: Well, if you marry all this stuff together, you know, from the external use of things you have—assuming the internet comes into it—everything is attached. And you can watch the things you do with it, as well as what you're saying, how you interact with people over the net, the conversations you have with them, and how you start to think. Then you can get a pretty good profile of how people will react under different circumstances. I mean, that's not hard to do. I used to do that against them too, by the way. [Laughs.] So! Not this—it was a different approach with other kinds of material, but it was the same concept, that's the point. I could read them like the back of my hand.

KS: How?

WB: Just based on how they operate. Looking and observing how they do things tells you a lot about a person.

KS: Okay. You're just using the same tools, okay? Am I right?

WB: Yeah. You're seeing not the same tools, but the same concepts.

KS: The same concepts, yes, exactly.

WB: Right. You know, all I'm saying is that the Internet of Things is only going to give you a greater depth of information to look at to do that. So, I disconnect everything. Except the computer! To talk to you, yes? [Laughs.]

KS: Do you think that an external artificial system which is collecting information from us based on biometric data and so on, will soon be able to know everything about us, read all our thoughts, then manipulate us and—finally—erase us in this whole process?

WB: Yeah, well that's what we've just been talking about, yes, Yup.

KS: So, at the end of the day, we're going be like cockroaches? Just a really unnecessary element in the whole process. So how can we deal with that? How can we defend ourselves? Do you see any solution here? Not using the internet at all? Not using the mobile? Or just going into the woods like Theodore Kaczynski? [Laughs.]

WB: Yes, well, I think what you're really getting at is what I've been trying to point out over here in different ways. That, you know, the systems they're putting together are really beginning to know more about you as a person and how you operate than even you recognize. Because, because each of us is kind of cluttered by our emotions, you know? Now, over here, when it comes to President Trump, there are so many people that want to get him out of office any way they can. They're manufacturing evidence against him. Trying to. And so, when I got asked about that position when I came out against the "Russia-gate" simply because it was a forensically proveable fabrication in a court of law, I was prepared to do that. Well, I got called a conspiracy theorist and all that. And the only thing I could do was say, "Well, these people are just showing how weak and baseless their argument is, and they're basically, fundamentally people who are mentally impaired by their emotions." And that's the problem with people. Most people—their emotions kind of cover up what they really are all about, and that's what they go to psychologists for, and psychiatrists, right? To try to figure out what's really their problem because it's covered up by emotions. And so, that's fundamentally what these systems will do, see through that emotion.

KS: See through emotions?

WB: Yes. Well, because what they're doing is trying to figure out what exactly you'll do, and how you operate—and to be able to recognize how you operate to see what exactly you will do under certain circumstances, no matter what your emotions are. Those are kinda on the side. This is at the core of what you are as a human being, how you operate, basically, without emotion covering it up. It's a very dangerous process. So, I disconnect everything. I don't want them having any of this. If they want to do something, they're going to have to come to me and ask. [Chuckles] Otherwise, it's destroying you as an individual, you know? They're basically coming back to you to control you. Then we'll put you into, "I'm a category A person, I'm a category B person, I'm category C." You know? You are allowed into category A, B, or C, and you're not allowed to deviate, so stay there. And that basically destroys the creativity, innovation, and what-have-you that people have, because they can't break out of their box. I was going to say, look at the cases we already know about. Look at the KGB and the Soviet Union. Look at what they did. They stagnated a lot, and people got drunk all the time, you know. I mean, they're still suffering from that. Look at East Germany, under the Stasi. You know, nobody wanted to do creative things anyway, because they were afraid to. So, this is what this kind of control does. It destroys creativity and innovation, and that in turn, stigmatizes and stymies civilization from growing.

KS: So, it is forcing us to become robots or something, like automatons?

WB: Automation. Automatic people.

KS: Do you think that in some ways we are being remotely controlled by social engineering, algorithms, and so on? And it's going to go further and further?

WB: Well, I think a good deal of that is true. I don't think we're completely there yet, by any means. I mean, there's a number of us over here who're still kind of rebelling against what's happening. So, you know, we still have some of the ability to speak up. It just takes a lot to shape up the vast members of the country. Most people like to just drift along to get along, you know. They keep going to work, they live their daily lives. *Don't bother me, I won't bother you,* that kind of thing. And I always say, there are basically three reasons why we shouldn't simply accept the "I'm not a—" statement, where you say *I don't care, I'm not doing anything wrong,* so I don't care if they understand or know anything. But number one basically says, I don't care if you violate my privacy rights. You can see all of my secrets and everything. And I think most people would not want that to happen. For example, would you give all your passwords up, to all your devices, and bank accounts? No! Things like that. The second one is what you think as a person is irrelevant. It is not relevant to anything. It's only a matter of what the government thinks. And third, Goethe gave a good point. How did it go? It's, it's a really important one to say the right way: "No one is more hopelessly enslaved than those who falsely believe they are free." It's exactly where we are.

KS: What is your advice for people to deal with that kind of scenario?

WB: My advice is, sue the bastards! So what I'm doing right now, is I've taken some of the stolen materials, since I helped build all that, you know? So, I've taken some of that and used it as exhibits in a lawsuit we have against the United States government for violating the constitutional rights of U.S. citizens. And I wrote up these things in the exhibits, even though they claim they're still classified, and you're not allowed to talk about it. So, even Clapper, the Director of National Intelligence—after I started talking about it in public, at the Freedom Law School in Florida and Westchester University—a week after I started that, he came out with this declaration that no current or former employees of the Intelligence community are allowed to talk about any of the material released. So I addressed him in a national press club in Washington, D.C. All the major media were right there. NBC, ABC, CBS. You know, all of them. And I said— with this declaration that the Director of National Intelligence, Clapper, had just issued to all current and former employees of the intelligence community—*I,*

Mr. Clapper, do not give up my First Amendment right to talk about anything in the public domain, thank you. And so, I just told him to get lost. Those—none of those news organizations published any of that. Yeah. And so it's how you control the narrative. If you don't let anybody know, they don't know this is going on. It's like, for example, National Security issued by FBI agents around the United States—just to get all the data from anybody—it's done with an FBI agent's signature. Not a judge's approval or anything. So, it's not a warrant, a signed warrant. They've been handing these things out to different companies. "Oh, you have to turn over all the data you have on this person or that person." They've been doing it for years. Finally, somebody challenged them in federal court. Because in there, it says you can't talk to anybody about the fact you've received this national security letter. You can't talk about it under penalty of law. Well, there's no such law, okay? In fact, it's a direct violation of the First Amendment of the Constitution to have freedom of speech. So, this guy challenged and took it right into the Second Circuit Court of Appeals, the next court down from the Supreme Court, and challenged it on constitutional grounds. And on that basis, he won. It was declared unconstitutional by the Second Circuit Court of Appeals. So, the FBI dropped it like a hot potato and ran away and said absolutely nothing further about it. And nobody else said too much about it either. Because that means, in the entire United States, all these national security letters are unconstitutional. That means if you get one, you can talk about it and just ignore it, okay? So that's what the FBI didn't want anybody to know. And the media kinda went along with that to keep knowledge of it out of the court, out of the system and the knowledge of the public. So, I keep blabbing it all over the place, everywhere I am, you know? Because these people are just criminals.

Joe Lauria, who's the editor of *Consortium News,* said he was really worried about Mr. Barr becoming the new Attorney General, because he believes in mass incarceration. So I said, "What is wrong with mass incarceration! If he goes down there and arrests all those criminals in Washington, D.C., that's all to the good." Because we'll mass incarcerate all of 'em. Put 'em in jail. Because I've been arguing they're all criminals. I've been pointing out why, and nobody's addressing the why except for me. And that's what I'm gonna do in federal court if I can ever get my foot in there, you know? So that's why I have my lawsuits. I've got two other lawsuits I'm supporting and advising on. I give them that information and advice, all in federal court—one in the Ninth Circuit, one in the Eleventh Circuit, one in the Third Circuit. So. I'm getting around as best I can. So, sue the bastards!

KS: Sue the bastards. Big advice, I would say. Huge advice.

WB: Do it collectively, too. Get together, do it. You don't have to be alone in this, you know.

KS: But people *are* still thinking they have to deal with this alone.

WB: They don't. That's the point. There are other people who feel the same way. Get together, talk about it, decide what you want to do.

Interviewee Biographies

ALEKSANDR DUGIN is a Russian political scientist, philosopher, and traditionalist. A former advisor to the Kremlin, Dugin is one of the best-known writers and political commentators in post-Soviet Russia, and is considered to have direct influence on the thought of Vladimir Putin. A Soviet dissident in the 1980s, he has been a leading theorist of "Eurasianism," authoring more than 30 books, among them *The Fourth Political Theory* and *Foundations of Geopolitics* (1997). His works have been used as textbooks in the Academy of the General Staff of the Russian military. Alexander Dugin is considered to be one of the most contentious thinkers of the modern world.

ALAIN de BENOIST is a French journalist, political philosopher, and founder of the (GRECE) and the larger cultural movement, the European New Right, launched in 1968. Alain de Benoist has authored such books as *The Problem of Democracy, Beyond Human Rights, Carl Schmitt Today, Manifesto for a European Renaissance, On the Brink of the Abyss, The Indo-Europeans, Runes and the Origins of Writing*, and *View from the Right* (vol. I, vol. II). He received the Grand Prix de l'Essai from the Académie Française for his book *Vu de droite* [View from the Right] in 1978. He has been the editor of the journals *Nouvelle Ecole* and *Krisis*, while his works have also been published in a various journals such as *Mankind Quarterly, Telos, The Scorpion, The Occidental Quarterly*, and *Tyr*. For over forty years Benoist has had a massive impact on the philosophical and ideological understanding of the political situation in Europe.

ANDREI RAEVSKY is a Swiss-born military analyst. He worked as a civilian consultant for the Swiss Strategic Intelligence Service (SND) writing strategic analyses, primarily about the Soviet/Russian military. He also worked as a specialist for the operational-level training of the General Staff of Swiss armed forces and with the UN Institute for Disarmament Research (UNIDIR) where he specialized in peacekeeping tactics and operations. His last work at UNIDIR concerned psychological operations and intelligence in peacekeeping. Raevsky is the author of a widely read blog called The Vineyard of the Saker. He is also the author of such books as *The Essential Saker: From the trenches of the emerging multi-polar world, The Essential Saker II: Civilizational Choices and Geopolitics: The Russian challenge to the Hegemony of the AngloZionist Empire*, and *The Essential Saker III: Chronicling the tragedy, farce and collapse of the Empire in the era of Mr MAGA*.

CARINE HUTSEBAUT is a Belgium psychotherapist, criminologist, and author of the books *Child Hunters: Requiem of a Child-killer, Profile of a Serial Killer, Little Sinners: The Church and Child Trafficking, Profession: Profiler*, and *He is still amongst us*. Hutsebaut is a Founder of the International Centre for Molested and Abducted/Adopted Children and a Member of the Academy of Behavioural Profiling. She has surveyed numerous "profiling" training courses at the FBI centre in Quantico, USA (made famous by the film *The Silence of the Lambs*). As a profiler, she gained entry into prisons with the worst serial criminals in order to better understand their behaviours, thought processes, and feelings. Her work has been the basis and inspiration for the making of multiple movies.

CATHERINE AUSTIN FITTS is the president of Solari, Inc., publisher of the Solari Report, and managing member of Solari Investment Advisory Services, LLC. Catherine served as managing director and member of the board of directors of the Wall Street investment bank Dillon, Read & Co. Inc., as Assistant Secretary of Housing and Federal Housing Commissioner at the United States Department of Housing and Urban Development in the first Bush Administration, and was the president of Hamilton Securities Group, Inc. Catherine has designed and closed over $25 billion of transactions and investments to date and has led portfolio and investment strategy for $300 billion of financial assets and liabilities. Catherine has a BA from the University of Pennsylvania, an MBA from the Wharton School, and studied Chinese at the Chinese University of Hong Kong. She publishes a column, Mapping the Real Deal, in Scoop Media in New Zealand. She is also the author of the book *Dillon Read and the Aristocracy of Stock Profits*.

DOUGLAS RUSHKOFF is an American writer, lecturer, columnist, media theorist, graphic novelist, and documentarian, named by MIT as one of the "World's ten most influential intellectuals." Rushkoff has written twenty books, ten of which are on media, technology, and culture. Amid his other publications are his most recently published *Team Human*, which is based on his podcast, as well as the bestsellers *Present Shock, Throwing Rocks, The Google Bus*, and *Media Virus*, among others. A Professor of Media Theory and Digital Economics, he is also a research fellow of the Institute for the Future and the founder of the Laboratory for Digital Humanism at CUNY/Queens. Rushkoff earned his PhD in

New Media and Digital Culture from Utrecht University and has been a columnist for *Medium*. Rushkoff has served as an advisor to the United Nations Commission on World Culture and makes regular appearances on TV shows, from the Colbert Report and Bill Maher to NBC Nightly News and Larry King.

ERIK DAVIS is best known for his book *Techgnosis: Myth, Magic, and Mysticism in the Age of Information*. An American writer, scholar, journalist, and public speaker, he has contributed articles and essays to various periodicals, including *Arthur, Artforum, Slate, Gnosis, Rolling Stone, LA Weekly, Spin,* and *The Village Voice,* among others. Davis has given talks at media art conferences, festivals, and universities around the world. He has taught seminars at UC Berkeley, UC Davis, California Institute of Integral Studies, and Rice University, as well as conducted workshops at the New York Open Centre. He has been interviewed by CNN, NPR, the *New York Times,* and the BBC, and has had appearances in a number of documentaries. His other books include *Nomad Codes: Adventures in Modern Esoterica* (Yeti, 2010) and the 33 -1/3 volume *Led Zeppelin IV* (Continuum, 2005).

SHEIKH IMRAN NAZAR HOSEIN is an Islamic scholar, philosopher and author who has specialized in Islamic eschatology, world politics, economics, and modern socio-economic/political issues. A graduate of the Aleemiyah Institute in Karachi, he has studied at many institutions of higher learning, among them the University of Karachi, the University of the West Indies, Al Azhar University, and the Graduate Institute of International Relations in Switzerland. He is author of *The Qur'an Dajjal and the Jasad, Constantinople in the Qur'an, Methodology for the Study of the Qur'an,* and *Jerusalem in the Qur'an.* While living in New York for ten years he served as the Director of Islamic Studies for the Joint Committee of Muslim Organizations of Greater New York and, since the age of 29, he has ceaselessly and expansively travelled around the world giving Islamic lecture-tours since graduating from the Aleemiyah Institute of Islamic Studies in 1971.

RABBI JOEL DAVID BAKST is a teaching rabbi and scholar of the Talmud and Kabbalah who studied and taught in Orthodox yeshivot while living in Jerusalem for 20 years. Joel comes from a rich family lineage of rabbis. Growing up in a conservative Jewish home in Southern California, at the age of 20 he became ba'al teshuva (newly religious), fulfilled his family's circle, and joined their long line of rabbis. He is the eighth generation of Rabbi Avraham Ragoler of Skhlov, brother of Rabbi Elijah, the famous Gaon of Vilnius whose teachings and School of Kabbalah were the subject of Joel's own esoteric research. Rabbi Bakst is the author of the book series *Torah, Kabbalah, and Consciousness.* This includes the two volumes of *The Secret Doctrine of the Gaon of Vilna—Volume I:*

The Messianic Role of Torah, Kabbalah, and Science, and *Volume II: The Josephic Messiah, Leviathan, Metatron, and the Sacred Serpent.* The third volume is *The Jerusalem Stone of Consciousness: DMT, Kabbalah, and the Pineal Gland.* His fourth book is *Beyond Kabbalah: The Teachings That Cannot Be Taught.* He has a global reach and has lectured and taught in Israel, the United States, and India.

JACK RASMUS studied economics at Berkeley and took his doctorate at the University of Toronto (1977). He is Associate Adjunct Professor of Economics at St. Mary's College in Moraga, California. His work focuses on economic inequities and he has written for many publications, including *The European Financial Review, World Review of Political Economy, World Financial Review,* and *Z Magazine,* among others, on economic, political, and labor issues. Dr. Jack Rasmus has authored many books on the USA's and global economy, including *Systemic Fragility in the Global Economy* (2015) and *The Scourge of Neoliberalism: U.S. Economic Policy from Reagan to Trump* (2020), soon forthcoming in Chinese.

JOHN PERKINS is an American author best known for his book *Confessions of an Economic Hit Man* (2004). His book spent over 70 weeks on the *New York Times* bestseller list and has been published in at least 32 languages worldwide. In *Confessions...,* Perkins lays claim to have played a role in the process of the economic colonization of Third World countries on behalf of banks, corporations, and the United States government. As Chief Economist at a major international consulting firm, Perkins has advised the United Nations, IMF, the World Bank, Fortune 500 corporations, the U.S. Treasury Department, and leaders of countries in Latin America, Asia, the Middle East, and Africa. Lecturing at over 50 universities, including Harvard and Oxford, he is the author of eight books on global economics and indigenous cultures. Perkins has been featured on ABC, NBC, CNN, CNBC, NPR, A&E, and the History Channel, as well as in publications such as the *New York Times,* the *Washington Post, Cosmopolitan,* and many others, on top of featuring in a plethora of documentaries. He was awarded the Rainforest Action Network Challenging Business As Usual Award, 2006 as well as the Lennon Ono Grant for Peace, 2012.

MIKHAIL A. LEBEDEV, PhD is an award-winning scientist in the fields of Neurophysiology and Brain-Computer Interfaces. Having earned his PhD at the University of Memphis, he currently holds the positions of Scientific Head and Chief Research Scientist for the Centre for Bioelectric Interfaces at the Institute of Cognitive Neuroscience for National Research, University Higher School of Economics, in Moscow, Russia, and Senior Research Scientist at Duke Medical Centre. He has conducted research into neurophysiology and motor control around the world—at the Institute for Information Transmission Problems, Moscow; the University of Tennessee, Memphis; La Scuola Internazionale Superiore di Studi Avanzati, Trieste; and the National Institute of Mental Health, Bethesda. Mikhail's research interests lie in the areas of electrocorticography, neurophysiology of cortex and basal ganglia, neural prostheses, primate motor control and cognition, and brain-machine interfaces. He has developed brain-machine interfaces and written over 100 papers, as well as edited journals and books. His success in his chosen fields has culminated in him receiving the Spotlight Award and a Megagrant from the Russian government.

PAUL CRAIG ROBERTS is an American economist, author, and former associate editor at *The Wall Street Journal*. Roberts also held the position of the United States Assistant Secretary of the Treasury for Economic Policy under President Ronald Reagan. After leaving government, he went on to hold the William E. Simon chair in economics at the Centre for Strategic and International Studies, serving on several corporate boards. Roberts' articles have appeared in *The New York Times* and *Harper's*, and in 1987 he was inducted into the Legion of Honour at the rank of chevalier (knight) by President of France, François Mitterrand. Roberts has also been the recipient of the United States Treasury's Meritorious Service Award and the International Journalism Award for Political Analysis from the Mexican Press Club. Currently he is chairman of The Institute for Political Economy and has authored numerous books, such as *The Neoconservative Threat to World Order, How America Was Lost,* and *The Failure of Laissez Faire Capitalism*. These books have been translated into over four languages including a Russian edition of *How America Was Lost*.

RICHARD FALK is an international law and international relations scholar who taught at Princeton University for forty years. In 2008 he served a six-year term as the UN Special Rapporteur on Palestinian human rights. He received his BS from the Wharton School, University of Pennsylvania; LLB from Yale Law School; and JSD from Harvard University. He is the author or co-author of numerous books, including *Religion and Humane Global Governance; Human Rights Horizons; On Humane Governance: Toward a New Global Politics; Explorations at the Edge of Time; Revolutionaries and Functionaries; The Promise of World Order; Indefensible Weapons; Human Rights and State Sovereignty; A Study of Future Worlds; This Endangered Planet;* co-editor of *Crimes of War*. He serves as Chair of the Nuclear Age Peace Foundation's Board of Directors and as honorary vice president of the American Society of International Law. He has been annually nominated for the Nobel Peace Prize since 2008 and his recent books include

Power Shift: On the New Global Order, Palestine Horizon: Toward a Just Peace, and a book of poems, *Waiting for Rainbows.*

TIM DRAPER is an American venture capital investor and founder of Draper Associates, DFJ, and the Draper Venture Network, a global network of venture capital funds. Draper has an investment portfolio that includes Baidu, Hotmail, Skype, Tesla, SpaceX, AngelList, SolarCity, Ring, Twitter, DocuSign, Coinbase, and Robinhood. He is a leading spokesperson for Bitcoin, Blockchain, ICOs, and cryptocurrencies, creating Draper University of Heroes, a residential and online school based in San Mateo, CA, which helps extraordinary people accomplish their life-long missions. The recipient of various awards and honours, among which is the World Entrepreneurship Forum's "Entrepreneur of the World," Draper has been listed as one of the top 100 most powerful people in finance by *Worth Magazine*. Tim Draper has often been regarded as one of the most successful venture capitalists of all time, as well as one of the most instrumental and prominent people in Silicon Valley today.

THOMAS CAMPBELL is a nuclear physicist who began researching altered states of consciousness with Bob Monroe (author of *Journeys out of the Body, Far Journeys,* and *The Ultimate Journey*), at Monroe Laboratories during the early 1970s. A former NASA physicist, Campbell gained his master's degree in physics from Purdue University, beginning his career working in the nuclear technology industry. An international lecturer and author of the *My Big TOE* trilogy, Campbell presently, and for the past 20 years, has been at the core of the development of the U.S. missile defence systems, working with the U.S. government.

WILLIAM BINNEY is former Technical Director of National Security Agency (NSA) and whistle-blower who worked for them for over 36 years. A former NSA crypto-mathematician, Binney completed his mathematics degree at Pennsylvania State University. Binney has worked in the operations side of intelligence for many years, specializing in Russia, and starting as an analyst before ending up as a Technical Director, then going on to become a geopolitical world Technical Director. In the 1990s, Binney co-founded a unit on automating signals intelligence with NSA research chief Dr. John Taggart. His NSA career led him to becoming Technical Leader for intelligence in 2001. He has expertise in intelligence analysis, traffic analysis, systems analysis, knowledge management, and mathematics (including set theory, number theory, and probability). After retiring from the NSA, Binney, together with fellow NSA whistleblower J. Kirk Wiebe, founded Entity Mapping, LLC., a private intelligence agency which markets their analysis programs to government agencies.

Index

A

Abraham, 87, 114, 117
Adorno, Theodor, 75
Ain Sof, 109
Al-Masih ad-Dajjal, 92, 97
Ali, Ben, 187
alienation, 3, 21, 180
Allah, 92–3, 95, 97, 99
Allison, Graham, 177
Antichrist, 7, 13, 14, 82, 87–8, 90, 92–3, 94–7, 100–2
Apocalypse, 12, 103, 115
Arab, 9, 14, 27–30, 34, 92, 95, 102, 147, 169, 171, 178–80
Ark of the Covenant, 111
artificial intelligence (AI), 2, 8, 10–2, 15, 46, 69, 80–3, 91, 95, 97, 138, 144, 149, 150–2, 155, 156–7, 159, 167, 182, 193–5, 202, 208
  external AI-based systems, 209
Attali, Jacques, 17

B

Bank of International Settlements, 64
banks, 57–8, 64, 123, 125–8, 131, 134–5, 139, 144, 161, 184, 192, 219, 235
Bannon, Steve, 16
Beaudrillard, Jean, 22
Benoist, Alain de, v, 18, 231

Bernanos, Georges, 21
Beyond Kabbalah, 108
Bezos, Jeff, 69
biodiversity, 178, 180
bioelectronics, 59, 60
biogenetics, 13, 82
Bitcoin, 64, 135, 178, 192–5, 221, 236
Black Budget, 164–6, 181
blockchain, 64–5, 178, 192–5, 236
Bolsonaro, Jair, 185
brain-machine interface nanotechnology, 59
Brave New World, 65, 182
A Brief History of the Future, 17
Bush, George W., 129–30, 137
Butterfly Effect, 106, 114
Byzantium, 93

C

Caliphate, 9
Cantor, Georg, 110
carbon-based computer, 206
Celente, Gerald, 134
Central Intelligence Agency (CIA), 55, 60, 72, 164, 221, 224
Chaos Theory, 106
China, 12, 27, 28, 30–2, 34, 45, 60, 63, 67, 119, 123, 130–2, 135, 144, 160–2, 167, 175, 176–7, 189, 195

chip, 52, 55, 58–60, 65, 152, 167
Christians, 2, 5, 7, 10, 29, 30, 32, 37, 71, 87, 88, 92–4, 97, 99–102, 112, 116, 118, 146–7
  Orthodox, 2, 7, 29, 94, 99, 100–101
civil war, 8, 14, 32, 130, 189
civilization, iii, 30, 35, 51, 63, 93, 98, 100, 108, 121, 172, 184–5, 227, 232
Clarke, Arthur C., 108
climate change, 28, 84, 103, 141–2, 144, 148, 174, 178, 180, 182
Clinton, Bill, 137
COVID-19, 52, 55, 66, 171, 180, 185–8, 193, 195
coherent superposition, 110
Communists, 4
Consciousness, 11, 35, 74, 77–8, 84, 86–7, 89, 104–22, 130, 142–3, 145, 151, 152, 153, 188, 197–9, 201, 203–10, 212–4, 216, 221, 233–4, 236
Constantinople, 93, 94, 102, 233
cortex, 150–1, 210, 212–3, 235
Cusack, John, 65, 66
cyborgs, 10, 11

D
dark matter, 118
DARPA, 35
Dasein, 3–4, 6
data-driven health care, 194
David, King, 111
Dawkins, Richard, 76
Debord, Guy, 22–3
decentralization, 35, 64, 177–8
dehumanizing, 3
democracy, 10, 32, 173–4, 176, 178, 180, 231
Department of Defense, 55, 59–60
depression, 34, 126–7, 134–5, 142
Die Welt, 3

digital currency, 52, 135
digital dissidents, 65, 66
digital yuan, 63
Dimethyltryptamine, 112, 121
diversity, vii, 21, 25
divine, 45, 86, 91, 106, 109, 110
DNA, 12, 41, 54, 203, 225
Dolan, Richard, 57
dollar, 31–2, 51–3, 56–8, 64, 66–7, 69, 126, 128, 131–2, 135–6, 162
Dome of the Rock, 111, 121
Dugin, Aleksandr, v, 1, 80, 82–4, 86–7, 231

E
Ecclesiastes, 108
economy, vii, 6, 8, 12, 19, 20–1, 25, 30, 32, 49, 57, 61, 65, 67, 88, 123–32, 134–9, 141, 144–5, 147–8, 158, 160–2, 175, 177, 191, 194, 234
Einstein, Albert, 156
Eisenhower, Dwight David, 161
Enlightenment, 2
Europe, 8–12, 14, 15, 18, 25–6, 30, 32, 38, 51–2, 71–2, 88, 95, 123–5, 129, 131–3, 136–7, 139, 147, 154, 158, 169, 172–3, 176–7, 179, 184, 186, 218, 219, 221, 231, 234
Evola, Julius, 4, 16

F
Facebook, 21, 23, 68, 72–3, 82, 218
Farrell, Joseph, 61
Federal Reserve, 124, 127–28, 135
fetish, 1, 19
finance, 4, 27, 57, 128-31, 164-5, 193-4, 222, 236
Floyd, George, 187–8
Foundation Stone, 111–3, 121–2
fractal process, 198

Index

freedom, vii, 6–7, 32, 45–6, 64, 66–7, 72, 95, 161, 180, 182, 193, 199, 202, 228–9
Fukuyama, Francis, 25, 164, 176, 180
Fundamental ontology, 3

G

Gomorrah (book), 51, 184
Gaon of Vilna, 113–4, 233
Gates, Bill, 8, 45, 46, 59–60, 65, 143, 160
gender, 19
   politics, 2, 10
   identity, 10
genetic engineering, 183
geopolitics, vii, 167, 176, 177–8, 231
Giordano James, 35
Girard, René, 74
Glazyev, Sergey, 144
globalisation, 2, 6, 19, 21, 25
Globalist, 8–9, 17, 72
   agenda, game, model, 1, 7, 33
God, 1–2, 4–7, 10–4, 17, 32, 37, 41, 63, 69, 70, 76, 81, 83–7, 92, 93–100, 102, 105–6, 109–10, 112–4, 116, 118, 120, 149, 151–3, 168, 210, 212–3
Gog and Magog, 94, 96–7, 102–3, 114–5, 117
Golden Dome, 11, 112
Goldman Sachs, 130
Gorbachev, Mikhail, 180
Great Replacement, 8
Groening, Matt, 75
guaranteed income, 19, 158, 161
Guenon, Rene, 4, 16

H

Harari, Noah Yuval, 60, 191
Hedges, Chris, 173
Hegel, Georg Wilhelm Friedrich, 110
Heidegger, Martin, 3–4

Hezbollah, 27, 29, 34, 171–2
Holy dread, 105, 107
Hollywood, 1, 2, 14, 102
Horkheimer, Max, 76
human rights, 21, 231, 235
Huxley, Aldous, 12, 65, 182

I

Immortality, 11, 78
individualism, 19, 24, 33
Infinity of infinities, 110
International Monetary Fund (IMF), 72, 132, 234
   Special Drawing Right (SDR), 162
Internet of Things, 224–6
Iran, 27, 28, 31, 34, 136, 162, 168–9, 171–2, 179
Islam, 8–9, 14, 20, 27–9, 32, 82, 83, 87, 92–3, 95–6, 99–100, 102, 112, 146–7, 172, 233
Islamic State, 9, 27

J

Jerusalem, 92–4, 97–9, 102–3, 107, 111–4, 118, 121, 168, 233–4
   Temple Mount, 113
Jesus, 93–4, 97, 99, 100–2
Jews, Orthodox, 103, 116, 233
Jihad, 100
Joy, Bill, 76
Jünger, Georg Friedrich, 22
Jung, Carl, 46

K

Kaczyński, Theodor, 76
Kaspersky, Natalya, 221
Kelly, Kevin, 88
Keynes, John Maynard, 126
King, Martin Luther (Jr.), 173
Krugman, Paul, 134

Khrushchev, Nikita, 101
Ku Klux Klan, 189
Kurzweil, Ray, 149, 155

L
Latouche, Serge, 21
Lauria, Joe, 229
Lefort, Claude, 19
Leftism, 4
Lenin, Vladimir, 32, 178–9
liberalism, 2, 4, 10, 13, 33
Lieber Research Group, 59
Lieber, Charles, 59, 65
Logos, 3
Lorenz, Edward, 106
Lukács, Georg, 19
Lynch, David, 13

M
Macron, Emmanuel, 18
mafia, 51, 184–5
Malabou, Catherine, 153
Malcolm X, 173
Marx, Karl, 19, 28, 32, 159, 163
Matrix, 6, 8–11, 16, 74, 82, 162
Mayim, Chayim, 112–3
McKenna, Terence, 88
megacities, 34–5, 65, 183
Messiah, 82, 94, 97, 105, 107–8, 111, 113–6, 234
metaphysical
  alternative, 4
  destiny, 3
  dimension, 112
  evil, 16
  explanation, 112
  idea, 14
  lies, 5
  problem, 2
  systems, 83

way of thinking, 3
  metaphysically based, 7
Metzinger, Thomas, 86, 150
Meyer, Thomas, 48
migrant crisis, 8
military, 18, 27-8, 30, 32, 35, 60, 64–5, 67, 98–9, 101–2, 143, 154, 159, 161, 165, 166–8, 171–2, 174–6, 178, 180-1, 183-4, 192, 231
Mind of Moses, 108
modernity, 1, 2, 5, 7, 9–11, 17, 19, 77, 85, 86, 88, 90, 180, 184
Mubarak, Hosni, 179, 180
Musk, Elon, 9, 17, 45, 46, 73–4, 151, 213
Muslim, 2, 7, 8–11, 27, 29–30, 92, 97, 99, 102, 180, 233

N
nanotechnology, 52, 59–61, 67
nationalism, 4, 72, 83–4, 88, 166–7, 177, 185–6
National Security Agency (NSA), 51, 59–60, 217–20, 222, 224, 236
NBIC, vii, 153
neoliberalism, 123, 134, 136–8, 234
Netanyahu, Benjamin, 60
neural networks, 11, 13, 151, 204–5
neuroweapons, 35
New World, 65
  Government, 6
  Order, 37, 165
Nietzsche, Friedrich, 5
Noah, 60, 117, 191
nuclear war/weapons, 28, 144, 164, 167–9, 174, 181, 202

O
Obama, Barack, 8, 129, 139, 146, 173, 175
Oculus Quest, 194
Olam, HaBah, 119

Index

Operation Warp Speed, 59–60, 65, 67
Orange Revolution, 7
Orwell, George, 12

P

pandemic, 31, 33, 123, 141–2, 148, 174, 178, 180, 185–7, 189–90, 194
Panter, Gary, 75
Peale, Vincent Norman, 211
philosophy, vii, 1, 4, 7, 74, 79, 85
pineal gland, 111–3, 121, 234
politics, 2, 10, 15, 25, 85, 92, 116, 130, 131, 144, 174–5, 179–80, 186–7, 189
population, 8, 20, 35, 81, 142, 152, 158, 171, 184, 186, 200
Post-humanism, 5
Prophet Muhammad, 92, 93
Proverbs, 108
Putin, Vladimir, 15, 172, 144

Q

quantum, 74, 109, 117, 215
Quran, 93–5, 97–9, 102
Queen of Sheba, 108

R

rabbit hole, viii
racism, 4, 34, 174, 188–9
radical subject, 11
Rappoport, John, 48, 52
recession, 125–7, 131–2, 134–5
rectification, 108, 114
religion, vii, 20, 21, 73, 85, 87, 100–2, 147, 168, 209, 235
robots, 8–11, 46, 65, 69, 74, 82, 83, 144–5, 151, 153, 157–8, 168, 181, 183, 227
Rose, Geordie, 152
Russia, 1, 7, 9–10, 14–6, 26–8, 30–2, 34, 59, 72, 94, 98–102, 136, 142, 144, 148–50, 161–2, 177, 180, 217, 225, 227, 231–2, 234–6

S

Salafi Islam, 8
movement, 99, 100
Sanders, Bernie, 174–5
Satan, 2, 4, 13, 17, 28, 71, 74, 107
Satanic, 1, 2, 10
agenda, 1, 16
concept, 6
grip, 175
ideology, 32
matrix, 6, 16, 74
mechanism, 2
paradigm, 2
plan, 1, 4–7
purposes, 13
themes, 6
Saviano, Roberto, 51, 184
Seven Sciences, 110
Shakespeare, William, 182
Shamsie, Kamila, 173
sharing economy, 8, 12, 49, 160
Sheldrake, Rupert, 45
Shelley, Mary, 182
Silicon Valley, 73, 76, 191–2, 236
simulacrum, 4, 12
simulation, vii, 25, 106, 197, 205, 207, 210, 212, 214–5
singularity, 73, 90, 117, 119
Sloterdijk, Peter, 68
Smart Contracts, 193–5
Snowden, Edward, 31
sociology, vii
Solomon, King, 108, 111, 121
Soros, George, 4
Soviet Union, 12, 48, 98, 101, 142, 176, 180, 227
Spitzer, Eliot, 219
standardisation, 21, 23
Stasi, 221–2, 227
Steiner, Rudolf, 87
surveillance capitalism, 59

T

Tarantino, Quentin, 14
terrorism, 20, 34, 72, 88, 99–100, 145, 166, 170, 177, 224
thought police, vii
Tiller, Bill, 63
tipping point, 115, 117, 119, 120
totalitarianism, 12, 79, 84, 180
traditionalism, 1, 4, 88
transhumanism, 78–9, 180–2, 184
Tree of Life, 109, 113, 116, 122
Trump, Donald, 7–8, 14–6, 59, 72, 124–5, 129–31, 136–7, 142, 145–6, 163, 165–6, 171, 174–6, 179–80, 185–6, 188–9, 219, 227, 234
Twitter, 73, 179, 236

U

Ullman, Tracy, 75
United Nations (UN), 72, 116, 165, 169, 187, 234
  Commission on World Culture, 233
  Institute for Disarmament Research (UNDIR), 27
  Security Council, 168, 170
  Special Rapporteur for the Middle East, 164, 235
urban guerrillas, 34

V

venture capitalists, 191, 236
virtualisation, 22
virus, 31, 34, 54, 59, 60, 82, 107, 109–10, 114–6, 118–21, 124–6, 128, 130–2, 137, 141, 152, 193–4, 221, 232

W

Wall Street, 48, 175, 219, 232
  The Wall Street Journal, 157, 235
warfare, 49, 55, 99, 141, 183

Western civilization, 93, 98, 100
Western Wall, 111
wet lab, 194
World Health Organization (WHO), 186, 189

Z

Zizek, Slavoy, 2, 4, 75, 80, 153
Zuckerberg, Mark, 69